THE MOST
TRUSTED NAME
IN TRAVEL

Frommer's®

shortcut

KAUAI

by Jeanne Cooper &
Shannon Wianecki

D0721348

FrommerMedia LLC

Published by

FROMMER MEDIA LLC

Copyright © 2016 by Frommer Media LLC, New York City, New York. Frommer Media LLC is not associated with any product or vendor mentioned in this book.

ISBN 978-1-62887-220-0 (paper), 978-1-62887-221-7 (e-book)

Editorial Director: Pauline Frommer
Editor: Alexis Lipsitz Flippin
Photo Editor: Dana Davis and Meghan Lamb
Cartographer: Roberta Stockwell
For information on our other products or services, see www.frommers.com. Frommer Media LLC also publishes its books in a variety of electronic formats.

Manufactured in China

5   4   3   2   1

HOW TO CONTACT US

In researching this book, we discovered many wonderful places—hotels, restaurants, shops, and more. We're sure you'll find others. Please tell us about them, so we can share the information with your fellow travelers in upcoming editions. If you were disappointed with a recommendation, we'd love to know that, too. Please write to: Support@FrommerMedia.com

FROMMER'S STAR RATINGS SYSTEM

Every hotel, restaurant and attraction listed in this guide has been ranked for quality and value. Here's what the stars mean:

★ Recommended
★★ Highly Recommended
★★★ A must! Don't miss!

CONTENTS

Officially Noted

1-12-21
slight moisture damage @ bottom
kg

LIST OF MAPS

ABOUT THE AUTHORS

Jeanne Cooper fell in love with the real Hawaii on her first visit in 1998, after growing up with enchanting stories and songs of the islands from her mother, who had lived there as a girl. The former editor of the *San Francisco Chronicle* travel section, Jeanne writes frequently about Hawaii for the newspaper and its website, SFGate.com, home of her Aloha Friday column and Hawaii Insider blog, and for magazines such as *Sunset* and *Caviar Affair*. She has also contributed to guidebooks on her former hometowns of Boston, Washington, D.C., and San Francisco.

Shannon Wianecki grew up in Hawaii swimming in waterfalls, jumping off of sea cliffs, and breakfasting on ripe mangoes. An award-winning writer and editor, she writes feature stories for numerous travel and lifestyle magazines. Having served 8 years as food editor for *Maui No Ka 'Oi Magazine,* she knows the island's restaurant scene as well as her own kitchen. She once won the Maui Dreams Dive Company's pumpkin-carving contest.

ACKNOWLEDGEMENTS

I would like to thank my editor, Alexis Lipsitz Flippin, and my husband, Ian Hersey, for their support, and all those in Hawaii who have shared their knowledge and aloha with me.

—Jeanne Cooper

Thanks to Gabe Marihugh for driving the Jeep through mudbogs in Lanai.

—Shannon Wianecki

INTRODUCTION

by Jeanne Cooper

Time has been kind to Kauai, the oldest and northernmost of the Hawaiian Islands. Millions of years of erosion have carved fluted ridges, emerald valleys, and glistening waterfalls into the flanks of Waialeale, the extinct volcano at the center of this near-circular isle. Similar eons have created a ring of enticing sandy beaches and coral reefs. Kauai's wild beauty sometimes translates to rough seas and slippery trails, but with a little caution, anyone can safely revel in the island's natural grandeur.

ESSENTIALS
Arriving

BY PLANE A number of North American airlines offer regularly scheduled, nonstop service to Kauai's main airport in Lihue (airport code: LIH) from the Mainland, nearly all from the West Coast. (*Note:* From Los Angeles, flights generally take about 5½ hours heading to Kauai, but only 4½ hours on the return, due to prevailing winds.)

United Airlines (www.united.com; ✆ 800/225-5825) flies nonstop to Kauai daily from Los Angeles, San Francisco, and Denver. **American Airlines** (www.aa.com; ✆ 800/433-7300) and **Delta Airlines** (www.delta.com; ✆ 800/221-1212) each have nonstop flights from Los Angeles. **US Airways** (www.usairways.com; ✆ **800/428-4322**), which at press time was slowly merging with American Airlines, flies nonstop from Phoenix. American also code-shares on some routes of **Alaska Airlines,** which flies nonstop to Lihue from San Jose, Oakland, and San Diego in California as well as Portland and Seattle in the Pacific Northwest. *Tip:* Upgrading to first class is often easiest and cheapest on Alaska.

Other carriers' service varies by season. **WestJet** (www.westjet.com; ✆ **888/937-8538**) offers its most frequent nonstop flights between Vancouver and Lihue December to March. From late May to mid-September, **Hawaiian Airlines** (www.hawaiian airlines.com; ✆ **800/367-5320**) flies nonstop to Lihue four times a week from Los Angeles and thrice weekly from Oakland.

You can also travel to Lihue via Oahu and Maui. **Hawaiian Airlines** (see above) flies to Kauai up to 19 times a day from Honolulu and four times a day from Kahului, Maui. The Honolulu route lasts about 35 minutes; the Maui route, about 10 minutes more, both using Boeing 717s that seat around 120. **Island Air** (www.islandair.com; ✆ **800/652-6541**) flies twin-engine turboprops, with 64 passengers, from Honolulu six times a day; flights take about 45 minutes.

Note: The view from either side of the plane as you land in Lihue, 2 miles east of the center of town, is arresting. On the left side, passengers have a close look at Haupu Ridge, separating the unspoiled beach of Kipu Kai (seen in "The Descendants") from busy Nawiliwili Harbor; on the right, shades of green demarcate former sugarcane fields, coconut groves, and the ridgeline of Nounou ("Sleeping Giant") to the north.

BY CRUISE SHIP   Several cruise lines call in Kauai's main port of Nawiliwili, but **Norwegian Cruise Lines** (www.ncl.com; ✆ **866/234-7350**) is unusual in offering weekly Hawaii itineraries that include overnight stays on Kauai and Maui, allowing for multiple excursions.

Visitor Information

Before your trip begins, visit www.gohawaii.com/kauai, the website of the **Kauai Visitors Bureau** (✆ **800/262-1400**) and download or view its free "Kauai Vacation Planner." (**Note:** The bureau's location in Lihue's Watumull Plaza, 4334 Rice St., Suite 101, is not the most convenient area for drop-bys, but it's open 8am–3pm weekdays.) Before and during your

Napali Coast cliffs.

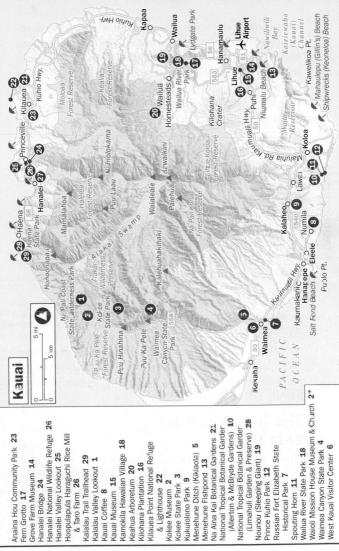

Kauai

5 mi

5 km

PACIFIC OCEAN

Na Pali Coast State Wilderness Park

Na Pali-Kona Forest Reserve

Alakai Swamp

Alakai Wilderness Preserve

Waimea Canyon State Park

Koke'e State Park

Pu'u Ka Pele Forest Reserve

Moloaa Forest Reserve

Keaila Forest Reserve

Lihue-Koloa Forest Reserve

Waialeale

Mamalahoa
Halelea
Namolokama
Kewalkini
Kalehuahakihaki
Palehua
Pihea
Pu'u Laau
Pu'u Ka Pele
Pu'u Hinahina
P'u Ka Pele

Kekaha
Waimea
Hanapepe
Eleele
Salt Pond Beach
Puolo Pt.
Numila
Kalaheo
Lawai
Koloa
Puhi
Lihue
Hanamaulu
Lihue Airport
Wailua
Wailua Homesteads
Wailua River Park
Lydgate Park
Kapaa
Princeville
Kilauea
Hanalei
Ha'ena
Ha'ena State Park
O'haena

Nawiliwili Bay
Niumalu Beach
Kalewewaho (Kauai) Channel
Mahaulepu (Gillin's) Beach
Shipwrecks (Keoneloa) Beach
Kawelikoa Pt.

Kilohana Crater
Waita Reservoir

Kuhio Hwy.
Kaumualii Hwy.
Maluhia Rd.
Olohena Rd.
Honoonapali

Kuamo'o Rd.

Roads: 56, 50, 51, 520, 540, 550, 530, 583

trip, consult the authoritative **Kauai Explorer** website (www.kauaiexplorer.com) for detailed descriptions of 18 of the island's most popular beaches (with or without lifeguards), plus a daily ocean report, surf forecasts, and safety tips. Hikers will also want to read Kauai Explorer's notes on 10 island trails, from easy to super-strenuous. Click on the "Visiting" link of **Kauai County**'s homepage (www.kauai.gov), for links to Kauai Explorer, the Visitors Bureau, bus schedules, camping information, local park and golf facility listings, a festival and events calendar, farmers' market schedules, and more.

The **Poipu Beach Resort Association** (www.poipubeach.org; © **888/744-0888** or 808/742-7444) highlights accommodations, activities, shopping, and dining in the Poipu area; follow the "Contact Us" link to receive a free map of the Koloa and/or Mahaulepu heritage trails.

Check out **Midweek Kauai** (www.midweekkauai.com) online before you arrive and look for a free copy, distributed on Wednesday, once you're on Kauai, to take advantage of the latest entertainment listings and dining specials. The **Garden Island daily** newspaper (http://thegardenisland.com) also publishes events listings, found under the online "Visitors" link.

The Island in Brief
EAST SIDE

Home to the airport, the main harbor, most of the civic and commercial buildings on the island, and the majority of its residents, Kauai's East Side has nevertheless preserved much of its rural character, with green ridges that lead to the shore, red-dirt roads crossing old sugarcane fields, and postcard-pretty

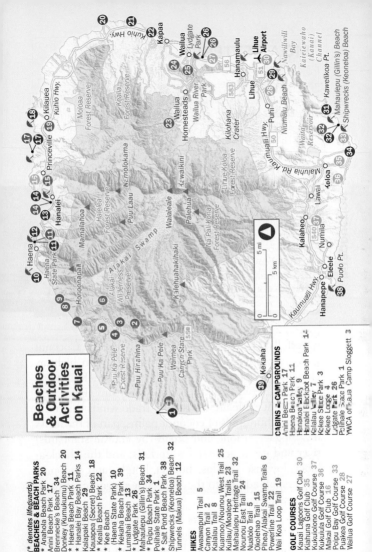

Beaches & Outdoor Activities on Kauai

MOA BETTER: chickens & roosters

One of the first things visitors notice about Kauai is the unusually large number of wild chickens. Mostly rural, Kauai has always had plenty of poultry, including the colorful jungle fowl known as *moa*, but after Hurricane Iniki blew through the island in 1992, they soon were everywhere, reproducing quickly and, in the case of roosters, crowing night and day. While resorts work tirelessly to trap or shoo them away, it's impossible to ensure you'll never be awakened by a rooster; if you're staying outside a resort, it's pretty much guaranteed you will. Light sleepers should bring earplugs.

waterfalls. Heading east from Lihue into the Coconut Coast strip of Wailua and Kapaa, the main highway changes its name and number from the Kaumualii Highway (Hwy. 50) to Kuhio Highway (Hwy. 56). More noticeable are the steady trade winds that riffle fronds of hundreds of coconut palms, part of the area's royal legacy; a long and broad (by Hawaii standards) river and easily accessed waterfalls; and the chock-a-block low-rise condos, budget hotels, and shopping centers, all adding to the East Side's significant rush-hour traffic jams.

LIHUE Bargain hunters will appreciate the county seat's many shopping, lodging, and dining options, but Lihue also boasts cultural assets, from the exhibits at the **Kauai Museum ★★** to hula shows, concerts, and festivals at the **Kauai War Memorial Convention Hall** and **Kauai Community College's Performing Arts Center.** Nearby outdoor attractions include **Kalapaki Beach ★★**, next to the cruise port of Nawiliwili; ATV, ziplining, hiking, and tubing excursions, the latter on old sugarcane irrigation flumes; and kayaking on **Huleia River** past the historic Menehune Fish Pond.

WAILUA **Wailua Falls ★** (seen in the opening credits of "Fantasy Island"), the twin cascades of **Opakeaa Falls ★★**, and a riverboat cruise to **Fern Grotto ★★** are highlights of this former royal compound, which includes remains of stone-walled *heiau* (places of worship), birthstones, and other ancient sites. Kayakers flock to Wailua River, which also offers wakeboarding and water-skiing; the municipal **Wailua Golf Course ★★** is routinely ranked as one of the top in the state; and hikers can choose from three trailheads to ascend **Nounou (Sleeping Giant) mountain.** Highway 56 also passes by the decaying structures of the Coco Palms resort, featured in Elvis Presley's "Blue Hawaii," closed after being damaged by Hurricane Iniki in 1992, and still awaiting restoration at press time. The family-friendly destination of **Lydgate Park ★** connects with one leg of the popular **Ka Ala Hele Makalae coastal path ★★**.

KAPAA The modern condos, motels, and shopping strips of Wailua and Waipouli along the Kuhio Highway eventually segue into **Old Kapaa Town,** where funky boutiques and cafes share plantation-era buildings with mom-and-pop groceries and restaurants. An all-ages hostel and other inexpensive lodgings attract international and budget travelers, including scruffy hikers returning from Kalalau Valley, all of whom seem equally grateful for the laundromat, taquerias, and other signs of civilization. There are sandy beaches here, but they're hidden from the highway until the road rises past **Kealia Beach Park ★**, a boogie-boarding destination and northern terminus of the coastal bike path.

ANAHOLA Just before the East Side becomes the North Shore, the highway dips and passes through this predominantly Native Hawaiian community near Kalalea Mountain, more widely known as **King Kong Mountain,** or just Kong, for its famous profile. Farm stands, a convenience store with homemade goodies, and the roadside **Duane's Ono Char-Burger ★★** can supply provisions for a weekday picnic at **Anahola Beach Park ★**; weekends draw local crowds. (Give the poles and nets of local fishermen a wide berth.)

NORTH SHORE

On a sunny day, there may be no more beautiful place on earth than Kauai's North Shore. It's not half-bad even on a rainy day (more frequent in winter), when waterfalls almost magically appear on verdant mountains; once the showers stop, rainbows soar over farms, taro patches, and long, curving beaches. The speed limit, and pace of life, slow down dramatically as the Kuhio Highway traverses a series of one-lane bridges, climaxing at a suitably show-stopping beach and the trailhead for the breathtaking **Napali Coast.** Two quaint towns—one home to a lighthouse and a seabird preserve—plus the island's most luxurious resort provide ample lodging, dining, and shopping options to match the natural wonders. But it's far enough from the South Shore (minimum 1½ hr. away) that day-trippers may wish they had relocated for a night or two.

KILAUEA A right turn going north on Kuhio Highway brings you to this village of quaint stone buildings and the plantation-vintage **Kong Lung Historic Market Center ★**, a cozy den of cafes, crafts makers, and boutiques. Kilauea Road heads *makai* (seaward) to **Kilauea Point National Wildlife Refuge ★★★**, a sanctuary for nene (the goose-like state bird) and other endangered species, and home to the stubby, red-topped **Kilauea Lighthouse,** built in 1913. Shortly before the preserve is the turnoff for scenic but not-so-secret **Kauapea (Secret) Beach ★★**, a 15-minute hike from a dirt parking lot. Ben Stiller owns a home on the cliffs here; numerous farms, the island's only mini-golf course, and the extensive **Na Aina Kai Botanical Gardens ★★** are the immediate area's other claims to fame. Two miles north, a 5-minute detour off the highway leads to **Anini Beach ★★★**, where a 2-mile fringing reef—the longest on Kauai—creates a shallow, pond-like setting for swimmers, snorkelers, and (when conditions permit) wind-surfers. The long beach is narrow but borders a grassy park with showers, restrooms, picnic tables, and campsites, across from a former polo field.

PRINCEVILLE This 11,000-acre resort and residential development is home to two 18-hole golf courses, steep trails to pocket beaches, and gorgeous views of crescent-shaped Hanalei Bay

Kilauea Lighthouse.

Hanalei.

and iconic **Makana,** the mountain that portrayed Bali Hai in "South Pacific." The **Princeville Shopping Center** holds a few bargain eateries as well as supplies for those staying in one of the many condo or timeshare units; money is generally no object for guests at the **St. Regis Princeville ★★**, Kauai's most luxurious hotel (formerly the Princeville Hotel), with elevator service to the beach below. Just before the highway drops into Hanalei Valley, a **vista point** offers a photo-worthy panorama of the Hanalei River winding through wetland taro patches under towering green peaks.

HANALEI Waiting to cross the first of nine one-lane bridges on the northern stretch of the Kuhio Highway (now Hwy. 560) is a good introduction to the hang-loose ethos of the last real town before road's end. The fringing green mountains share their hue with the 1912 **Waioli Huiia Church ★** and other vintage wooden buildings, some of which house unique shops and moderately priced restaurants. Nearby, the beaches along 2-mile-long, half-moon **Hanalei Bay ★★★** attracts surfers year-round; during the calmer summer conditions, children splash in the water while parents lounge on the sand (a la "The Descendants"). Three county beach parks offer various facilities, including several lifeguard stations; the southernmost **Black Pot Beach Park ★★**, renowned for its 300-foot-long pier, allows camping on weekends and holidays.

HAENA Homes modest and grand hide in the lush greenery of Haena on either side of the Kuhio Highway as it undulates past rugged coves, tranquil beaches, and immense caves, finally dead-ending at **Kee Beach ★★★**, gateway to the Napali Coast and a popular destination for snorkelers (when the surf permits) and campers. **Limahuli Garden & Preserve ★★**, the northern outpost of the National Tropical Botanical Garden, explains Haena's legends, rich cultural heritage, and ecological significance to visitors able to navigate its steep terraces in the shadow

Koloa eucalyptus tree tunnel.

of Mount Makana. Food trucks at **Haena Beach Park** ★★★ supplement the meager if popular dining options, such as Mediterranean Gourmet at the **Hanalei Colony Resort** ★★ (p. 134), the only North Shore resort with rooms right on the sand.

NAPALI COAST ★★★ Often written as Na Pali ("the cliffs"), this dramatically crenellated region that bridges the North Shore and West Side begins not far from where the road ends. Hardy (and some foolhardy) hikers will cross five valleys as they follow the narrow, 11-mile **Kalalau Trail** to its end at beautiful **Kalalau Valley,** with tempting detours to waterfalls along the way. The less ambitious (or more sensible) will attempt shorter stretches, such as the 2-mile hike to Hanakapiai Beach. In summer, physically fit kayakers can spend a day exploring Napali's pristine reefs, sea caves, and hidden coves, which also come into view on catamaran and motorized raft tours (almost all departing from Kauai's West Side); helicopter tours from Lihue, Port Allen, or Princeville offer the quickest if most expensive way to explore Napali's stunning topography (see "Organized Tours," p. 59).

SOUTH SHORE

After a short drive west from Lihue on Kaumualii Highway, a well-marked left turn leads to a mile-long **tree tunnel** of eucalyptus trees, planted in 1911. The well-shaded Maluhia Road is ironically the primary entrance to the sunniest of Kauai's resort areas, Poipu; the South Shore also generally has the calmest ocean conditions in winter. Among outdoor attractions are the geyser-like **Spouting Horn** ★★, the McBryde and Allerton gardens at the **National Tropical Botanical Garden** ★★, family-friendly **Poipu Beach Park** ★★★, and other sandy beaches, including those in rugged **Mahau-lepu ★★**. Pocket coves, surf breaks, and dive sites also make the area ideal for watersports. The only downside: The North Shore is at least 1½ hours away.

POIPU   Three of Kauai's best hotels—the lavish **Grand Hyatt Kauai Resort & Spa ★★★**, the family-friendly **Sheraton Kauai Resort ★★**, and the luxury boutique **Koa Kea Hotel & Resort ★★★**—punctuate the many low-rise condos and vacation homes in the master-planned **Poipu Beach Resort.** Landlubbers can enjoy tennis, 36 holes of golf, and numerous options for dining and shopping, including those at the **Shops at Kukuiula** just outside the resort proper. (To access another 18 holes of golf and the island's best spa, both located in the luxurious Kukuiula residential community, you'll need to stay in one of its $1,000-plus-a-night **Club Cottages ★★**.)

KOLOA   Before the Poipu Bypass Road (Ala Kinoiki) was built, nearly every South Shore beachgoer drove through Hawaii's oldest sugar plantation town, founded in 1835. If you're staying elsewhere, it would be a shame not to visit at least once, to browse the shops and restaurants in quaint storefronts under towering monkeypod trees. Historical plaques on each building give glimpses into the lives of the predominantly Japanese American families who created the first businesses there. Those staying in South Shore condos may find themselves making multiple trips, especially to stock up on produce at the "sunshine market" at noon Mondays, to buy fresh seafood from the **Koloa Fish Market ★**, or purchase other groceries from two local supermarkets; several food trucks also hang out here.

KALAHEO & LAWAI These more residential communities on either side of the main highway are just a 15-minute drive to Poipu Beach Park. On the way, you'll pass through the green fields of rural Omao along Koloa Road (Hwy. 530). Visitors en route to or from Waimea Canyon often refuel at the locally oriented restaurants here; others find lodgings in the relatively inexpensive (but often unlicensed) bed-and-breakfasts. (Keep in mind higher elevations are mistier, with wild chickens roaming even more freely than on the resorts below.) Savvy golfers savor the views and discount fees at upcountry **Kukuiolono Golf Course ★★**. On the west edge of Kalaheo, look for the turnoff for **Kauai Coffee ★★**, whose 3,100 acres produce a dizzying variety of coffees, with free samples at the visitor center.

WEST SIDE

This arid region may have the fewest lodgings, destination restaurants, or swimmable beaches, but the twin draws of **Waimea Canyon State Park ★★★** (rightly hailed as the "Grand Canyon of the Pacific") and the **Kalalau Overlook ★★★** in Kokee State Park make up for the long drive (80 min. to the latter from Poipu). Most Napali snorkel tours are also based here, not to mention two swinging bridges, a weekly art festival, and other good excuses to pull over. Those who can manage the bumpy, unpaved 5-mile road to **Polihale State Park ★★** are rewarded with views of Niihau and Napali, as well as a 17-mile stretch of sand (including the restricted-access **Barking Sands Beach** on the Pacific Missile Range Facility).

ELEELE & PORT ALLEN The main highway from Kalaheo passes by Eleele's plantation homes and several miles of coffee trees before the intersection with Waialo Road. Turn *makai* (seaward) and the road dead-ends a few blocks later at Port Allen, the island's second largest commercial harbor; nearly all boat tours launch from here. Although the area is fairly industrial—and its once-vaunted "Glass Beach" by the oil tanks no longer has enough polished sea glass left to recommend it—the affordable dining and shopping options in Port Allen and adjacent **Eleele Shopping Center** are worth exploring post-snorkel or pre-sunset cruise.

NIIHAU   Just 17 miles across the Kaulakahi Channel from the West Side of Kauai lies the arid island of Niihau (pronounced *"nee-ee-how"*), nicknamed "The Forbidden Island." Casual visitors are not allowed on this privately owned isle, once a cattle and sheep ranch that now supports fewer than 200 full-time residents, all living in the single town of Puuwai, and nearly all Native Hawaiians. Nonresidents can visit on hunting safaris (starting at $1,750) and half-day helicopter tours ($385 per person, five-person minimum) departing from Kauai's West Side. Helicopter tours include lunch and several hours of beach time. You're more likely to see the endangered Hawaiian monk seal than Niihauans, which is how they like it; see **www.niihau.us** for safari and tour details. For more about Niihau culture, visit **www.niihauheritage.org**.

HANAPEPE   An easy detour off Kaumualii Highway, Hanapepe looks like an Old West town, with more than 2 dozen art galleries and quaint stores, plus a couple of cafes, behind rustic wooden facades that inspired Disney's "Lilo and Stitch." Musicians, food trucks, and other vendors truly animate the quiet town during the Friday night festival and artwalk from 6 to 9pm. The other daytime attraction is the **swinging footbridge** ★ over Hanapepe River (rebuilt after 1992's Hurricane Iniki, and marked by a large sign of Hanapepe Rd.). On the other side of the highway, family-friendly **Salt Pond Beach ★★** is named for the traditional Hawaiian salt pans in the red dirt, which gives the salt *('alae)* its distinctive color and flavor.

Hanapepe swinging footbridge.

WAIMEA Hawaii's modern history officially begins here with the landing of British explorer Capt. James Cook on Dec. 20, 1778, 2 days after his ships sailed past Oahu. Despite Cook's orders to the contrary, his sailors quickly mingled with native women, introducing venereal disease to a long-isolated population. Foreigners kept coming to this enclave at the mouth of the Waimea ("reddish-water") River, including a German doctor who tried to claim Kauai for Russia in 1815, and American missionaries in 1820. Today Waimea is attuned to its more recent history of plantation and *paniolo* (cowboy) culture, as well as its Native Hawaiian roots, all of which can be explored at the **West Kauai Visitor Center ★**. Waimea Canyon and Kokee State Park hikers flock to Waimea's shave ice stands and moderately priced dining choices in the late afternoon, while locals seek out **Waimea Theater,** one of the island's few places to catch a movie or concert.

KEKAHA Travelers heading to or from Waimea Canyon may be tempted to go via Kokee Road (Hwy. 55) in Kekaha as a change of pace from Waimea Canyon

Road. Don't bother. There's not much to see in this former sugar town, whose mill operated for 120 years before shutting down in 2000, other than **Kekaha Beach Park,** a long, narrow strand with little sand and often-rough waters. You do have to pass through Kekaha on the way to **Polihale State Park ★★**; if the latter's access road is impassable, stop by Kekaha for a striking view of **Niihau,** 17 miles offshore, or a brilliant sunset. But plan on heading back to Waimea (or farther) for dinner.

GETTING AROUND

Unless you're on a fairly leisurely schedule, you'll need a car or other motorized vehicle to see and do everything on Kauai, which has one major road—one lane in each direction, in most places—that rings the island except along the Napali Coast. During rush hour, from about 6 to 9am and 3 to 6pm, the road between Lihue and Kapaa—the central business district—can turn into a giant parking lot, even with a third, "contra-flow" lane whose direction is determined by time of day. Bypass roads in Kipu (when heading north from Poipu) and Kapaa (when heading south) can alleviate some of the stress, but plan accordingly.

Note: The top speed is 50mph, with many slower sections in residential and business areas. Addresses in this chapter will use Kaumualii Highway for Hwy. 50 and Kuhio Highway for Hwy. 56/560, following local convention. Some addresses use a single number before a dash, which simply indicates one of five island divisions. Since highway addresses can be hard to spot (if marked at all), directions may be given with mile marker numbers, cross streets, and/or the descriptors mauka (toward the mountains) and makai (toward the sea).

The official mailing address of sites in and around Poipu Beach is Koloa, which GPS devices may require. This chapter lists them as "Poipu," as most guides do, to distinguish them from Old Koloa Town and environs.

BY CAR   All of the major car-rental agencies are represented on Kauai. At the airport baggage claim, cross the street to catch one of the frequent shuttle vans to the rental lots. **Avis** (www.avis.com; © **800/230-4898**) also rents cars from the Grand Hyatt Kauai and the Princeville Airport. Be sure to book early for peak periods. **Discount Hawaii Car Rental** (www.discount hawaiicarrental.com; © **800/292-1939**) may have cheaper options for last-minute bookings; it also offers free pickup for cruise passengers.

BY MOTORCYCLE, MOPED, OR SCOOTER   Riders 21 and older with a heavyweight motorcycle license can rent a "hog" from **Kauai Harley-Davidson** (www. kauaiharley.com; © **888/690-6233** or 808/212-9469) outside Lihue. Rates start at $179 for 24 hours, with unlimited mileage. Lihue's **Kauai Mopeds** (www. kauai-mopeds.com; © **808/652-7407**) offers two-person scooters with similar age and license restrictions; daily rates start at $75 for models with a top speed of 52mph, and $110 for those reaching 75mph. For cruising back roads (directions provided), those 18 or older with a driver's license can rent a single-person moped with a top speed of 30mph for $65 a day.

BY TAXI OR SHUTTLE   Set by the county, taxi meter rates start at $3, with an additional $3 per mile; it's about $50 to Poipu and $90 to Princeville from the airport, plus 40¢ per item of luggage, and $4 per bulky item. You can also arrange private tours by taxi starting at $120 for 2 hours. Call **Kauai Taxi Company** (www. kauaitaxico.com; ☎ **808/246-9554**) for taxi, limousine, or airport shuttle service. From the airport, solo travelers will find it cheaper ($42 to Poipu, $72 to Princeville) to take the shared-ride **SpeediShuttle** (www.speedishuttle.com; ☎ **877/242-5777**), but be aware it may make multiple stops. **Pono Express** (http://ponoexpress.com; ☎ **800/258-6880**) offers private airport shuttles and sightseeing tours in vans accommodating one to 14 passengers; rate is by vehicle or by hour. Once in Poipu, book a free ride on the **Aloha Spirit Shuttle** (☎ 808/651-9945); the 12-person open-air tram—a former Disneyland people-mover—shuttles locals and visitors around resorts and restaurants from 5 to 10pm daily.

BY BUS **Kauai Bus** (www.kauai.gov/transportation; ☎ **808/246-8110**) continues to expand bus service between Kekaha and Hanalei daily, including stops near several Poipu and Lihue hotels, the central Kapaa hotel corridor, the Princeville Shopping Center, and Hanalei. *Note:* There's also an airport stop, but suitcases, large backpacks, and surfboards are not allowed on the bus. The white-and-green buses, which have small bike racks in front, run more or less hourly from 5:30am to 10:30pm weekdays, and 6:30am to 6pm on weekends and holidays. The fare (exact change only) is $2 for adults and $1 for seniors and children 7 to 18.

BY BIKE Due to narrow (or nonexistent) shoulders along much of the main highway, relying on bicycles for transportation is generally unsafe. For recreational routes, including the coastal **Na Ala Hele Makalae** bike path, see "Biking," p. 96.

[FastFACTS]

Dentists Emergency dental care is available from **Dr. Mark A. Baird,** 4–9768 Kuhio Hwy. (at Keaka Rd.), Kapaa (*(C)* **808/822-9393**), and **Dr. Michael Furgeson,** 4347 Rice St., Lihue (*(C)* **808/246-6960**).

Doctors Walk-ins are accepted from 8am to 7pm weekdays and 8am to 4pm weekends at the **Kauai Medical Clinic's Urgent Care Clinic** (*(C)* **808/245-1532**), 4484 Pahee St., Lihue. The clinic's nonurgent-care facility (*(C)* **808/245-1500**), part of the Wilcox Memorial Hospital complex at 3-3420 Kuhio Hwy., Lihue (makai side, at Ehiku St.), is open for appointments 8am to 5pm weekdays and 8am to noon Saturday. Kauai Medical Clinic also has branches, with

varying hours, in **Koloa,** 5371 Koloa Rd. (*(C)* **808/742-1621**); **Kapaa,** 4-1105 Kuhio Hwy., mauka side, in the **Kapaa Shopping Center** (*(C)* **808/822-3431**); and **Eleele,** 4392 Waialo Rd. (*(C)* **808/335-0499**). **Hale Lea Medicine,** 2460 Oka St. (at Kilauea Rd.), in **Kilauea** (*(C)* **808/828-2885**), serves the North Shore, with appointments offered 9am to 5pm weekdays and 9am to 1pm Saturday.

Emergencies Dial *(C)* **911** for police, fire, and ambulance service.

Hospitals **Wilcox Memorial Hospital,** 3-3420 Kuhio Hwy. (makai side, at Ehiku St.), Lihue (*(C)* **808/245-1100**), has emergency services (*(C)* **808/245-1010**) available 24 hours a day, as do the smaller

Mahelona Memorial Hospital, 4800 Kawaihau Rd., Kapaa (*(C)* **808/823-4166**), and **Kauai Veterans Memorial Hospital,** 4643 Waimea Canyon Dr., Waimea (*(C)* **808/338-9431**).

Internet Access Numerous cafes (including Kauai's four **Starbucks** outlets; www.starbucks.com) offer free Wi-Fi hotspots; many hotels offer free Wi-Fi in public areas or for a fee in rooms. All Hawaii public libraries have free Wi-Fi but require a library card ($10 nonresidents, good for 3 months). Kauai's branches are in Hanapepe, Kapaa, Koloa, Lihue, Princeville, and Waimea; all are closed Sunday. See http://libraries hawaii.org for details on locations, hours, and reserving a personal computer with Wi-Fi (click on "Services").

Police   For non-emergencies, call ©️ **808/241-1711.**

Post Office   **The main post office** is at 4441 Rice St., Lihue, open 8am to 4pm weekdays and 9am to 1pm Saturday; hours vary at the 14 other offices across the island. To find the one nearest you, visit www.usps.com or call ©️ **800/275-8777.**

Weather   For current weather conditions and forecasts, call the **National Weather Service** at ©️ **808/245-6001.** For the daily ocean report, including surf advisories, visit **www.kauaiexplorer.com/ocean_report**.

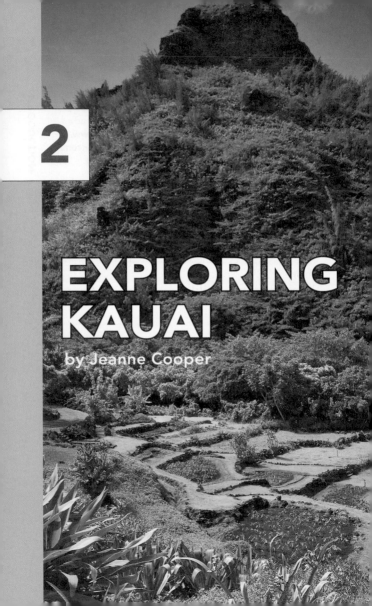

EXPLORING KAUAI

by Jeanne Cooper

A WEEK ON KAUAI

Because much of the Garden Island, including the Napali Coast, is inaccessible to cars, a week will *just* suffice to view its beauty. To save driving time, split your stay between the North and South shores (detailed below) or stay on the East Side.

DAY 1: Arrival, Lunch & a Scenic Drive ★★★

From the airport, stop by **Hamura's Saimin Stand** (p. 159) or another **Lihue** lunch counter (see "Plate Lunch, Bento & Poke," p. 160) for a classic taste of Kauai, before driving through the bustling Coconut Coast on your way to the serenity of the rural **North Shore** (p. 39). Soak in the views at the **Kilauea Point National Wildlife Refuge & Lighthouse** (p. 42), and then poke around Kilauea's **Kong Lung Historic Market Center** (p. 186).

Kayaking in Hanalei River.

FACING PAGE: **The Makana Mountain Range at Limahuli Tropical Botanical Garden and Preserve**

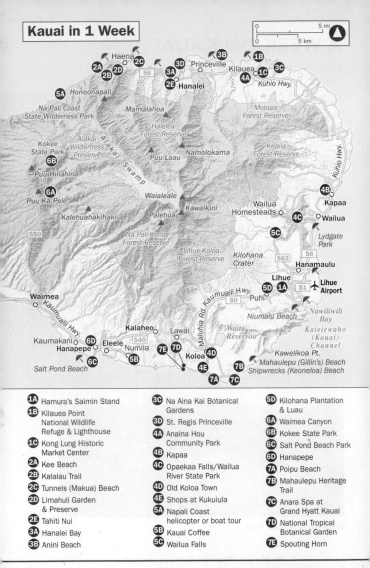

Kauai in 1 Week

0 — 5 mi	
0 — 5 km	

Haena
2A **2B** **2D** **2C**
Honoonapali
5A
Na Pali Coast State Wilderness Park

3D **3A** **3B** Princeville
2E Hanalei
Kilauea **1B** **1C** **3C**
4A Kuhio Hwy.

56

Mamalahoa
Halelea Forest Reserve
Puu Laau
Namolokama

Moloaa Forest Reserve

Alakai Wilderness Preserve
Alakai Swamp

Kokee State Park
6B
Puu Hinahina

Kealia Forest Reserve

Waialeale
Kawaikini

Wailua Homesteads
4C **4B** Kapaa
Wailua
5C
Lydgate Park

6A
Puu Ka Pele
Kalehuahakihaki
Palehua
Na Pali-Kona Forest Reserve
Lihue-Koloa Forest Reserve
Kilohana Crater

583
56
Hanamaulu
Lihue
5D **1A** Lihue Airport
Puhi
51

Waimea
Kaumualii Hwy.
50 Kaumualii Hwy. Maluhia Rd.
Niumalu Beach
Nawiliwili Bay
Kaieiewaho (Kauai) Channel

Waita Reservoir
Kalaheo
Lawai
Kaumakani
Hanapepe **6D** Eleele Numila **5B** **7E** **7D** **4D** Koloa **4E** **7B** **7C**
6C
Salt Pond Beach
7A
Kawelikoa Pt.
Mahaulepu (Gillin's) Beach
Shipwrecks (Keoneloa) Beach

26

1A Hamura's Saimin Stand
1B Kilauea Point National Wildlife Refuge & Lighthouse
1C Kong Lung Historic Market Center
2A Kee Beach
2B Kalalau Trail
2C Tunnels (Makua) Beach
2D Limahuli Garden & Preserve
2E Tahiti Nui
3A Hanalei Bay
3B Anini Beach

3C Na Aina Kai Botanical Gardens
3D St. Regis Princeville
4A Anaina Hou Community Park
4B Kapaa
4C Opaekaa Falls/Wailua River State Park
4D Old Koloa Town
4E Shops at Kukuiula
5A Napali Coast helicopter or boat tour
5B Kauai Coffee
5C Wailua Falls

5D Kilohana Plantation & Luau
6A Waimea Canyon
6B Kokee State Park
6C Salt Pond Beach Park
6D Hanapepe
7A Poipu Beach
7B Mahaulepu Heritage Trail
7C Anara Spa at Grand Hyatt Kauai
7D National Tropical Botanical Garden
7E Spouting Horn

DAY 2: Hike & Snorkel the North Shore ★★★

Thanks to the time difference, you'll have a head start driving across the nine one-lane bridges on the way to the end of the road and popular **Kee Beach** (p. 71). If conditions permit, hike at least a half hour out on the challenging **Kalalau Trail** (p. 40), for glimpses of the stunning **Napali Coast,** or tackle the first 2 miles to **Hanakapiai Beach,** 3 to 4 hours round-trip. After (or instead of) hiking, snorkel at **Kee** and equally gorgeous **Tunnels (Makua) Beach** (p. 73), accessed from **Haena Beach Park** (p. 73). Eat lunch in Haena, and then spend time in the jewel-box setting of **Limahuli Garden and Preserve** (p. 43). Return to Hanalei to explore shops and galleries; after dinner, enjoy live Hawaiian music at the venerable **Tahiti Nui** (p. 195).

DAY 3: Adventures in Hanalei ★★★

The day begins on **Hanalei Bay, kayaking, surfing,** or **snorkeling** (see "Watersports," p. 79) or just frolicking at one of the three different beach parks. If waves are too rough, head instead to lagoon-like **Anini Beach** (p. 68). In the afternoon, try ziplining (p. 115) or horseback riding (p. 110) amid waterfalls and green mountains; the less adventurous (who've booked in advance) can tour delightful **Na Aina Kai Botanical Gardens** (p. 44). Savor views of Hanalei Bay and "Bali Hai" over cocktails at the **St. Regis Princeville** (p. 135) before dinner at **Bar Acuda** (p. 163).

DAY 4: Nature & Culture En Route to Poipu ★★

After breakfast, head south. Visit Kilauea's **Anaina Hou Community Park** (p. 33) for Kauai-themed mini-golf in a botanical garden or a hike or bike along the scenic Wai Koa loop trail. Stop for a bite at a funky cafe in **Kapaa,** and then drive to **Opaekaa Falls** and see the cultural sites of **Wailua River State Park** (p. 37). After crossing through busy Lihue, admire the scenery on the way to **Old Koloa Town** (p. 188), where you can browse the quaint shops before checking into your Poipu lodgings. Pick a dinner spot from the many choices in the **Shops at Kukuiula** (p. 195).

DAY 5: Napali by Boat or Helicopter ★★★

Splurge on a **snorkel boat** or **Zodiac raft tour** (p. 79) to the **Napali Coast,** or a **helicopter tour** (p. 59) for amazing views of Napali, Waimea

Na Pali Coast viewed from helicopter.

Canyon, waterfalls, and more. After your boat returns, hoist a draft beer at **Kauai Island Brewery & Grill** (p. 195). For helicopter tours, most of which depart from Lihue, book a late-morning tour (after rush hour); have lunch in Lihue, and then drive to **Wailua Falls** (p. 36) before perusing the shops, tasting rum, or riding the train at **Kilohana Plantation** (p. 34).

DAY 6: Waimea Canyon & Kokee State Park ★★★

Start your drive early to "the Grand Canyon of the Pacific," **Waimea Canyon** (p. 56). Stay on the road through forested **Kokee State Park** (p. 52) to the **Kalalau Valley Lookout** (p. 46), and wait for mists to part for a magnificent view. Stop by the **Kokee Museum** (p. 109) for trail information for a hike after lunch at **Kokee Lodge** (p. 179). Or hit the waves at **Salt Pond Beach** or stroll through rustic **Hanapepe** (p. 77), home to a **Friday night art walk** (p. 196).

DAY 7: Beach & Spa Time in Poipu ★★★

Spend the morning at glorious **Poipu Beach** (p. 75) before the crowds arrive, and then head over to **Shipwrecks (Keoneloa) Beach** (p. 76) to hike along the coastal **Mahaulepu Heritage Trail** (p. 108). Later, indulge in a spa treatment at **Anara Spa** at the Grand Hyatt Kauai (p. 140) or take a tour (booked in advance) at the **National Tropical Botanical Garden** (p. 43). Check out the flume of **Spouting Horn** (p. 51) before sunset cocktails at **RumFire Poipu Beach** in the **Sheraton Kauai** (p. 142) and dinner at **The Beach House** (p. 169) or **Red Salt** (p. 172).

ATTRACTIONS & POINTS OF INTEREST

EAST SIDE

Fern Grotto ★★ NATURAL ATTRACTION The journey as much as the destination has kept this tourist attraction popular since 1946, when the Smith family first began offering boat trips 2 miles up the Wailua River to this lava-rock cave with lush ferns hanging from its roof. The open-air barge cruises past royal and sacred sites of antiquity, noted by a guide, until it arrives at a landing that's a short walk from the grotto. Although you can no longer enter the cave, an observation deck provides a decent view, as well as the stage for a musician and hula dancer to perform the "Hawaiian Wedding Song" (made famous by Elvis Presley's 1961 film "Blue Hawaii," filmed nearby at the Coco Palms.) The tour, a total of 80 minutes, includes music and hula on the return trip down Hawaii's longest river (see "Wailua River State Park," below.) **Note:** Kayakers may visit Fern Grotto on their own, as long as their arrival or departure doesn't overlap with those of the tour boats; see "Kayaking" on p. 83 for rental information. **Kamokila Hawaiian Village** (see below), across the river from the grotto, also offers guided outrigger canoe tours and kayak rentals.

2 miles inland from Wailua Marina State Park, south side of Wailua River off Kuhio Hwy. Tours via **Smith's Motor Boats** (www.smithskauai.com; ✆ **808/821-6895**) depart at 9:30 and 11am, and 2 and 3:30pm. $20 adults, $10 children 3–12 (book online for 10% off).

Grove Farm Museum ★ HISTORIC SITE/ MUSEUM AOL cofounder Steve Case may own Grove Farm now, but little else has changed at the

100-acre homestead of George N. Wilcox. The son of missionaries in Hanalei, Wilcox bought the original 900-acre Grove Farm from a German immigrant in 1864 and turned it into a successful sugar plantation. Two-hour guided tours start at the original plantation office and include the two-story main home, still furnished with vintage decor and Hawaiiana, plus extensive gardens and intriguing outbuildings, such as a Japanese teahouse built in 1898. *Note:* Tours may be canceled on rainy days. Contact the museum about its free rides on restored, plantation-era steam trains near the old Lihue Sugar Mill, usually offered the second Thursday of each month. 4050 Nawiliwili Rd. (Hwy. 58), at Pikaka St., Lihue. http://grove farm.org. © **808/245-3202.** Admission $20 adults, $10 children 11 and under. Open only for guided tours Mon and Wed–Thurs at 10am and 1pm; reservations required.

Kamokila Hawaiian Village ★ CULTURAL ATTRACTION   This family-run 4-acre compound of thatched huts and other replica structures, opened in 1979 on the site of an ancient village, always looks in need of more upkeep. Nevertheless, it serves as a pleasantly low-key introduction to traditional Hawaiian culture, especially for families. Peacocks and wild chickens roam around huts designated for healing, sleeping, eating, birthing, and more, all part of a self-guided tour, with displays inside some huts. You're also welcome to sample fruit hanging from the many labeled trees, including mountain apple, guava, and mango. A stand-in for an African village in the 1995 movie "Outbreak," Kamokila is known as having the fastest (and cheapest) access for paddling to **Uluwehi (Secret) Falls** ★★, **Fern Grotto** ★★, and several swimming holes. Off Kuamoo Rd. (Hwy. 580), Kapaa. Look for sign across from Opaekaa Falls, 2 miles inland from Kuhio Hwy.; entrance road is steep. http://villagekauai.com. © **808/823-0559.** Admission

Fern Grotto.

$5 adults, $3 children 3–12. Daily canoe and kayak rentals $35 adults, $30 children 3–12. Guided outrigger canoe rides: **Secret Falls** $30 adults, $20 children 3–12; **swimming hole** $20 adults, $15 children 3–12; **Fern Grotto** $20 adults, $15 children 3–12. Daily 9am–5pm.

Kauai Museum ★★ MUSEUM   The fascinating geological and cultural history of Kauai and Niihau are well-served in this compact museum that's just a little too good to save for a rainy day. Visitors enter through the Wilcox Building, the former county library built in 1924 with a somewhat incongruous Greco-Roman facade on its lava rock exterior. Inside are temporary exhibitions, a gift shop with an extensive book selection, and the Heritage Gallery of koa-lined cases brimming with exquisite Niihau shell lei and beautifully carved wooden bowls (*umeke*) and other furnishings that once belonged to royalty. (There's even a display of Iolani Palace china no doubt coveted by the Honolulu site's curators.)

The adjacent Rice Building, a two-story lava rock structure opened in 1960, tells "The Story of Kauai." The main floor's exhibits focus on the island's volcanic origins through the arrival of Polynesian voyagers and the beginning of Western contact, including the whalers and missionaries who quickly followed in Capt. Cook's wake. Rare artifacts include a torn piece of a Niihau makaloa mat, a highly prized bed covering and art form that was essentially abandoned in the late 19th century. On the second floor, the story shifts to that of the plantation era, when waves of immigrants fomented the complex stew known as "local" culture, and continues through World War II. One display illuminates the little-known story of the Japanese pilot who crashed on Niihau during the Pearl Harbor attack, took captives, and was eventually overpowered by several Native Hawaiian islanders after others had rowed to Kauai to alert authorities.

Tip: Try to time a visit on the first Friday of the month, when the museum holds a traditional pa'ina (feast) with a plate lunch, live music, and hula in the courtyard at 11:30am; admission is $20, reservations recommended.

4428 Rice St., Lihue. www.kauaimuseum.org. © **808/245-6931.** Admission $10 adults, $8 seniors, $6 students 13–17, $2 children 6–12 (free admission to gift shop). 1st Sat of every month admission $8 adults, $6 seniors, $2 students 13–17, $1 children 6–12. Mon–Sat 10am–5pm. Guided tours Mon–Fri 10:30am free with admission. Check "Events" listings online for frequent crafts workshops and festivals.

Keahua Arboretum ★ GARDEN Part of the Lihue-Koloa Forest Reserve, this grove of rainbow eucalyptus (named for its colorful bark), monkeypod, and mango trees may not be well-maintained from an arborist's standpoint, but it's a nifty, family-friendly place to picnic and dip in a cool stream, particularly after a hike on the nearby **Kuilau Trail** (p. 106). A short loop trail leads to a "swimming hole" with a rope swing; be sure to wear mosquito repellent. Facilities include picnic tables, pavilions, and composting toilets. Part of the fun is getting here: The main parking area and picnic tables are across a spillway at the paved end of Kuamoo Road, about 5 miles inland from Opaekaa Falls. (Please use good judgment when deciding if it's safe to ford the stream.) This is also where adventurers will find the trailhead for the 13-mile **Powerline Trail** (p. 107), which ends near Princeville, and the extremely rugged, unpaved Wailua Forestry Management Road, the start of much more challenging treks to the "Jurassic Park" gates (just poles now) and Waialeale's "Blue Hole."

End of Kuamoo Rd., Kapaa. 7 miles inland from intersection with Kuhio Hwy., Wailua. www.dlnr.hawaii.gov/forestry/frs/reserves/kauai/lihue-koloa. © **808/274-3433.** Free admission. Daily during daylight hours.

Kilohana Plantation ★★ FARM/ATTRACTIONS Longtime Kauai visitors might remember this 105-acre portion of a former sugar plantation for the unique shops tucked into a handsome 1930s mansion, its luau, or the courtyard **Gaylord's** restaurant, named for original owner Gaylord Wilcox. While all of those elements are still there, so many changes have happened in recent years that few should skip a visit here. In addition to sampling the wares of the **Mahiko Lounge,** the 2013 conversion of the mansion's former living room (see "Kauai Nightlife," p. 194), tipplers ages 21 and up can create their own mini mai tai

Kilohana Plantation.

around a gleaming wood bar in the **Koloa Rum Co.**'s tasting room (www.koloarum.com; © **808/246-8900**). There's a 16-person maximum per free, half-hour tasting (see website for the varying hours), while an all-ages store sells the locally made spirits as well as non-alcoholic gifts.

The first new railroad to open on the island in almost 100 years, the **Kauai Plantation Railway** (www.kauaiplantationrailway.com; © **808/245-7245**) uses a restored diesel locomotive to pull open-sided cars with trolley-style bench seats around a 2½-mile track. The train passes by Kilohana's gardens growing 50 varieties of fruit and vegetables and through flowering fields and forest on a 40-minute narrated tour that includes a stop to feed goats, sheep, and wild pigs (watch your hands). It departs five times daily between 10am and 2pm. Tickets are $18 for adults and $14 for kids 3 to 12; reservations are not required, but you can receive a 15% Web discount by calling ahead and requesting it. On weekdays, you can also combine a train ride that starts at 9:30am with an easy hike, lunch, and orchard tour that costs $75 for adults and $65 for kids 3 to 12 (ask for the 15% Web discount when reserving).

On Tuesday and Friday, the railway offers an "express train" package with **Luau Kalamaku** (www. luaukalamaku.com; ✆ **808/833-3000**), a theatrical-style show with dinner buffet in a specially-built theater-in-the-round near the Wilcox mansion. The train-luau package is $113 for adults and $83 for teens 13 to 18, and $59 kids 3 to 12 (ask for Web discount of 10% when reserving). For the luau dinner and show only, it's $95 for adults, $65 for teens, and $45 for children.

3-2087 Kaumualii Hwy., Lihue, just north of Kauai Community College and a half-mile south of Kukui Grove Shopping Center. www.kilohanakauai.com. ✆ **808/245-5608.** Mansion opens at 10:30am daily; restaurant, lounge, and shop hours vary.

Lydgate Park ★ PARK   This is one of the rare beach parks in Hawaii where the facilities almost outshine the beach. Hidden behind the Aston Aloha Beach Resort, **Lydgate Beach ★** (p. 67) offers two rock-walled ponds for safe swimming and snorkeling. But many families also gravitate to the 58-acre, half-mile-long park for the immense **Kamalani Playground,** a sprawling wooden fantasy fortress decorated with ocean-themed ceramics. It was built by 7,000 volunteers in 1994; many returned 7 years later for the **Kamalani Kai Bridge** expansion, an equally whimsical structure that leads to observation decks and small pavilions in the dunes. Stroller pushers, joggers, and cyclists also pick up the 2.5-mile southern leg of the **Ka Ala Hele Makalae coastal path** here; Lydgate's northern end is next to **Hikinaakala Heiau,** part of Wailua River State Park (below). Facilities include picnic tables, restrooms, showers, pavilions, and campgrounds.

Leho Dr. at Nalu Rd., Wailua. From intersection of Kuhio Hwy. and Hwy. 51 outside of Lihue, head 2½ miles north to Leho Dr. and turn right. Turn right again on Nalu Rd. and follow to parking areas. Free admission. Daily during daylight hours

Wailua River State Park ★★ PARK/HISTORIC SITE   Ancients called the Wailua River "the river of the great sacred spirit." Seven temples once stood along this 20-mile river, Hawaii's longest, fed by the some 450 inches of rain that fall annually on Waialeale at the island's center. The entire district from the river mouth to the summit of Waialeale was once royal land, originally claimed by Puna, a Tahitian priest said to have arrived in one of the first double-hulled voyaging canoes to come to Hawaii.

Cultural highlights include the remains of four major temples; royal birthing stones, used to support female alii in labor; a stone bell used to announce such births; and the ancient stone carvings known as petroglyphs, found on boulders near the mouth of the Wailua River when currents wash away enough sand. Many sites have **Wailua Heritage Trail** markers; go to www.wailuaheritagetrail.org for map and details. The **Hawaii State Parks website** (www.hawaiistate parks.org) also has downloadable brochures on two heiau (temples) that each enclosed an acre of land: Just north of Lydgate Park, next to the mouth of the Wailua River, **Hikinaakala Heiau** once hosted sunrise ceremonies; its name means "rising of the sun." Now reduced to its foundation stones, it's part of a sacred oceanfront complex that also appears to have been a place of refuge (puuhonua). Two miles up

Kuamoo Road (Hwy. 580) from the main highway, **Poliahu Heiau** shares its name with the goddess of snow (admittedly a weather phenomenon more common to the Big Island). The 5×5-feet lava rock walls—attributed to menehune, and most likely erected by the 1600s—may have surrounded a luakini, used for human sacrifice. (Please don't stand on the rock walls, enter the center of the heiau, or leave "offerings," which is considered disrespectful.)

Across the road from Poliahu is an ample parking lot and sidewalk leading to the overlook of 40-foot-wide, 151-foot-tall **Opaekaa Falls ★★**. Named for the "rolling shrimp" that were once abundant here, this twin cascade glistens under the Makaleha ridge—but don't be tempted to try to find a way to swim beneath it. The danger keep out signs and wire fencing are there because two hikers fell to their deaths from the steep, slippery hillside in 2006.

You're allowed to wade at the base of the 100-foot **Uluwehi Falls ★★**, widely known as Secret Falls, but first you'll need to paddle a kayak several miles to the narrow right fork of the Wailua River, and then hike about 30 to 45 minutes on a trail with a stream crossing. Many kayak rental companies offer guided tours here (see "Kayaking," p. 83).

Also part of the state park, but at the end of Maalo Road (Hwy. 583), 4 miles inland from the main highway in Kapaia, is equally scenic **Wailua Falls ★**. Pictured in the opening credits of "Fantasy Island," this double-barreled waterfall drops at least 80 feet (some say 113) into a large pool. Go early to avoid crowds and enjoy the morning light. *Note:* The state has also installed fencing here to block attempts at a hazardous descent.

Opaekaa Falls and **Poliahu Heiau:** Off Kuamoo Rd., 2 miles inland from intersection with Kuhio Hwy. just north of Wailua River Bridge. **Hikinaakala Heiau:** South side of Wailua River mouth; access from Lydgate Park (p. 507). **Wailua Falls:** end of Maalo Rd. (Hwy. 583), 4 miles north (inland) of intersection with Kuhio Hwy. in Kapaia, near Lihue. www.hawaiistateparks.org/parks/kauai. © **808/274-3444.** Free admission. Daily during daylight hours.

NORTH SHORE

Anaina Hou Community Park ★ GARDEN/ATTRACTIONS Anywhere else, a mini-golf park might be easily dismissed as a tourist trap. On Kauai, it's a wonderful introduction for families to the Garden Island's tropical flora and cultural history, and just one of several visitor attractions in this inviting park. The well-landscaped, 18-hole **Kauai Mini Golf & Botanical Gardens** (www.kauaiminigolf.com; © **808/828-2118**) showcases native species, Polynesian introductions, plantation crops, Japanese and Chinese gardens, and modern plantings. Open daily, it's quite popular on weekends, as are the adjacent mini skate park and playground. For a more natural experience, walk or mountain bike along the park's 5-mile **Wai Koa Loop Trail.** This unpaved, rolling path starts in a forest of albizia and Cook Island pines and passes through a working farm and mahogany orchard before reaching the highlights of the Kalihiwai Lagoon reservoirs and stone dam lookout. The trail is open during daylight hours and access is free, but because it crosses private property, you're asked to sign a waiver at the golf course's **Namahana Cafe,** a pleasant cafe and gift shop where you can also rent a mountain bike for the day or longer. Donated by the founder of E-Trade and his wife, Bill and Joan Porter, the 500-acre community park also offers skateboard ramps, a dog park, and farmer's markets (Sat 9am–1pm, Mon 4pm–dusk).

5-2723 Kuhio Hwy., Kilauea. Heading north from Lihue, pass the Shell station at Kolo Rd. turnoff to Kilauea; entrance is 500 yards farther on the left, at Kauai Mini Golf sign. www.anaina hou.org. © **808/828-2118. Anaina Hou Community Park:** Free admission. **Kauai Mini Golf:** Daily 10am–8pm (last golfers start at 7:30pm); admission $18 ages 11 and up, $10 children 5–10, free for children 4 and under. **Wai Koa Loop Trail:** Free admission.

Haena State Park ★★ NATURAL ATTRACTIONS

Besides snorkeling at pretty **Kee Beach ★★★** (p. 71), in the shadow of jutting Makana (Bali Hai) mountain, or camping, the main allure of this state park is that it's at the end of the road, the perfect place to witness sunset after a leisurely drive to the North Shore. It's also the start of the 11-mile **Kalalau Trail** (p. 45), meaning its large parking area can still fill up quickly—if so, just turn around and you'll find overflow parking farther away. At the western end of Kee Beach, an uphill path leads to an ancient hula platform and temple *(heiau)*, where hula *halau* (schools) still conduct formal ceremonies; please be respectful by covering up before hiking up here, and leave any offerings undisturbed. Before the road's end, you'll also want to stop for a look at two **wet caves,** former sea caves left high but not dry when the ocean receded; chilly water percolates into them from a spring that's affected by the nearby tides. The larger **Waikanaloa** is just off the road, with parking in front. From there it's a short, uphill walk to the craggier **Waikapalae,** seen as the entrance to the Fountain of Youth in "Pirates of the Caribbean: On Stranger Tides." Note that swimming is neither allowed nor considered safe.

Northern end of Kuhio Hwy., Haena. www.hawaiistateparks.
org/kauai. © **808/274-3444.** Free admission. Daily during
daylight hours.

**Hoopulapula Haraguchi Rice Mill & Taro
Farm ★★** FARM/MUSEUM Many of the green
taro patches seen from the Hanalei Valley Overlook
belong to the 30-acre **Haraguchi Farm,** where fifth-
generation farmer Lyndsey Haraguchi-Nakayama,
family members, and other laborers tend Hawaii's
revered staple by hand. When the Haraguchis bought
the farm in 1924, the wetlands were rice paddies,
planted by Chinese immigrants in the 1800s. With the
purchase came a wooden rice mill that stayed in oper-
ation until 1960, the only such structure left in the
state. Restored several times after fire and hurricanes,
the **Hoopulapula Haraguchi Rice Mill** is now a
nonprofit "agrarian museum" and, like the farm, is
open to visitors only as part of a weekly guided tour.
Adults will appreciate hearing Haraguchi-Nakayama's
stories from the family's rice-growing days, when children would be tasked with keeping grain hungry birds
away; she'll also point out the endangered birds in this
corner of the **Hanalei National Wildlife Refuge.**
Current challenges include frequent floods and large
apple snails that eat young shoots. Once you've begun
to appreciate the hard work of cultivating *kalo,* as the
Hawaiians call taro, it's time to sample fluffy, freshly
pounded taro rolled in coconut. The tour begins at the
family's roadside stand in Hanalei with a taro smoothie
and ends there with a tasty lunch.
Check in at Hanalei Taro & Juice stand, 5-5070 Kuhio Hwy.,
Hanalei, 1¼ miles west of Hanalei Bridge. www.haraguchirice
mill.org. © **808/651-3399.** Tours $87 adults, $52 children 5–12;
Wed 9:45am by reservation only.

Kilauea Point National Wildlife Refuge & Lighthouse ★★★ NATURE PRESERVE/LIGHTHOUSE   Two miles north of Kilauea's historic town center is a 200-acre headland habitat—the island's only wildlife refuge open to the public—that includes cliffs, two rocky wave-lashed bays, and a tiny islet serving as a jumping-off spot for seabirds. You can easily spot red-footed boobies, which nest in trees and shrubs, and wedge-tailed shearwaters, which burrow in nests along the cliffs between March and November (they spend winters at sea). Scan the skies for the great frigate bird, which has a 7-foot wingspan, and the red-tailed tropicbird, which performs aerial acrobatics during the breeding season (March–Aug). Endangered nene, the native goose reintroduced to Kauai in 1982, often stroll close to visitors, but please don't feed them. Mounted telescopes and loaner binoculars from the refuge's visitor center may bring into view the area's marine life, from spinner dolphins, Hawaiian monk seals, and green sea turtles year-round to humpback whales on their winter migrations. Nevertheless, the primary draw for many of the refuge's half-million annual visitors is the **Kilauea Point Lighthouse** (www.kilauealighthouse.org), built in 1913 and listed on the National Register of Historic Places. The 52-foot-tall white lighthouse wears a jaunty red cap above its 7,000-pound Fresnel lens, whose beam could be seen from 20 miles away before it was deactivated in 1976. Docents offer free tours of the beacon, officially renamed the Daniel K. Inouye Lighthouse in 2013, in memory of the state's late senator.

End of Kilauea Rd., Kilauea. www.fws.gov/refuge/kilauea_ point. ✆ **808/828-1413.** Admission $5 ages 16 and up; free for ages 15 and under. Tues–Sat 10am–4pm. Heading north on Kuhio Hwy., turn right on Kolo Rd., just past mile marker 23, then left on Kilauea Rd. and follow 2 miles to entrance.

Limahuli Garden and Preserve ★★ GARDEN
Out on Kauai's far North Shore, beyond Hanalei and the last wooden bridge, there's a mighty cleft in the coastal range where ancestral Hawaiians lived in what can only be called paradise. Carved by a waterfall stream known as Limahuli, the lush valley sits at the foot of steepled cliffs that Hollywood portrayed as Bali Hai in "South Pacific." This small, almost secret garden, part of the National Tropical Botanical Garden, is ecotourism at its best. Here botanists hope to save Kauai's endangered native plants, some of which grow in the 1,000-acre Limahuli Preserve behind the garden, an area that is off-limits to visitors. The self-guided tour encourages visitors to walk slowly up and down the garden's .75-mile loop trail (resting places provided) to view indigenous and "canoe" plants, which are identified in Hawaiian and English, as well as plantation-era imported flowers and fruits. From taro to sugarcane, the plants brought over in Polynesians' voyaging canoes (hence their nickname) tell the story of the people who cultivated them for food, medicine, clothing, shelter, and decoration; note the traditional hut with a thatched roof made from the indigenous loulu palm. The tour booklet also shares some of the fascinating legends inspired by the area's dramatically perched rocks and Makana mountain, where men once hurled firebrands (*'oahi*) that floated far out to sea. You'll learn even more on one of the daily 2½-hour guided tours, but be sure to reserve well in advance.

5-8291 Kuhio Hwy., Haena, ½-mile past mile marker 9. www.
ntbg.org/gardens/limahuli.php. © **808/826-1053.** Self-guided tour $20 adults, $10 college students with ID, free for
children 18 and younger with paying adult; Tues–Sat 9:30am–
4pm. Guided tour $40 adults, $20 college students with ID, free
for children 10–18 with paying adult (younger children not
recommended); Tues–Sat 10am by reservation only, credit card
required.

**Na Aina Kai Botanical Gardens & Sculpture
Park ★★** GARDEN Off the North Shore's beaten
path, this magical garden and hardwood plantation
covers 240 acres, sprinkled with 70 life-size (some
larger-than-life-size) whimsical bronze statues. It's the
place for avid gardeners, as well as people who think
they don't like botanical gardens. It has something for
everyone: a poinciana maze, an orchid house, a lagoon

Na Aina Kai Botanical Gardens.

with spouting fountains, a Japanese teahouse, a streamside path to a hidden beach—even re-creations of traditional Navajo and Hawaiian compounds. A host of different tours is available, from 1½ hours ($35) to 5 hours ($85) long, ranging from casual, guided strolls and rides in small covered trams to treks from one end of the gardens to the ocean. Currently, these tours are open only to adults and children 13 and older. Younger kids are invited on tours of the wonderful "Under the Rainbow" garden, featuring a gecko hedge maze, a tropical jungle gym, a pint-size railroad, a treehouse in a rubber tree, and a 16-foot-tall Jack-and-the-Beanstalk giant with a 33-foot wading pool below. The 2 hour tour is $35 for adults and $20 for kids 13 and under, and includes the maze and koi pond in the formal gardens. *Tip:* Most tours are limited to eight or nine guests, and the gardens are closed weekends and Monday, so book a tour before you arrive. Families should note the last Saturday of each month is usually Keiki (Children's) Day, when the children's garden is open from 9am to noon for just $10; check the website for other seasonal family activities.

4101 Wailapa Rd., Kilauea. www.naainakai.org. ✆ **808/828-0525.** Tours Tues–Fri; most tours start at 9 or 9:30am, with some repeated at 1 or 1:30pm; $35–$85. Dec–April birdwatching tours: Wed 8:30am; $60. Reservations strongly recommended. From Lihue, drive north on Kuhio Hwy. past mile marker 21 and turn right on Wailapa; from Princeville, drive south 6½ miles and take the 2nd left past mile marker 22 onto Wailapa. At road's end, drive through iron gates to visitor center on the right.

Napali Coast State Wilderness Park ★★★

PARK This 15-mile-long crown of serrated ridges and lush valleys is the most impressive of Kauai's

45

natural features—and also its most inaccessible. Only hardy, well-equipped hikers should attempt the full length of the 11-mile **Kalalau Trail,** which begins at Kee Beach and plunges up and down before ending at **Kalalau Valley.** The area's last Hawaiian community lived in this 3-mile-wide, 3-mile-deep valley until the early 1900s. The valley, which can also be viewed from an overlook in **Kokee State Park ★★★** (p. 52), is the setting for Jack London's 1912 short story "Koolau the Leper," based on a true tale of a man who hid from authorities determined to exile him to Molokai. (Today, the bohemian squatters bedevil rangers and others determined to protect the valley's cultural treasures.) Most visitors just huff and puff 4 miles round-trip from Kee Beach to scenic but unswimmable **Hanakapiai Beach,** or make it a daylong adventure by adding a 4-mile, boulder-hopping slog to Hanakapiai Falls (see "Hiking," p. 108).

In late spring and summer, kayakers may explore the sea caves and oceanside waterfalls of Napali, but landing is only allowed at Kalalau and Milolii beaches; Kalalau requires a camping permit, while Milolii allows day use (see "Kayaking," p. 83). **Nualolo Kai,** the lower, seaside portion of another valley, has many archaeological sites, some under restoration, but only motorized raft (Zodiac) tours may land here (see "Boat & Raft [Zodiac] Tours," p. 79). The natural arch at **Honopu Beach** is a highlight of the snorkel cruises passing by, but may be examined closely only by the few capable of swimming here from Kalalau or a moored kayak—a dicey proposition much of the year.

The easiest, and most expensive, way to survey Napali's stunning land- and seascape is by helicopter (see "Helicopter Tours," p. 59). However you experience it, though, you'll understand why Napali remains the star of countless calendars, postcards, and screen savers.

Between Kee Beach and Polihale State Park. www.hawaiistate parks.org/parks/kauai/napali.cfm. © **808/274-3444.**

Waioli Mission House Museum and Church ★

HISTORIC SITE/MUSEUM   Many visitors passing through Hanalei pull over for a photo of **Waioli Huiia Church** (www.hanaleichurch.org; © **808/826-6253**), a 1912 American Gothic wooden church with a steep roof, forest-green walls, and belfry reflecting the shape and hues of the mountains behind it. Nearby is the timber-and-plaster **Mission Hall,** built in 1841 and the oldest surviving church building on Kauai. Hidden by a grove of trees behind it is the two-story **Mission House,** erected in 1837 by the area's first missionaries, who traveled from Waimea via outrigger canoe.

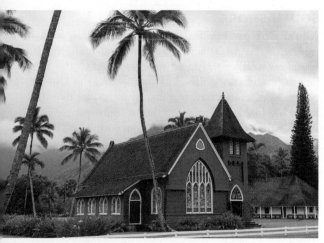

Waioli Huiia Church.

Teachers Abner and Lucy Wilcox and their four sons moved to this two-story, surprisingly airy home in 1846; four more sons were born here while the Wilcoxes instructed native students in English and the newly transliterated Hawaiian language. The homespun Americana—well-thumbed Bibles, braided rugs, and a spinning wheel—is complemented by Hawaiian elements such as ohia wood floors, a lava rock chimney, and lanais. Restored in 1921, the house is open for first-come, first-served guided tours 3 days a week; you'll leave your shoes on the lanai and stay about 30 minutes.

5-5363 Kuhio Hwy., Hanalei. Heading north from Hanalei Bridge, pass Waioli Huiia Church and turn left on the dirt road just before Hanalei School. A dirt parking area is about 150 hundred yards (137 meters) on the left, with a footpath to the house. www.grovefarm.org/waiolimissionhouse. ℂ **808/245-3202.** Requested donation $10 adults, $5 children 5–12. Tours on demand Tues, Thurs, and Sat 9am–3pm.

SOUTH SHORE

Kauai Coffee ★★ FARM Some 4 million coffee trees grow on 3,100 acres of former sugarcane fields from Lawai Valley to Eleele, making Kauai Coffee the largest producer of coffee in Hawaii—and the United States. Kona coffee fans might sniff at the fact that the beans are machine-harvested, but it's surprisingly sustainable for such massive production, with 2,500 miles of drip-irrigation tubes, water recycling, cherry-pulp mulching, and other practices. You can learn all about the coffee growing and roasting process on a free short, self-guided or guided tour, or from a video and displays in the free tasting area behind the gift shop on a covered porch. Let's face it, everyone heads to the latter first: How better to determine the difference between coffee varietals such as Blue Mountain, yellow catuai, or red catuai beans (to name a few) in an equally wide array of roasts and blends? A small snack bar in the tasting room helps take the edge off all that caffeine.

870 Halewili Rd. (Hwy. 540), Kalaheo. www.kauaicoffee.com. © **808/335-0813.** Free admission. Daily 9am–5pm (until 5:30pm Sept–May). Free guided tours daily 10am, noon, and 2 and 4pm. From westbound Kaumualii Hwy., drive through Kalaheo and look for Hwy. 540 on left just outside of town. From that intersection, it's 2½ miles to the visitor center. Hwy. 540 rejoins Kaumualii Hwy. another 1½ miles west.

Kukuiolono Park ★ HISTORIC SITE/GARDEN Hawaiians once lit signal fires atop this Kalaheo hillside, perhaps to aid seafarers or warn of invaders. Most visitors are still in the dark about this unusual park, created by pineapple magnate Walter McBryde and then bequeathed to the public after his death in 1930. A mile off the main highway, the park includes the 9-hole **Kukuiolono Golf Course** ★★ (p. 103) and lively clubhouse restaurant **Birdie's;** a Japanese garden, where you might see weddings being held; a collection of intriguing Hawaiian lava rock artifacts, and several miles of jogging paths. A meditation pavilion and stone benches also provide excuses to enjoy the views.

854 Puu Rd., Kalaheo. © **808/332-9151.** Free admission. Gates open daily 7am–6pm. From Lihue, take Kaumualii Hwy. west into Kalaheo, turn left on Papalina Rd. and drive mostly uphill for about a mile; look for sign at right—entrance has huge iron gates and stone pillars—and continue uphill to park.

National Tropical Botanical Garden ★★ HISTORIC SITE/GARDEN Formerly owned by the McBryde Sugar Company, which bought the land from Hawaii's Queen Emma in 1886, this lush swath of Lawai Valley contains three separate gardens worth visiting, as well as the headquarters and research facilities of the National Tropical Botanical Garden. The

186-acre **McBryde Garden,** open for self-guided tours, boasts the largest collection of rare and endangered Hawaiian plants in the world, plus numerous varieties of palms, tropical fruit trees, heliconias, orchids, and other colorful flowers. Its Spice of Life trail, which includes cacao and allspice trees, meanders past picturesque Maidenhair Falls. The accessible Diversity Trail, opened in late 2014, follows a 450-million-year timeline as it passes through a misty tunnel and ends at a new pavilion with restrooms and a cafe. Allow at least 90 minutes to explore this garden; note that most of the trails are unpaved.

Open only to guided tours, the captivating formal gardens of adjacent **Allerton Garden** are the legacy of wealthy Chicagoan Robert Allerton and his companion John Gregg, whom Allerton later adopted. Allerton bought the land from McBryde in 1938 and with

Allerton Garden.

Gregg designed a series of elegant outdoor "rooms," where fountains and European statuary bracket plants collected from Southeast Asia and the Pacific. Allerton Garden tours last about 2½ hours; the 3-hour sunset tours end with a peek inside the oceanfront Allerton estate (normally off-limits), accompanied by appetizers and drinks served on the lanai.

Both the Allerton and McBryde garden tours require a tram ride down to the valley, and reservations (by credit card) are required. It's free, however, to tour the well-labeled **Southshore Visitors Center Garden,** where the trams depart. Its several acres include separate areas for ornamental flowers and trees, plants evocative of a plantation era home garden, Hawaiian native plants, and the profusion of color and textures known as the Gates Garden, at the entrance. The well-stocked gift shop, where tour members check in, includes cuttings and seeds cleared for export, as well as nature-inspired local art, crafts, and food.

NTBG Southshore Visitors Center, 4425 Lawai Rd. (across the street from Spouting Horn), Poipu. www.ntbg.org. ℂ **808/742-2623. Visitors Center Garden:** Self-guided tours daily 8:30am–5pm; free admission **McBryde Garden:** Self-guided tours daily 9:30am–5pm, admission $20 adults, $10 children 6–12, free for children 5 and under. Trams leave hourly on the half-hour, last tram 3:30pm. **Allerton Garden:** Guided tours daily 9 and 10am, and 1, 2, and 3pm; admission $40 adults, $15 children 6–12, free for children 5 and under. All tours require reservations and check-in 30 min. in advance.

Spouting Horn ★★ NATURAL ATTRACTION Hawaii's equivalent to Old Faithful—at least in regularity, if not temperature—is an impressive plume of seawater that jettisons anywhere from 10 to 50 or so feet into the air above the rocky shoreline (fenced for safety reasons). The spout comes from the force of ocean swells funneling waves through a lava tube, with the most spectacular displays winter and other high-surf days. The *whoosh* of the spraying water is often followed by a loud moaning sound, created by air pushing through from another nearby hole. There's an ample parking lot (as well as restrooms) on the site, but if you spot large tour buses in attendance, don't try to compete with the crowds for a Spouting Horn photo. Instead, browse the vendors of arts, crafts, and jewelry (from $5 bangles to Niihau shell leis costing hundreds of dollars) under the tents along the bluff, or watch the wild chickens put on a show, until the buses pull out 15 to 20 minutes later. Keep an eye out for spouting whales December through April.

Ocean side of Lawai Rd., Poipu, 2 miles west of the traffic circle with Poipu Rd. Free admission. Daily during daylight hours.

WEST SIDE

Kokee State Park ★★★ PARK It's only 16 miles from Waimea to Kokee, but the two feel worlds apart: With 4,345 acres of rainforest, Kokee is another climate zone altogether, where the breeze has a bite and trees look quite continental. This is a cloud forest on the edge of the Alakai Swamp, the largest swamp in Hawaii, on the summit plateau of Kauai. Days are cool and wet, with intermittent bright sunshine, not unlike Seattle on a good day. Bring your sweater, and, if you're staying over, be sure you know how to light a fire (overnight lows dip into the 40s/single digits Celsius).

While invasive foreign plants such as strawberry guava, kahili ginger, and Australian tree ferns have crowded out native plants, the forest still holds many treasures, including several species that only grow on Kauai: mokihana trees, whose anise-scented green berries adorn the island's signature lei; iliau, a spiky

A PRINCE OF A prince

With his name gracing half of Kauai's main highway as well as a popular beach and busy avenue in Waikiki, you could say **Prince Jonah Kuhio Kalanianaole** is all over the map, just as he was in life. The nephew and adopted son of King David Kalakaua and Queen Kapiolani, Prince Kuhio studied in California and England before the American-backed overthrow of the monarchy in 1893. He spent a year in prison after being arrested in 1895 for plotting to restore the kingdom, and later fought with the British in the Boer War. In 1903, he was elected as a territorial delegate to the U.S. Congress, where he served until his death in 1922, at age 50.

Along the way, Prince Kuhio founded the first Hawaiian Civic Club, restored the Royal Order of Kamehameha, created the Hawaiian Home Lands Commission (which awards long-term leases to Native Hawaiians), established national parks on Maui and the island of Hawaii, opened his Waikiki beachfront to the public, and popularized outrigger canoe racing—just to name a few of the reasons "the people's prince" is so revered. His March 26 birthday is a state holiday, which his home island of Kauai marks with 2 weeks of **festivities** (www.princekuhio.net).

His birthplace in Poipu is part of **Prince Kuhio Park,** a small, grassy compound off Lawai Road, not far from where surfers navigate "PK's," a break also named for the prince. The park holds the foundations of the family home, a fish pond that's still connected by a culvert to the sea, the remains of a heiau (shrine), and a monument that still receives floral tributes. *Note:* It's considered disrespectful to sit on the rock walls, as tempting as it might be to picnic or don snorkel gear for the nearby cove.

plant similar to Maui's silversword; and the endangered white hibiscus, one of the few of its kind to have a fragrance.

Before exploring the area, though, be sure to stop by the **Kokee Natural History Museum ★★** (www. kokee.org; © **808/335-9975;** daily 9am–4:30pm). It's right next to the restaurant/gift shop of the Lodge at Kokee, in the meadow off Kokee Road (Hwy. 550), 5 miles past the first official Waimea Canyon lookout. Admission is free, but it deserves at least the $1 donation requested per person. This is the best place to learn about the forest and Alakai Swamp. The museum shop has great trail information as well as local books and maps, including the official park trail map; a .1-mile nature walk with labeled plants starts just behind the museum.

Another 2.7 miles up the road from Kokee Lodge is **Kalalau Overlook ★★★**, the spectacular climax of your drive through Waimea Canyon and Kokee— unless the gate is open to the Puu O Kila Lookout 1 mile farther, the true end of the road. The latter lookout is usually closed in inclement weather, which is frequent: Nearby Waialeale is playing catch for clouds that have crossed thousands of miles of ocean. The view from Kalalau Overlook can be Brigadoon-like, too, but when the mists part, it's breathtaking. Shadows dance cross the green cliffs dappled with red and orange, white tropicbirds soar over a valley almost 4,000 feet below, and the turquoise sea sparkles on the horizon. Just below the railing, look for the fluffy red 'apapane honeycreepers darting among the scarlet-tufted ohia lehua trees. Mornings tend to offer the clearest views.

With so many trails to hike up here, including the boardwalk through the Alakai Swamp (p. 52), some choose to stay overnight, either by pitching a tent in

View from Kalalau Overlook.

one of several campsites (by permit only) or opting for one of the cabins run by the Lodge at Kokee or the YWCA's Camp Sloggett (see "Where to Stay," p. 151). You'll need to plan carefully, though, when it comes to food and drink: The lodge's restaurant (see "Where to Eat," p. 179) is open only from 9am to 2:30pm, with takeout until 3pm, but I've found it closes early when business is slow. In the late afternoon, your best hope may be a snack vendor at a Waimea Canyon overlook; otherwise, it's a winding 15-mile drive down to Waimea. Kokee Rd., 7 miles north of its merge with Waimea Canyon Rd. (Hwy. 550). www.hawaiistateparks.org/parks/kauai. © **808/274-3444.** Free admission. Daily during daylight hours.

Russian Fort Elizabeth State Historical Park ★
HISTORIC SITE   To the list of those who tried to conquer Hawaii, add the Russians. In 1815, a German doctor tried to claim Kauai for Russia. He even supervised the construction of this fort in Waimea, named

Russian Fort Elizabeth.

for the wife of Czar Alexander I (spelled "Elisabeth" on some signage), but he and his handful of Russian companions were expelled by Kamehameha I a couple of years later. Only the walls remain today, built with stacked lava rocks in the shape of a star. If the grounds have been recently mowed, you can easily follow a path around the fort's perimeter to the oceanside entrance to the interior; see the interpretive sign by the parking lot. The site also provides panoramic views of the west bank of the Waimea River, where Captain Cook landed, and the island of Niihau. **Note:** Tidy restrooms make this a convenient pit stop.

Ocean side of Kaumualii Hwy., Waimea, just after mile marker 22, east of Waimea River. www.hawaiistateparks.org/parks/kauai. ℰ **808/274-3444.** Free admission. Daily during daylight hours.

Waimea Canyon State Park ★★★ PARK/ NATURAL ATTRACTION   Often called "The Grand Canyon" of the Pacific—an analogy attributed to Mark Twain, although there's no record he ever visited— Waimea Canyon is indeed spectacular, albeit on a smaller scale. A mile wide, 3,600 feet deep, and 14 miles long, depending on whom you ask, Kauai's counterpart to Arizona's icon deserves accolades for its beauty alone. A jumble of red-orange pyramids, striped with gray bands of volcanic rock and stubbled with green and gold vegetation, Waimea Canyon was formed by a series of prehistoric lava flows, earthquakes, and erosion from wind and water, including the narrow Waimea River, still carving its way to the sea. You can stop by the road and look at the canyon, hike into it, admire it from a downhill bicycle tour, or swoop through it in a helicopter. (For more information, see "Organized Tours" and "Other Outdoor Activities," below.)

By car, there are two ways to visit Waimea Canyon and reach Kokee State Park, 15 miles up from Waimea. From the main road of Kaumualii Highway, it's best to head up Waimea Canyon Drive (Hwy. 550) at Waimea town. You can also pass through Waimea and turn up Kokee Road (Hwy. 55) at Kekaha, but it's steeper—one reason the twice-daily downhill bike tours prefer that route—and its vistas, though lovely, are not as eye-popping as those along Waimea Canyon Drive, the narrower rim road. The two routes merge about 7 miles up from the highway and continue as Kokee Road.

The first good vantage point is **Waimea Canyon Lookout,** between mile markers 10 and 11 on Kokee Road; there's a long, gently graded paved path for those who can't handle the stairs to the observation area. Far across the canyon, two-tiered **Waipoo Falls** cascades 800 feet, while you might spot a nimble mountain goat clambering on the precipices just below. From here, it's about another 5 miles to Kokee. A few more informal and formal lookout points along

Waimea Canyon.

the way also offer noteworthy views. **Puu Ka Pele Lookout,** between mile markers 12 and 13, reveals the multiple ribbons of water coursing through Waipoo Falls. **Puu Hinahina Lookout,** between mile markers 13 and 14, actually has two different vista points, one with a sweeping view of the canyon down to the Pacific, and another of Niihau, lying 17 miles west. Waimea Canyon Drive and Kokee Road, Waimea. www.hawaii stateparks.org/parks/kauai. © **808/274-3444.** Free admission. Daily during daylight hours.

West Kauai Visitor Center ★ MUSEUM/ ATTRACTION Although its hours are limited, this center's two free weekly activities and the small but well-curated cultural exhibitions merit a stop here before or after your Waimea Canyon expedition. The **"Keepers of the Culture"** displays include vintage photos, artifacts, and panels on Waimea's natural and cultural history, from traditional Hawaiian practices such as salt-making and herbal medicine to the arrival of Captain Cook, the sugar plantation era, *paniolo* (cowboy) culture and the modern Pacific Missile Range Facility. Kids will more likely enjoy the **lei-making class,** which takes place at 9.30am Friday from March to mid-November (when fresh blossoms are available); it's free, but you need to reserve by phone no later than noon the Thursday before. On Monday, a free **guided walking tour** of historic Waimea Town explores its ancient Hawaiian roots and modern history with stops at the Captain Cook monument, missionary churches, and picturesque Waimea Pier. It starts at 9:30am and lasts about 3 hours; reservations are required by 4pm the Friday before.

9565 Kaumualii Hwy. (*mauka* side) at Waimea Canyon Rd., Waimea. Parking is in rear, with lot entrance only from Kaumualii Hwy. www.westkauaivisitorcenter.org. © **808/338-1332.** Free admission. Mon–Fri 10am–4pm.

Organized Tours

Farms, gardens, historic houses, and other points of interest that may be open only to guided tours are listed under "Attractions & Points of Interest," above. For boat, kayak, bicycle, hiking, and similar tours, see listings under "Other Outdoor Activities" in chapter 3.

HELICOPTER TOURS ★★★

If you forgo touring Kauai by helicopter, you'll miss seeing the vast majority of its untouched ridgelines, emerald valleys, and exhilarating waterfalls. Yes, the rides are expensive ($200–$300 per person), but you'll take home memories—not to mention photos, videos, and/or a professional DVD—of the thrilling ride over

Napali Coast viewed from helicopter.

Waimea Canyon, into Kalalau Valley on Kauai's wild Napali Coast, and across the green crater of Waialeale, laced with ribbons of water.

Most flights depart from Lihue, last about 55 to 75 minutes, and, regardless of advertising, offer essentially the same experience: narrated flights, noise-canceling headphones with two-way communication, and multi-camera videos of your ride or a pre-taped version (often a better souvenir). The risks are also about the same—Kauai's last crash involving a sightseeing helicopter was in 2007, with many thousands of flights safely flown since. (If your pilot chooses to bypass Waialeale due to bad weather, appreciate his or her caution.) So how to distinguish among the half-dozen major operators?

Given the noise inflicted on residents, wildlife, and tranquillity-seeking hikers by flights that hover as low as 500 feet, I recommend touring with the most eco-friendly of the bunch, and most luxurious: **Blue Hawaiian**★★★(www.bluehawaiian.com;✆**800/745-2583** or 808/245-5800). Its American Eurocopter

HOLLYWOOD loves KAUAI

More than 50 major Hollywood productions have been shot on Kauai since the studios discovered the island's spectacular natural beauty. Two of Kauai's most recent star turns were 2015's "Jurassic World" (an update of 1993's "Jurassic Park") and 2011's "The Descendants." The latter includes several scenes in Hanalei and the breathtaking overlook of Kipu Kai. You can visit a number of Kauai locations that made it to the silver screen—including the settings of such TV classics as "Fantasy Island" and "Gilligan's Island"—on the **Hawaii Movie Tour** from **Roberts Hawaii** (www.roberts hawaii.com/island/kauai;

© **800/831-5541**). Offered daily except Sunday, the narrated minibus tour features singalongs and video clips that play between sightseeing stops. You'll likely see more of Kauai on this 6-hour tour, which includes exclusive access to the shuttered Coco Palms resort, than you could on your own. Tickets are $110 for adults and $57 for children 4 to 11 (free for 3 and under, if seated on adult's lap); prices include lunch at a restaurant and pickup/drop-off ($10 extra for Princeville lodgings). **Tip:** Book online for discounted fares—$99 adults, $51 children—and reserve early.

Eco-Star choppers have a unique tail design that reduces noise and fuel use, while the roomy interior has six business-class-style leather seats with premium views. The best seats are the two next to the pilot, but the raised row of rear seats won't disappoint (keep in mind seating is usually determined by weight distribution.) The 55-minute "Eco Adventure" ride from Lihue costs $239 ($211 when booked online at least 5 days in advance), which also makes Blue Hawaiian the best value.

For those staying on the North Shore, it may be more convenient to arrange a tour with **Sunshine Helicopters ★★** (www.sunshinehelicopters.com; © **866/501-7738** or 808/270-3999). Its 40- to 50-minute flights from Princeville Airport are in quiet, roomy Whisper Star models, similar in design to Blue Hawaiian's Eco-Stars (it flies different craft out of Lihue.) Tours cost $289 for open seating, $364 if you want to reserve an even roomier "first class" seat in the front row; it's $249 and $324, respectively, if you book online, with an extra $10 off on flights before 8:30am or after 2pm.

Although its aircraft are not as quiet as those of Blue Hawaiian and Sunshine, two other companies have unique itineraries deserving of consideration. **Island Helicopters** (www.islandhelicopters.com; © **800/829-5999** or 808/245-8588) has exclusive rights to land at remote 350-foot Manawaiopuna Falls, nicknamed "Jurassic Falls" for its movie cameo. During your 25 minutes on the ground, you'll hear about the geological history and rare native plants in this area of Hanapepe Valley, which like Niihau is owned by the Robinson family. In part due to landing fees and fuel costs, Island's 75- to 85-minute **Jurassic Falls Tour ★** costs $324 (plus 4% if using a credit card); it leaves from Lihue Airport. **Safari Helicopters** (www.safari helicopters.com; © **800/326-3356** or 808/246-0136) offers the 90-minute **Kauai Refuge Eco-Tour ★★**, which includes a 30- to 40-minute stopover at an otherwise inaccessible Robinson-owned site overlooking vast Olokele Canyon; Keith Robinson is occasionally on hand to explain his efforts to preserve rare, endemic plants here (which your landing fees subsidize). The tour costs $304 ($252 booked online) and departs from Lihue.

ACTIVE KAUAI

by Jeanne Cooper

Kauai's nearly 70 beaches include some of the most beautiful in the world, and all are open to the public, as required by state law. They are also in the middle of the vast, powerful Pacific, where currents and surf patterns are often quite different than those of Mainland beaches. The North Shore sees the highest surf in winter (Oct–Apr), thanks to swells originating in the Arctic that can also wrap around the West Side and turn the East Side's waters rough. In summer, Antarctic storms can send large swells to the South Shore that wrap around the West Side and churn up the East Side.

Note: You'll find relevant sites on the "Kauai" map, p. 5.

The good news is there's almost always a swimmable beach somewhere: You just need to know where to look. Start by asking your hotel concierge or checking the daily ocean report on **Kauaiexplorer.com** to find out current conditions. Nine beaches—all of them county or state parks—have lifeguards, who are keen to clue you in on safety.

Below are highlights of the Garden Isle's more accessible beaches. For detailed listings, including maps and videos, of virtually all strands and coves, see **www.kauaibeachscoop.com**.

PREVIOUS PAGE: **Surfer into the sunset.**

Safe Swimming on Kauai

"When in doubt, don't go out" is the mantra of local authorities, who repeat this and other important safety tips on a video loop at the Lihue baggage claim and on a local TV channel for visitors. That refers to going into unsafe waters, walking on slippery rocks and ledges that may be hit by high surf, or other heedless acts, such as disregarding beach closed signs in winter. Many of the unguarded beaches have waters that should only be enjoyed from the sand, or during calm conditions, which can change rapidly; large waves may come in sets as much as 20 minutes apart. While you might see locals seemingly ignoring the warning signs that note hazards such as strong currents, steep drop-offs, dangerous shorebreak, and the like, keep in mind they've had years to acclimatize. Don't be afraid to ask for their advice, though, since they'll tailor it for newcomers. By all means, *do* go out to Kauai's beaches; just bring ample prudence with you.

East Side
ANAHOLA BEACH ★

Anahola is part of the Hawaiian Home Lands federal program, meaning that much of the land here is reserved for long-term leases by Native Hawaiians; you'll pass their modest homes on the road to this secluded, mostly reef-protected golden strand. The 1½-acre **Anahola Beach Park** on the south end feels like the neighborhood's back yard, particularly on weekends, with kids learning to surf or bodyboarding, a hula class on the grass, and picnickers. It's better to explore here during the week, when you might share it with just a few fishermen and campers (who may also be locals). There are sandy-bottomed pockets for swimming and reefy areas for snorkeling, safe except in high surf. The Anahola River, usually shallow enough to walk across, bisects the beach. Facilities include picnic tables, restrooms, campsites, and lifeguards.

From Kuhio Hwy. heading north, turn right on Anahola Rd. (between mile markers 13 and 14) and head ¾-mile to the beach park. You can also park north of the Anahola River by taking a right on Aliomanu Rd. ½-mile past Anahola Rd., just after Duane's Ono Char-Burger (p. 167).

DONKEY (KUMUKUMU) BEACH ★★

When the only way to reach this beach was by a down-hill hike through sugarcane fields near a donkey pasture, nude sunbathers took full advantage of its seclusion. Now it's bordered by large luxury estates and the **Ka Ala Hele Makalae** coastal path, connecting it to Kealia Beach, 1.5 miles south; the 10-minute walk down to the ocean is mostly paved, and even starts at a parking lot with restrooms. So keep your clothes on, but do enjoy the soft golden sand at this tree-lined beach, also known as Paliku ("vertical cliff") and Kuna Bay. The water is too rough for swimming or snorkeling, but you may see advanced surfers and bodyboarders here. The north side has a shallow cove that's safe for wading in calm conditions.

From Kapaa, take Kuhio Hwy. north past mile marker 11; parking lot is on right, marked by sign with two hiking figures on it. Footpath to beach starts near parking lot entrance.

KALAPAKI BEACH ★★

This quarter-mile-long swath of golden sand may seem like a private beach, given all the lounge chairs on its border with the Kauai Marriott Resort, which towers behind. But there's generally plenty of room to find your own space to sunbathe, while the jetty stretching across much of Kalapaki Bay offers a protected place to swim or paddle; body-surfing and surfing are also possible at a small break. The view of the mossy-green Haupu Ridge rising out of Nawiliwili Bay is entrancing, as is watching massive cruise ships and Matson barges angle their way in and out of the nearby harbor. The water is a little murkier here, due to stream run-off. Facilities include restrooms and showers, with numerous shops and restaurants within a short walk.

From Lihue Airport, turn left onto Hwy. 51 to Rice St., turn left and look for Kauai Marriott Resort entrance on the left. Free beach access parking is in the upper lot, past the hotel's porte-cochère.

KEALIA BEACH ★

Only very experienced surfers and bodyboarders should try their hands on the usually powerful waves here, but everyone else can enjoy the show from the broad golden sand, a picnic table, or the nearby coastal multiuse path. The lifeguards can advise you if it's calm enough to go for a swim and where to do it. When the wind is up, which is often, you might see kite flyers. The 66-acre **Kealia Beach Park** is just off the main highway, often with food trucks and coconut vendors in the parking lot, making it a convenient place for an impromptu break. Facilities include restrooms and picnic shelters.

Off Kuhio Hwy. in Kapaa, just north of Kapaa River and Mailihuna Rd.

LYDGATE BEACH ★

Part of the family oasis of 58-acre **Lydgate Park ★** (p. 36) on the south side of the Wailua River mouth, Lydgate Beach has two rock-walled ponds that create the safest swimming and best snorkeling on the East Side—unless storms have pushed branches and other debris into the pond, which can take several days to clear. Families also gravitate here for the immense wooden play structure known as the **Kamalani Playground** and access to a 2.5-mile stretch of the **Ka Ala Hele Makalae coastal path,** suitable for strollers and bikes. Facilities include a pavilion, restrooms, outdoor showers, picnic tables, barbecue grills, lifeguards, campsites, and parking.

Leho Dr. at Nalu Rd., Wailua. From the intersection of Kuhio Hwy. and Hwy. 51 outside of Lihue, head 2½ miles north to Leho Dr. and turn right, just before Aston Aloha Beach Resort. Turn right again on Nalu Rd. and follow to parking areas.

North Shore

ANINI BEACH ★★★

Anini is Kauai's safest beach for swimming and windsurfing, thanks to one of the longest, widest fringing reefs on Kauai, among the very largest in all of Hawaii. With shallow water 4 to 5 feet deep, it's also a good snorkel spot for beginners (although the coral and varieties of fish are sparse closer to shore). In summer months, divers are attracted to the 60-foot dropoff near the channel in the northwest corner of the nearly 3-mile-long reef. In winter, this channel creates a very dangerous rip current, although the near-shore waters generally stay calm; it can be fun to watch breakers pounding the distant reef from the bath-like lagoon. The well-shaded, sinuous beach is very narrow in places, so keep walking if you'd like more privacy. The 13-acre **Anini Beach Park** on the southwestern end has restrooms, picnic facilities, a boat-launch ramp, campsites, and often a food truck or two.

From Lihue, follow Kuhio Hwy. past Kilauea to the 2nd Kalihiwai Rd. exit on right (the 1st Kalihiwai Rd. dead-ends at Kalihiwai Beach). Head downhill ½-mile to a left on Anini Rd.

Anini Beach.

HANALEI BEACH ★★★

Easily one of Hawaii's most majestic settings, unbelievably just a few blocks from the main road, Hanalei Beach is a gorgeous half-moon of golden-white sand, 2 miles long and 125 feet wide. Hanalei means "lei-shaped," and like a lei, the curving, ironwood-fringed sands adorn Hanalei Bay, the largest inlet on Kauai. While the cliffside St. Regis Princeville dominates the eastern vista, the view west is lush and green; behind you, emerald peaks streaked with waterfalls rise to 4,000 feet. Renowned for experts-only big surf in winter (Sept–May), Hanalei attracts beginners and old hands with steady, gentler waves the rest of the year. In summer, much of the bay turns into a virtual lake, creating ideal swimming conditions for kids. The county manages three different beach parks here, two with lifeguards.

Black Pot Beach Park, near the historic, 300-foot-long pier, is particularly good for swimming, snorkeling, surfing, and fishing, while you'll also see kayakers and stand-up paddleboarders coming in from

DEADLY beauty: QUEEN'S BATH

With so many lovely places to hike, swim, or snorkel in relative safety on Kauai, it's hard to understand why so many visitors put themselves in jeopardy at Queen's Bath, an oceanfront "pond" in the lava rocks below the Princeville cliffs, where 29 recorded drownings and numerous injuries have occurred. The site is most dangerous from October to April, but even on seemingly calm summer days, rogue waves can knock the unwary off ledges, or surge across the pond and pull swimmers into the open ocean, where they can drown long before help arrives.

Others have broken limbs by falling on the steep, rough trail—which is extremely slippery when wet—or while trying to enter the rocky pond. (It doesn't help that local daredevils enjoy jumping into the turbulent water of a nearby inlet, which inspires numerous YouTube videos and hapless imitators.) Unlike the many blithe reviewers on TripAdvisor who happened to experience tranquil conditions, I cannot in good conscience direct visitors here. If nothing else will dissuade you, know that parking is tight and illegally parked cars can and will be booted.

the mouth of the Hanalei River; note that it can be difficult to find parking on weekends and during holiday periods. Facilities include restrooms, showers, picnic tables, and campsites. **Hanalei Pavilion Beach Park,** in the center of the bay, has wide-open swimming (in calm weather), surfing, and boogie-boarding, under the watchful eye of lifeguards; facilities include restrooms, showers, and pavilions (the local nickname for this surf spot). "Pine Trees" is the widely used moniker for **Waioli Beach Park,** shaded by ironwood trees towards the western edge of the bay. It's another popular surf spot—champions Andy and

Bruce Irons grew up riding the waves here, and started the children's Pine Trees Classic held here every April. Check with lifeguards in winter about possible strong currents; facilities include showers and restrooms.

From Princeville heading north on Kuhio Hwy., enter Hanalei and turn right at Aku Rd. just after Tahiti Nui, then right on Weke Rd. Hanalei Pavilion Beach Park will be on your left; the road dead-ends at parking lot for Black Pot Beach Park. For Waioli Beach Park (Pine Trees), take Aku Rd. to a left on Weke Rd., then right on Hee Rd.

KAUAPEA (SECRET) BEACH ★★

Not exactly secret, but still wonderfully secluded, this long, broad stretch of light sand below forested bluffs lies snugly between rocky points, with only a few cliff-top homes and Kilauea Point Lighthouse to the east providing signs of civilization. Although strong currents and high surf, especially in winter, make the water unsafe, tide pools at the west end invite exploration when the surf is low, creating beguiling mini-lagoons; a small artesian waterfall to the east is perfect for washing off salt water. **Note:** Despite its reputation as a safe haven for nudists (who hang out at the more remote eastern end), Kauai County does occasionally enforce the "no public nudity" law here. And as with all destinations where your car will be out of sight for extended periods, be sure to take your valuables with you. It's a 15-minute walk downhill to the beach.

Heading north on Kuhio Hwy., pass Kilauea and take first Kalihi-wai Rd. turnoff on right. Drive about 50 yards, then turn right on unmarked dirt road on right and follow to parking area. Trail at end of lot leads downhill to beach, about a 15-min. walk.

KEE BEACH ★★★

The road ends here at this iconic tropical beach, hugged by swaying palms and sheltering ironwoods, its pale dunes sloping into a cozy lagoon brimming with a kaleidoscope of reef fish. You could feel like a sardine during the peak summer period, when the ocean is at its most tranquil and the parking lot is full by 9am. To be fair, many cars are for hikers tackling all or part of the 11-mile **Kalalau Trail** (p. 45), whose trailhead is just before the beach, and some belong to campers. Kee (pronounced *"kay-eh"*) is also subject to high surf in winter, when rogue waves can grab unwitting spectators from the shoreline and dangerous currents form in a channel on the reef's western edge. It's best to avoid the channel year-round, and always check with the lifeguards about the safest areas for swimming or snorkeling. Part of **Haena State Park** (p. 40), Kee has restrooms and showers in the woodsy area east of the parking lot. This is also a spectacular place to observe sunset, but you won't be alone in that endeavor, either.

From Hanalei, take Kuhio Hwy. northwest about 7½ miles to the road's end.

LUMAHAI BEACH ★

Between lush tropical jungle of pandanus and ironwood trees and the brilliant blue ocean lie two crescents of inviting golden sand beach, separated by a rocky outcropping. Here is Kauai at its most captivating—and where you must exercise the most caution. Locals have nicknamed it "Luma-die," reflecting the sad tally of those drowned or seriously injured here. With no reef protection and a steeply sloping shore, the undertow and shorebreak are exceptionally strong, while the rocky ledges that seemingly invite exploration are often slapped by huge waves that knock sightseers into the tumbling surf and sharp rocks. Flash floods can also make the Lumahai River, which enters the ocean from the western beach, turn from a wading pool into a raging torrent. Plus, it has neither lifeguards nor facilities; parking is in a bumpy, unpaved area or along the narrow highway. So why would one even go here? When summer brings more tranquil surf, it's a gorgeous setting to stretch out on the sand—not too close to the shorebreak—and soak in the untamed beauty. **Note:** The eastern beach, reached by a short, steep trail from the highway, is where Mitzi Gaynor sang "I'm Gonna Wash That Man Right Outta My Hair" in "South Pacific."

From Hanalei, follow Kuhio Hwy. about 2½ miles west. Look for pullout on ocean side near mile marker 4 for trail leading to eastern beach. For western beach, continue west (downhill) to larger, unpaved parking area on *makai* side by mile marker 5.

TUNNELS (MAKUA) BEACH ★★★ & HAENA BEACH ★★★

Tunnels Beach, more properly known as Makua, takes its English name from the labyrinth of lava tubes that wind through its inner and outer reef, making this Kauai's premiere snorkeling and diving site. The reefs mean the water is safe to enter nearly year-round. But as fascinating as the rainbow of tropical fish and the underwater tunnels, arches, and channels may be, they're more than matched by the beauty of what's above water. The last pinnacle in a row of velvety green mountains, Makana (Bali Hai) rises over the western end of a golden curved beach with a fringe of ironwood trees. The only problem: Where to park? The handful of spots on dirt access roads fill up first thing, and residents vigilantly enforce "no parking" zones.

Fortunately, a quarter-mile up the sand is **Haena Beach Park,** a county facility with plenty of parking—plus restrooms, showers, picnic tables, campsites, and lifeguards. You might even pass a snoozing

Hawaiian monk seal along the way. During calm conditions, most frequent in summer, Haena Beach offers good swimming and some snorkeling, though not as enticing as at Tunnels. Winter brings enormous waves, rip currents, and a strong shorebreak, time to leave the water to the expert local surfers. Do walk across the road for a gander at **Maniniholo Dry Cave,** another former sea cave (see "Haena State Park," p. 40), but one where you can walk for yards and yards inside before it gets too dark and low (watch your noggin).

From Hanalei, Tunnels (Makua) is just after mile marker 8 on Kuhio Hwy., but not visible from the road. Continue ½-mile to Haena Beach Park and parking lot on right.

South Shore

MAHAULEPU BEACHES ★★

Not far from Poipu's well-groomed resorts is a magical place to leave the crowds—and maybe the last few centuries—behind. To reach the three different beaches of Mahaulepu, framed by lithified sand dunes, former sugarcane fields, and the bold Haupu ridge, you'll have to drive at least 3 miles on an uneven dirt road through private land (gates close at 6pm), or hike the fascinating Mahaulepu Heritage Trail (p. 108). The first tawny strand is **Mahaulepu Beach,** nicknamed Gillin's Beach after the former Grove Farm manager whose beach house is the only modern structure you'll see for miles; it's available for rent starting at $3,450 a week (www.gillinbeachhouse.com). Windsurfing is popular here; strong currents means it's generally not safe for swimming or snorkeling. If you're lucky, the sea will have swept away the sand normally covering the petroglyphs in Waiopili Stream at the beach. Around the point is **Kawailoa Bay,** also a windsurfing destination, with a rockier shoreline great

Mahaulepu Beach.

for beachcombing and fishing. Wedged between dramatically carved ledges, **Haula Beach** is a picturesque pocket of sand with a rocky cove, best for solitude. *Note:* The coastline here can be very windy, and subject to high surf in summer.

By car: From Poipu Rd. in front of Grand Hyatt Kauai, continue on unpaved road 3 miles east, past the golf course and stables. Turn right at the T intersection, go 1 mile to big sand dune, turn left, and drive ½ mile to a small lot under the trees to reach **Mahaulepu Beach.** You can continue on dirt road (high-clearance 4WD recommended) another ¼-mile to **Kawailoa Bay,** then another ½-mile to short trail to **Haula Beach. By foot:** Follow Mahaulepu Heritage Trail (www.hikemahaulepu.org) 2 miles from east end of Shipwrecks (Keoneloa) Beach; public access parking is just east of Grand Hyatt Kauai, on Ainako St.

POIPU BEACH ★★★

A perennial "best beach" winner, the long swath of Poipu is actually two beaches in one, divided by a tombolo, or sandbar point. On the left, a lava-rock jetty protects a sandy-bottom pool that's perfect for children most of the year; on the right, the open bay attracts swimmers, snorkelers, and surfers. (If the waves are up, check with the lifeguards for the safest place to swim.) The sandy area is not especially large, but 5½-acre **Poipu Beach Park** offers a spacious lawn for kids to run around, plus picnic shelters, play structures, restrooms, and showers. There are plenty of palm trees, but not much shade; bring a beach umbrella to stay cool. Given the resorts and condos nearby, Poipu understandably stays busy year-round, and on New Year's Eve, it becomes Kauai's version of Times Square, with a fireworks celebration. *Note:* A short walk east is **Brennecke's Beach,** a sandy cove beloved by body-surfers and boogie-boarders; be forewarned that waves can be large, especially in summer, and the rocky sides are always hazardous. Injuries do occur at Brennecke's, which has no lifeguard.

From Koloa, follow Poipu Rd. south to traffic circle and then east to a right turn on Hoowili Rd. Parking is on the left at intersection with Hoone Rd.

SHIPWRECKS (KEONELOA) BEACH ★

Makawehi Point, a lithified sand dune, juts out from the eastern end of this beach, whose Hawaiian name means "the long sand." Harrison Ford and Anne Heche jumped off Makawehi in "Six Days, Seven Nights" (don't try it yourself), while body-surfers and boogie-boarders find the roiling waters equally exhilarating. Novices should enjoy their antics from the shore, or follow the ironwood trees to the path leading to the top of Makawehi Point, which is also the start of the **Mahaulepu Heritage Trail** (p. 108). A paved beach path in front of the Grand Hyatt Kauai leads west past tide pools to the blustery point at Makahuena, perfect for photographing Shipwrecks and Makawehi Point.

Restrooms and showers are by the small parking lot on Ainako Street.

Public access from Ainako St., off Poipu Rd., just east of Grand Hyatt Kauai.

West Side

SALT POND BEACH ★★

You'll see Hawaii's only salt ponds still in production across from Salt Pond Beach, just outside Hanapepe. Generations of Hawaiians have carefully tended the beds in which the sun turns seawater into salt crystals, *pa'akai*. Tinged with red clay, *'alae*, the salt is used as a health remedy as well as for seasoning food and drying fish. While the salt ponds are off-limits to visitors, 6-acre **Salt Pond Beach Park** is a great place to explore, offering a curved reddish-gold beach between two rocky points, a protective reef that creates lagoon-like conditions for swimming and snorkeling (talk to the lifeguard first if waves are up), tide pools, and a natural wading pool for kids. Locals flock here on weekends for individual recreation and large family gatherings, so go during the week for more quiet enjoyment. Facilities include showers, restrooms, a campground, and picnic areas.

From Lihue, take Kaumualii Hwy. to Hanapepe, cross Hanapepe Bridge, and look for Lele Rd. on left (½-mile ahead). Turn left, and follow Lele Rd. to a right turn on Lokokai Rd. Salt Pond Beach parking lot is 1 mile ahead.

POLIHALE BEACH ★★

This mini-Sahara on the western end of the island is Hawaii's biggest beach: 17 miles long and as wide as three football fields in places. This is a wonderful place to get away from it all, but don't forget your flip-flops—the midday sand is hotter than a lava flow. The

Polihale State Park.

pale golden sands wrap around Kauai's northwestern shore from Kekaha plantation town, just beyond Waimea, to where the ridges of Napali begin. For military reasons, access is highly restricted for a 7-mile stretch along the southeastern end near the Pacific Missile Range Facility, including the famed **Barking Sands Beach,** known to Hawaiians as Nohili. You'll still have miles of sand to explore in 140-acre **Polihale State Park,** provided you (or your car) can handle the 5-mile, often very rutted dirt road leading there. (Avoid driving on the car-trapping sand, too.) The sheer expanse, plus views of Niihau and the first stark cliffs of Napali, make the arduous trek worth it for many. While strong rip currents and a heavy shorebreak make the water dangerous, especially in winter, **Queen's Pond,** a small, shallow, sandy-bottom inlet, is generally protected from the surf in summer. The park has restrooms, showers, picnic tables, campsites, and drinking water (usually), but no lifeguards or any other facilities nearby, so plan accordingly. As in all remote areas, don't leave any valuables in your car.

From Kekaha, follow Kaumualii Hwy. 7 miles northwest past Pacific Missile Range Facility to fork at Kao Rd., bear right, and look for sign on left to Polihale. Follow dirt road 5 miles to main parking area, bearing to right at forks.

WATERSPORTS

Several outfitters on Kauai not only offer equipment rentals and tours, but also give out expert information on weather forecasts, sea and trail conditions, and other important matters for adventurers. Brothers Micco and Chino Godinez at **Kayak Kauai** (www. kayakkauai.com; © **888/596-3853** or 808/826-9844) are experts on paddling Kauai's rivers and coastline (as well as hiking and camping), offering guided tours and equipment rentals at their store in the Wailua River Marina. You can also learn about ocean and reef conditions and recommended boat operators at **Snorkel Bob's** (www.snorkelbob.com) two locations in Kapaa and Poipu (see "Snorkeling," below). *Note:* Expect to tip $10 to $20 for the crew or guides on any tours.

Boat & Raft (Zodiac) Tours

One of Hawaii's most spectacular natural attractions is Kauai's **Napali Coast**. Unless you're willing to make an arduous 22-mile round-trip hike (see "Hiking" on p. 104), there are only two ways to see it: by helicopter (see "Helicopter Tours" on p. 59) or by water. Cruising to Napali may involve a well-equipped yacht under full sail, a speedy powerboat, or for the very adventurous, a Zodiac inflatable raft, in which you may explore Napali's sea caves or even land at one of Napali's pristine valleys—be prepared to hang on for dear life (it can reach speeds of 60 miles an hour) and get very wet. (For safety reasons, some boat and raft tours do not permit young children.)

Boogie boarding the Kauai surf.

You're almost guaranteed daily sightings of pods of spinner dolphins on morning cruises, as well as Pacific humpback whales during their annual visit to Hawaii from December to early April. In season, both sailing and powerboats combine **whale-watching** with their regular adventures. **Sunset cruises,** with cocktails and/ or dinner, are another way to get out on the water and appreciate Kauai's coastline from a different angle.

Note: In addition to Captain Andy's (details below), only two other companies have permits to land at Nualolo Kai, home to the ruins of an 800-year-old Hawaiian village below an elevated Napali valley: **Na Pali Explorer** (www.napali-explorer.com; ✆ **808/ 338-9999**), which may depart from Hanalei or Kekaha ($159), and **Kauai Sea Tours** (www.kauai seatours.com; ✆ **800/733-7997** or 808/826-7254), leaving from Port Allen ($139). All trips are on rigid-hull inflatables, which unlike larger boats can pass through the reef opening; tours with landings take place April through October, conditions permitting.

Captain Andy's Sailing Adventures ★ Captain Andy has been sailing to Napali since 1980, with a fleet that now includes two sleek 55-foot custom catamarans, the *Spirit of Kauai* and *Akialoa;* a luxurious 65-foot catamaran, the *Southern Star;* and the 24-foot zippy Zodiac, which holds about a dozen thrill-seekers. The 5½-hour **Napali catamaran cruise** costs $149 for adults and $109 for children 2 to 12 and includes continental breakfast, a deli-style lunch, snorkeling, and drinks; aboard the *Southern Star* ($169 adults, $119 children), a barbecue lunch replaces the deli fare. A 4-hour Napali Coast dinner cruise—which sails around the South Shore when Napali's waters are too rough, most often in winter—costs $119 for adults and $89 for children ($149/$109 on the *Southern Star*), with no snorkeling; all Napali catamaran cruises leave from Port Allen. The 2-hour **Poipu cocktail sunset sail** aboard the *Spirit of Kauai* or *Akialoa,* including drinks and *pupu* (appetizers), is $79 for adults and $59 for children; it sails Saturday only, from Kukuiula Small Boat Harbor near Poipu. **Napali Zodiac cruises** depart from Kikiaola Small Boat Harbor in Kekaha; the 4-hour version ($139 adults, $119 children 5–12) includes snorkeling and snacks, while the 6-hour version ($159/$119) adds a landing at Nualolo Kai (depending on conditions) and expands snacks to a picnic lunch. *Tip:* Book online for a $10-per-person discount.

www.napali.com. *©* **800/535-0830** or 808/335-6833.

Holo Holo Charters ★★★ A 50-foot catamaran called *Leila,* licensed for 45 passengers but limited to just 37, serves Holo Holo's 5-hour, year-round **Napali snorkel cruises:** They're $149 adults and $109 children 6 to 12, including continental breakfast and deli lunch, and post-snorkel beer and wine. The 65-foot *Holo Holo* power catamaran, the island's largest, was built specifically to handle the channel crossing between Kauai and Niihau, where passengers snorkel after Napali sightseeing on 7-hour trips, also with two meals and post-snorkel libations ($195 adults, $139 children 6–12). The 3½-hour **sunset cruise** ($115 adults, $99 children 5–12), also aboard the *Holo Holo,* offers heavy appetizers, cocktails, and, at sunset, a champagne toast. Both *Holo Holo* and *Leila* depart from Port Allen, April through November. Holo Holo Charters also offers Napali snorkel tours from Hanalei on Kauai's most comfortable inflatable "rafts," really speedboats with fiberglass hulls, twin motors, stadium seats, freshwater shower, and a marine toilet (not to be undervalued on a 4-hr. trip that includes drinks and lunch). These tours cost $189 for adults and kids 6 to 12. *Tip:* Book online at least 3 days ahead for $15 to $20 off per person. www.holoholokauaiboattours.com. © **800/848-6130** or 808/335-0815.

Liko Kauai & Makana Charters ★ Born and raised on Kauai, from a Native Hawaiian family with roots on Niihau, Captain Liko offers more than just a typical cruise; this is a 5-hour combination Napali Coast tour/snorkel/historical lecture/whale-watching extravaganza with lunch. It all happens on power catamarans: the 49-foot *Na Pali Kai,* limited to 32 passengers, and the 32-foot *Makana,* with just 12 on board, both narrow enough to go in the sea caves normally only visited by inflatable craft. The 5-hour tours cost $139 for adults and $95 for children 4 to 12 (10% discount with online bookings). Boats depart twice daily from Kikiaola Small Boat Harbor in Kekaha; check in at 4516 Alawai Rd., Waimea (from Kaumualii Hwy., turn right at Alawai just west of the Waimea River). www.tournapali.com. © **808/338-9980.**

Bodysurfing & Boogie Boarding

The best places for beginners' bodysurfing and boogie boarding are **Kalapaki Beach** and **Poipu Beach;** only the more advanced should test the more powerful shorebreak at **Kealia, Shipwrecks (Keoneloa),** and **Brennecke's** beaches (see "Beaches," p. 65). Boogie-board rentals are widely available at surf shops (see "Surfing," p. 93) and beachfront activity desks. On the South Shore, **Nukumoi Surf Shop** (www.nukumoi surf.com; © **808/742-8019**), right across from Brennecke's Beach at 2100 Hoone Rd., Poipu, has the best rates and selections ($6 a day; $20 a week). On the North Shore, **Hanalei Surf Co.** (www.hanaleisurf. com; © **808/826-9000**), rents boogie boards for $5 a day, $20 a week, or $7 with fins, $22 weekly (3- and 5-day discounts also available), it's in Hanalei Center (the old Hanalei School Building), 5–5161 Kuhio Hwy., *mauka* side, Hanalei

Kayaking

With Hawaii's only navigable river (some would say rivers), numerous bays, and the stunning Napali Coast, Kauai is made for kayaking. The most popular kayaking route is up the Wailua River to Uluwehi or Secret Falls (limited to permitted kayaks Mon–Sat), but you can also explore the Huleia and Hanalei rivers as they wind through wildlife reserves, go whale-watching in winter along the South Shore, or test your mettle in summer with an ultra-strenuous, 17-mile paddle from Hanalei to Polihale.

Kayak Kauai (www.kayakkauai.com; ✆ **888/596-3853** or 808/826-9844), the premiere outfitter for all kinds of paddling, offers a range of rentals and tours from its store in Wailua River Marina, 3-5971 Kuhio Hwy., Kapaa (just south of the Wailua River Bridge, mauka side). River kayak rental starts at $29 for a one-person kayak and $54 for a two-person kayak per day ($64 for Wailua River–permitted double kayaks), including paddles, life preservers, back rests, and car racks. Twice-daily, 5-hour guided Wailua River tours with a Secret Falls hike/swim and picnic lunch cost $85 for adults and $60 for children under 12; a 3-hour version that skips the waterfall hike but adds a swimming hole is $55 for adults and $45 for children. The 5-hour Blue Lagoon tour from the Hanalei River mouth includes a shuttle to/from the Wailua River Marina, snorkeling, bird-watching, and beach time; it's $95 for adults and $85 for children.

Kayak Kauai's Napali tours ($240, including lunch), offered April through September, are only for the very fit who also aren't prone to seasickness; the 12-hour tour requires 5 to 6 hours of paddling, often through large ocean swells, in two-person kayaks. Co-owner Micco Godinez calls it "the Everest of sea kayaking." Trips depart Haena Beach and end at Polihale, with lunch and a rest stop at Milolii Beach, with shuttle to/from Wailua. The 6-hour winter whale-watching tours ($145) along the South Shore are slightly less challenging but still a significant workout. Kayak Kauai also gives 90-minute kayak lessons in Wailua River for $75 per person (two-person minimum).

Headquartered in Poipu, **Outfitters Kauai** (www.outfitterskauai.com; ✆ **888/742-9887** or 808/742-9667) offers a similar variety of well-organized tours, from a Wailua kayak/waterfall hike ($106 adults, $86 children 5–14, including lunch) to a summer Napali tour ($234 ages 15 and older only) and a winter whale-watching paddle from Poipu to Port Allen ($156 adults, $126 children 10–14). The kid-friendly Hidden Valley Falls tour heads 2 miles downwind on the Huleia River and includes a short hike to a swimming hole and a picnic by a small waterfall, with the bonus of a motorized canoe ride back; it's $116 for adults and $96 for children 3 to 14.

Family-owned **Kayak Hanalei** (www.kayak hanalei.com; © **808/826-1881**) offers relaxed, informative guided tours of Hanalei River, with snorkeling in Hanalei Bay, at 8:30am weekdays for $106 adults, $96 children 5 to 12. Daily rentals start at $27 half-day for a single kayak to $81 full-day for a triple, all gear included. No hauling is required; you launch under the colorful "Dock Dynasty" sign behind the store, 5-5070A Kuhio Hwy., Hanalei (makai side, behind Hanalei Taro & Juice Co.).

Sailing

Kalapaki Bay and Nawiliwili Harbor provide a well-protected if bustling place to learn to sail or, with sufficient experience, take a spin around the harbor yourself. In addition to surfing and stand-up paddle-boarding lessons and rentals, **Kauai Beach Boys** (www.kauaibeachboys.com; © **808/246-6333**) offers 1-hour rides with an instructor ($39) and sailing lessons for $140 per hour on its two-person, 18-foot Hobie Tandem Island and six-person, 16-foot Hobie Getaway boats; skilled sailors can tool around Kalapaki Bay on their own for $95 an hour ($75 per additional hour, up to $195 a day), or go out on the ocean with an instructor.

Scuba Diving

Diving, like all watersports on Kauai, is dictated by the weather. In winter, when heavy swells and high winds hit the island, it's generally limited to the more protected South Shore. Probably the best-known site along the South Shore is **Caverns,** located off the Poipu Beach resort area. This site consists of a series of lava tubes interconnected by a chain of archways. A constant parade of fish streams by (even shy lionfish are spotted lurking in crevices), brightly hued Hawaiian lobsters hide in the lava's tiny holes, and turtles sometimes swim past.

In summer, the magnificent North Shore opens up, and you can take a boat dive locally known as the **Oceanarium,** northwest of Hanalei Bay, where you'll find a kaleidoscopic marine world in a horseshoe-shape cove. From the rare (long-handed spiny lobsters) to the more common (taape, conger eels, and nudibranchs), the resident population is one of the more diverse on the island. The topography, which features pinnacles, ridges, and archways, is covered with cup corals, black-coral trees, and nooks and crannies enough for a dozen dives.

Because the best dives on Kauai are offshore, including the crystal-clear waters off Napali and Niihau, I recommend booking a dive with **Bubbles Below Scuba Charters** (www.bubblesbelowkauai. com; ✆ **808/332-7333**), specializing in highly personalized small-group dives with an emphasis on marine biology. Based in Port Allen, the 36-foot Kaimanu is a custom-built Radon dive boat that comes complete with a hot shower, accommodating up to eight passengers; the 31-foot, catamaran-hulled Dive Rocket, also custom-built, takes just six. Standard two-tank boat dives cost $135 (if booked directly); it's $245 for the two-tank dive along the Mana Crack, an 11-mile submerged barrier reef, that includes a Napali cruise. Bubbles Below offers a three-tank trip, for experienced divers only, to more challenging locations such as the "forbidden" island of Niihau, 90 minutes by boat from Kauai, and its nearby islets of Lehua and Kaula; locations vary by time of year and conditions ($345). You should also be willing to share water space with the resident sharks. The all-day, three-tank trip costs $345 (booked directly), including tanks, weights, dive computer, lunch, drinks, and marine guide. Ride-alongs for nondivers and crustacean-focused twilight/night dives, as well as bottles of Nitrox, are also available.

On the South Shore, the highly regarded **Fathom Five Adventures** (www.fathomfive.com; © **800/972-3078,** 808/742-6991) offers customized boat dives for up to six passengers, starting at $130 for a two-tank dive up to $350 for a three-tank Niihau dive ($40 more for gear rental).

GREAT SHORE DIVES Spectacular shoreline dive sites on the North Shore include beautiful **Kee Beach,** where the road ends and the dropoff near the reef begs for underwater exploration (check with lifeguards first). **Cannons,** east of Haena Beach Park, has lots of vibrant marine life in its sloping offshore reef. Another good bet is the intricate underwater topography off **Tunnels Beach,** also known as Makua Beach. The wide reef here makes for some fabulous snorkeling and diving, especially during the calm summer months. (See "Beaches" on p. 65 for location details.)

On the South Shore, head to the right of the tombolo (sand bar) splitting **Poipu Beach** if you want to catch a glimpse of sea turtles; it's officially known as Nukumoi Point but nicknamed Tortugas (Spanish for "turtle"). The former boat launch at **Koloa Landing** has a horseshoe-shaped reef that's teeming with tropical fish. It's off Hoonani Road, about a quarter-mile south of Lawai Road near the Poipu traffic circle. **Sheraton Caverns,** located off the Sheraton Kauai, is also popular—its three large underwater lava tubes are usually filled with marine life.

If you want a guided shore dive, **Fathom Five Adventures** (see above) will take you out daily for $75 for one tank and $90 for two tanks at Koloa Landing; spring through fall, it also offers weekday, two-dive shore dives at Tunnels for $165, with a one-tank night version for $100.

Snorkeling

You can buy snorkel gear at any number of stores on the island, but with luggage fees going up, I find it easier just to rent. **Kauai Bound** (www.kauaibound store.com; © **808/320-3779**) provides top-quality snorkel sets, including carrying bags, fish ID card, and no-fog drops, for $7.50 a day or $28 a week (child's version $5 daily, $20 weekly) at its store in Anchor Cove Shopping Center, 3366 Waapa Rd., Lihue, open 8am to 5pm daily. You also can rent pro-level underwater cameras ($20–$30 a day), camera accessories, and other outdoor gear here.

Robert Wintner, the quirky founder of the state-wide chain **Snorkel Bob's** (© **800/262-7725;** www.snorkelbob.com), is a tireless advocate for reef protection, funding campaigns for more legislation through the Snorkel Bob Foundation. His two stores here rent a great variety of snorkel gear ($35 a week for adult

Sea turtles in Kauai waters.

sets, $22 for child sets), with the convenience factor of 24-hour and interisland drop-offs, plus discounts on reputable snorkeling cruises. The East Side location (© **808/823-9433**) is at 4-734 Kuhio Hwy., Kapaa, just north of Coconut Marketplace, while the South Shore outlet (© **808/712-2206**) is at 3236 Poipu Rd., just south of Old Koloa Town.

In general, North Shore snorkeling sites are safest in summer and South Shore sites in winter, but all are subject to changing conditions; check daily ocean reports such as those on **Kauaiexplorer.com** before venturing out. See "Boat & Raft (Zodiac) Tours" for snorkel cruises to the reefs off Napali and Niihau. The following shoreline recommendations apply in times of low surf (see "Beaches" on p. 65 for more detailed descriptions):

EAST SIDE The two rock-walled ponds at **Lydgate Park** south of the Wailua River are great for novices and children, if it hasn't rained heavily.

NORTH SHORE **Kee Beach,** located at the end of Kuhio Hwy., and **Tunnels (Makua) Beach,** about a mile before in Haena, offer the greatest variety of fish. **Anini Beach,** located off the northern Kalihiwai Road, between Kuhio Hwy. mile markers 25 and 26, south of Princeville, has the most protected waters.

SOUTH SHORE The right side of the tombolo, the narrow strip of sand dividing **Poipu Beach** into two coves, has good snorkeling but can be crowded. You can also follow the beach path west past the Waiohai Marriott to the pocket cove in front of Koa Kea Hotel; if the tide is high (and calm) enough, you can observe its teeming marine life. A boat ramp leads into the rocky cove of **Koloa Landing** (see "Scuba Diving," above), where on clear days you'll spot large corals, turtles, and plenty of reef fish. (**Note:** Rain brings in stream runoff, which turns the water murky.) Tour groups often visit rock-studded **Lawai Beach** off Lawai Road, next to the Beach House Restaurant; watch out for sea urchins as you swim among parrotfish, Moorish idols, and other reef fish.

WEST SIDE **Salt Pond Beach,** off Kaumualii Hwy. near Hanapepe, has good snorkeling amid hundreds of tropical fish around two rocky points.

Sport Fishing

DEEP-SEA FISHING Kauai's fishing fleet is smaller than others in the islands, but the fish are still out there, and relatively close to shore. All you need to bring is your lunch (no bananas, per local superstition) and your luck. **Sportfish Hawaii** (www.sportfish hawaii.com; **✆ 877/388-1376** or 808/396-2607), which inspects and books boats on all the islands, has prices starting at $790 for a 4-hour exclusive charter (six passengers maximum), up to $1,250 for 8 hours. Rates may be better, though, booking directly through local operators such as Captain Lance Keener at **Ohana Fishing Charters** (www.fishingcharters kauai.com; © **800/713-4682**); excursions on the wide and stable 30-foot *Hoo Maikai* out of Kapaa start at $140 per person for a 4-hour shared trip up to $1,250 for a private 8-hour trip (up to six passengers). Captain Harry Shigekane of **Happy Hunter Sport Fishing** (www.happyhuntersportfishing.com; © **808/639-4351**) offers 4-hour shared charters for $200 per person aboard his 41-foot Pacifica, the *Happy Hunter II,* out of Nawiliwili Small Boat Harbor. Private tours run $700 to $1,300; veterans, police officers and firefighters receive an extra hour of fishing.

FRESHWATER FISHING Freshwater fishing is big on Kauai, thanks to dozens of manmade reservoirs full of largemouth, smallmouth, and peacock bass (also known as *tucunare*). The **Puu Lua Reservoir**, in Kokee State Park, also has rainbow trout and is stocked by the state every year, but has a limited season, in recent years mid-June to the end of September.

Sportfish Hawaii (www.sportfishhawaii.com; © **877/388-1376** or 808/396-2607) offers guided bass-fishing trips starting at $265 for one or two people for a half-day and $375 for one person for a full day, beginning at 6:30am in Kapaa.

Whatever your catch, you're required to first have a **Hawaii Freshwater Fishing License,** available online through the **State Department of Land and Natural Resources** (http://freshwater.ehawaii.gov)

or through fishing-supply stores such as **Wal-Mart,** 3–3300 Kuhio Hwy., Lihue (© **808/246-1599**), or **Waipouli Variety,** 4–911 1-A Kuhio Hwy., Kapaa (© **808/822-1014**). A 7-day nonresident license is $10 (plus a $1 convenience fee if purchased online).

Stand-up Paddleboarding

Like everywhere else in Hawaii, stand-up paddle-boarding (SUP) has taken off on Kauai. It's easily learned when the ocean is calm, and still easier than traditional surfing if waves are involved. Lessons and equipment are generally available at all beachfront activity desks and the island's surf shops (see "Surfing," below), while Kauai's numerous rivers provide even more opportunities to practice. Kauai native and pro surfer Chava Greenlee runs **Aloha Stand Up Paddle Lessons** (www.alohasuplessonskauai.com; © **808/639-8614**) at Kalapaki Beach, where he first learned to stand-up paddle; the bay offers a large, lagoon-like section ideal for beginners, plus a small surf break for more advanced paddlers. He and his fellow instructors (all licensed lifeguards) also teach SUP in Poipu, just south of the Sheraton Kauai. Two-hour group lessons (eight-person maximum) cost $75 and include 30 minutes on land and 90 minutes on water, both with instructor; lessons are offered four times a day. Walk-ups are welcome, but reservations are recommended. **Kauai Beach Boys** (www.kauai beachboys.com) gives 90-minute lessons three times a day on the beach at Kalapaki (© **808/246-6333**) and Poipu (© **808/742-4442**); the $75 fee includes a board, leash, and a rash guard (which also helps prevent sunburn). Once you've got the hang of it,

Nukumoi Surf Shop, across from Brennecke's Beach (www.nukumoisurf.com; © **808/742-8019**), will rent you boards with paddles for $20 an hour, $80 a day, or $250 a week.

In Hanalei, you can launch directly into the river and head to the bay from **Kayak Hanalei** (www.kayak hanalei.com; © **808/826-1881**), 5 5070A Kuhio Hwy., makai side, behind Hanalei Taro & Juice. Rental boards are $43 daily, $32 half-day (offered daily); 90-minute lessons are available Mon–Sat., with group classes starting at $91 for ages 8 and up. Private sessions for ages 5 and up cost $139.

Outfitters Kauai (www.outfitterskauai.com; © **808/742-9667**) combines a SUP lesson with a 2-mile downwind paddle on the Hulcia River and hike to a swimming hole; a motorized outrigger brings you back up the river. The half-day trip starts at 7:45am and costs $126 for adults and $96 for kids 12 to 14.

Surfing

With the global expansion in surfing's popularity, the most accessible breaks around the island have plenty of contenders. Practice patience and courtesy when lining up to catch a wave, and ask for advice from local surf shops before heading out on your own. **Hanalei Bay**'s winter surf is the most popular on the island, but it's for experts only. **Poipu Beach** is an excellent spot to learn to surf; the waves are generally smaller, and— best of all—nobody laughs when you wipe out. To find out where the surf's up, go to **Kauai Explorer Ocean Report** (www.kauaiexplorer.com/ocean_report) or call the **Weather Service** (© **808/245-3564**).

Surfing near Poipu Beach.

Poipu is also the site of numerous surfing schools; the oldest and best is **Margo Oberg's School of Surfing** (www.surfonkauai.com; © 808/332-6100), at the Sheraton Kauai. A world surfing champion at age 15, Oberg founded the Poipu school in 1977 and now runs it with the help of eldest son Shane and friendly young pro instructors. Two-hour lessons cost $68, including 90 minutes of group instruction (up to six students) and 30 minutes of additional practice, with soft-topped boards for beginners and booties provided; private sessions are $125. If you want to keep practicing, it's easy to rent from **Nukumoi Surf Shop** (www.nukumoisurf.com; © 808/742-8019), right across from Brennecke's Beach at 2100 Hoone Rd., Poipu. Nukumoi charges $6 an hour, $25 a day, or $75 a week for soft boards; the hard (epoxy) boards, for experienced surfers, cost $8 an hour, $30 a day, or $90 a week.

If you're staying on the North Shore, consider a lesson from **Hawaiian Surfing Adventures** (www. hawaiiansurfingadventures.com; © 808/482-0749), which offers smaller group lessons (maximum of four students) that include 90 minutes of instruction, up to an hour of practice, and soft boards for $65. The exact surf spot in Hanalei will vary by conditions; check-in for lessons is at the **Hawaiian Beach Boys Surf Shop**, 5-5134 Kuhio Hwy. (makai side, just before Aku Rd. when heading north). It also offers daily rentals starting at $20 for soft boards and $25 for the expert epoxy boards, with discounts for longer periods, as does **Hanalei Surf Co.** (www.hanaleisurf.com/rentals; ✆ **808/826-9000**), 5–5161 Kuhio Hwy. (mauka side, in Hanalei Center), Hanalei.

Tubing

Back in the days of the sugar plantations, local kids would grab inner tubes and jump in the irrigation ditches crisscrossing the cane fields for an exciting ride. Today you can enjoy this (formerly illegal) activity by "tubing" the flumes and ditches of the old Lihue Plantation with **Kauai Backcountry Adventures** (www.kauaibackcountry.com; ✆ **888/270-0555** or 808/245-2506). Passengers are taken in 4WD vehicles high into the mountains above Lihue to look at vistas generally off-limits to the public. At the flumes, you will be outfitted with a giant tube, gloves, and headlamp (for the long passageways through the tunnels, hand-dug circa 1870). All you do is jump in the water, and the gentle flow will carry you through forests, into tunnels, and finally to a mountain swimming hole, where a picnic lunch is served. The 3-hour tours are $106, open to ages 5 and up (minimum height 43 in., maximum weight 300 pounds). Swimming is not necessary—all you do is relax and drift downstream—but do wear a hat, swimsuit, sunscreen, and shoes that can get wet, and bring a towel, change of clothing, and insect repellent. Tours are offered at 9 and 10am, and 1 and 2pm. *Tip:* The water is always cool, so starting midday, when it's warmer, might be more pleasant.

Windsurfing & Kite Surfing

With a long, fringing reef protecting shallow waters, the North Shore's Anini Beach is one of the safest places for beginners to learn windsurfing. Lessons and equipment rental are available at **Windsurf Kauai** (www.windsurf-kauai.com; ✆ **808/828-6838**). Owner Celeste Harzel has been teaching windsurfing on Anini Beach for decades, with special equipment to help beginners learn the sport; she and fellow teacher Lani White also offer novice and refresher classes on weekdays, and advanced classes by request. A 2-hour lesson is $100 and includes equipment and instruction. If you want to keep going, rent the equipment for $25 an hour.

Serious windsurfers and kitesurfers (that is, those who travel with their own gear) will want to check out **Haena Beach Park** and **Tunnels Beach** on the North Shore, and the **Mahaulepu** coastline (including Mahaulepu/Gillin's Beach and Kawailoa Bay) on the South Shore. See "Beaches," p. 65, for details.

OTHER OUTDOOR ACTIVITIES
Biking

Although the main highway has few stretches truly safe for cycling, there are several great places on Kauai for two-wheeling. The **Poipu** area has wide, flat paved roads and several dirt cane roads (especially around Mahaulepu), while the **East Side** has two completed legs of the **Ka Ala Hele Makalae** multi-use trail (www.kauaipath.org/kauaicoastalpath), eventually intended to extend from Anahola to the airport in Lihue. For now, the 2.5-mile Lydgate Park loop connects it with Wailua Beach, while another 4.1-mile leg links Kapaa's Lihi Park to Ahihi Point, just past Donkey (Kumukumu) Beach, 1.5 miles north of Kealia Beach Park. Mountain bikers can also ride the scenic 5-mile **Wai Koa Loop Trail** at the Anaina Hou Community Park (p. 39) in Kilauea, or attempt more challenging trails in actual mountains, if it's not too muddy.

Several places rent mountain bikes, road bikes, and beach cruisers, including helmets and locks, with sizeable discounts for multiday rentals. In Poipu, **Outfitters Kauai** (www.outfitterskauai.com; ☏ **888/742-9887** or 808/742-9667) charges $25 a day for hybrid bikes and $45 for Kona brand off-road and road bikes; reservations are recommended. The shop is at 2827 Poipu Rd., Poipu, in the Kukuiula Market strip, across from the fire station; look for the yellow mini-submarine out front. Outfitters Kauai also leads twice-daily, 4½-hour **downhill Waimea Canyon bicycle tours** ($106 adults, $86 kids 12 to 14) that follow the Kokee Road spur to Kekaha. Some find the experience memorable, but I think there are better places on Kauai to cycle, and certainly better ways to see the canyon.

Kapaa has choices for both adventurers itching to explore the single-track trails in the mountains and vacationers just wanting to pedal the coastal path for a couple of hours. **Kauai Cycle** (www.kauaicycle.com; ☏ **808/821-2115**) offers cruisers for $20 a day, but specializes in road and mountain bikes for $30 a day ($45 full-suspension), with maps and advice customized to abilities and current trail conditions. No reservations are needed; just walk in to its store and repair shop, which also sells clothing and gear, at 4-934 Kuhio Hwy., Kapaa, north of Ala Road, makai side (across from Taco Bell). Families in particular will want to take note of the shiny Trek beach cruisers, tandems, and trailers from **Coconut Coasters** (www.coconutcoasters.com; ✆ **808/822-7368**) at 4-1586 Kuhio Hwy., Kapaa, just north of Kou Street on the ocean side. Half-day rentals start at $18; reservations are recommended.

On the North Shore, **Pedal 'n Paddle** in Hanalei (www.pedalnpaddle.com; ✆ **808/826-9069**) rents beach cruisers for $15 a day and hybrids for $20; it's in the Ching Young Village Shopping Center, 5-5190 Kuhio Hwy., makai side, just past Aku Road. In Kilauea, the rental mountain bikes from **Namahana Cafe** (www.namahanacafe.org/bike-rentals; ✆ **808/828-2118**) in Anaina Hou Community Park can be used on the Wai Koa Loop Trail or taken elsewhere; the rate is $25 for 1 to 6 hours and $33 for 24 hours (discounts for longer rentals).

Birding

Kauai provides more than 80 species of birds—not counting the "wild" chickens seen at every roadside attraction. To identify what you're seeing, check out photographer Jim Denny's **www.kauaibirds.com** or buy his excellent "Birds of Kauai" handbook online or in local gift shops. Coastal and lowland areas, including the wildlife refuges at Kilauea Point (p. 42) and along the Hanalei River, are home to introduced species and endangered native waterfowl and migratory shorebirds; the cooler uplands of Kokee State Park

Red-crested cardinal.

shelter native woodland species, who were able to escape mosquito-borne diseases that killed off lowland natives. David Kuhn of **Terran Tours** (✆ 808/335-0398) leads custom bird-watching excursions that spot some of Hawaii's rarest birds, using a 4WD vehicle to access remote areas. Rates start at $300 for a half-day, with longer periods available; e-mail info@soundshawaiian.com.

Many pairs of endangered nene, the endemic state bird, call Princeville's **Makai Golf Club** home, as do nesting Laysan albatross in winter; for $40, you can ogle them and their carefully marked nests on a self-guided **sunset golf cart tour** (www.makaigolf.com; ✆ 808/826-1863).

Golfing

It's no wonder that Kauai's exceptional beauty has inspired some exceptionally beautiful links. More surprising is the presence of two lovely, inexpensive public courses: the 9-hole **Kukuiolono** on the South Shore, and the even more impressive 18-hole **Wailua Golf Course** on the East Side; see details below.

Value-seekers who don't mind occasionally playing next to a Costco and suburban homes—amid panoramas of several soaring green ridges—will appreciate **Puakea** (www.puakeagolf.com; ✆ **808/245-8756**), part of AOL founder Steve Case's Grove Farm portfolio. Greens fees for 18 holes are $99, $59 after 11am, and $35 after 3pm; it's $35 for 9 holes anytime. It's centrally located, at 4150 Nuhou St., off Nawiliwili Road, Lihue. (Greens fees in this section include cart rentals unless noted.)

Bargain hunters may also call **Standby Golf** (http://hawaiistandbygolf.com; ✆ **888/645-2665**) between 7am and 10pm daily for discounted greens fees of up to 30% off same-day or future golfing at **Kauai Lagoons** and **Kiahuna golf clubs,** described below. Standby Golf says it can guarantee same-day tee times, too, for last-minute types.

To play the newest course on the Garden Island, you'll need to be a guest in one of the $1,000-plus-a-night **Club Cottages and Club Villas at Kukuiula** (www.parrishkauai.com/kukuiula; ✆ **800/325-5701**) who along with members of **Kukuiula** (http://kukuiula.com; ✆ **855/742-0234**) have exclusive access to Tom Weiskopf's rolling 18-hole course through gardens, orchards, and South Shore grasslands. Money can't buy your way out of dealing with trade winds, wherever you play, so start early for best scores.

EAST SIDE

Kauai Lagoons Golf Club ★★ Jack Nicklaus designed the 18-hole Kiele Course in the late 1980s, and returned for a 2011 makeover that created a half-mile series of four oceanfront holes, said to be the longest such stretch in the state. Featuring beautiful mountain, harbor, and *moana* (ocean) views, they're now part of the **Kiele Moana Nine;** the former back 9 are named **Kiele Mauka Nine,** reflecting their *mauka* (toward the mountains) location, behind the Kauai Marriott Resort. Together they're known as the **Kiele Championship Course.** As part of the renovations, Nicklaus chose the top 9 holes from his former 18-hole Mokihana Course to create the **Kiele Waikahe Nine,** perfect for juniors or beginners, with lots of open fairways. There's a free shuttle from the airport, 5 minutes away. Facilities include a driving range, snack bar, a pro shop, practice greens, a clubhouse, and club and shoe rental.

3351 Hoolaulea Way, Lihue, next to Kauai Lagoons and Kauai Marriott Resort. www.kauailagoonsgolf.com. © **800/634-6400** or 808/241-6000. Greens fees $205 ($150 for Marriott guests, $165 for guests of other select hotels), $115–$135 after noon; nine holes $80–$105. Juniors 6–17 $60 anytime. From the airport, take Hwy. 51 south to a left on Rice Rd. Turn left at entrance to Kauai Marriott Resort and drive past hotel. Golf parking area is 500 yards ahead, on the left; golf shop and bag drop are on the right.

Wailua Golf Course ★★ Highly rated by both "Golf Digest" and the Golf Channel, this coconut palm–dotted, largely seafront course in windy Wailua has hosted three U.S. amateur championships. Spread along the *makai* (ocean) side of the main highway, the first 9 holes were built in the 1930s; the late Kauai golf legend Toyo Shirai designed the second 9 in 1961. Nonresident rates start at just $48 (plus $20 for a cart) for 18 holes. Facilities include the **Over Park** snack bar/restaurant and bar, locker room with showers, driving range, practice greens, and club rentals.

3-5350 Kuhio Hwy. (Hwy. 56), Wailua, 3 miles north of Lihue airport. www.kauai.gov/golf. © **808/241-6666.** Greens fees $48 weekdays, $60 weekends/holidays, half-price after 2pm or for back nine only in morning. Motorized cart $20 ($11 for 9 holes), pull cart $7 ($5 for 9 holes).

NORTH SHORE

Makai Golf Club ★★★ Now that Princeville's Prince Course has closed for renovations (from which it's expected to re-emerge as a private club), this gem of a course—the first on the island to be designed by Robert Trent Jones, Jr.—is sure to increase in popularity. It's already gained favor with non-golfers by offering self-guided **sunset golf cart tours** ($40; © 808/826-1863) with a map to memorable vistas, flora and fauna (including nesting Laysan albatross in winter). Jones returned in 2009 to redesign the 27 holes he created here in 1971, creating the 18-hole championship Makai Course, which winds around ocean bluffs and tropical forest with compelling sea and mountain views, and the family-friendly 9-hole Woods Course, in the sylvan setting its name suggests. There's a "time par" of 4 hours, 18 minutes, here, to keep golfers on track (otherwise they might be gawking at the scenery all day). Other facilities include a clubhouse, a pro shop, practice facilities, a restaurant, and club rentals. ***Note:*** Guests of the St. Regis and Westin Princeville Ocean Resort Villas should inquire at the golf shop or through their respective concierges about special discounts. 4080 Lei O Papa Rd., Princeville. www.makaigolf.com. © 808/826-1912. Greens fees $239; $179 after noon. Woods 9 $55 for adults; $28 for juniors 16–17 and children 6–15 unaccompanied by adult; free for children 6–15 with paying adult. From Lihue, take Kuhio Hwy. to the Princeville main entrance, turn right, go 1 mile and course is on the left.

SOUTH SHORE

Kiahuna Golf Club ★ This par-70, 6,353-yard course designed by Robert Trent Jones, Jr., is a veritable wildlife sanctuary, where black-crowned night herons, Hawaiian stilts, and moorhens fish along Waikomo Stream, and outcroppings of lava tubes by the second fairway hold rare blind spiders. Keep your eyes peeled for remains of a stone-walled *heiau* (temple) and a Portuguese home from the early 1800s, whose former inhabitants lie in a nearby crypt—and watch out for the mango tree on the par 4, 440-yard hole 6. Facilities include a driving range, practice greens, club rentals, and a restaurant, **Joe's on the Green,** popular with locals.

2545 Kiahuna Plantation Dr. (off Poipu Rd.), Koloa. www.kiahuna golf.com. ✆ **808/742-9595.** Greens fees $110, $75 after 2pm. $47 for juniors 17 and under with paying adult.

Kukuiolono Golf Course ★★   Although not on a resort, this 9-hole hilltop course has unbeatable views to match an unbeatable price: $9 for all day, plus $9 for an optional cart. The course is part of woodsy **Kukuiolono Park** (p. 49), which includes a Japanese garden and Hawaiian rock artifacts; both the garden and the course were developed by pineapple tycoon Walter McBryde, who bequeathed it to the public in 1930. The course is well maintained, given the price, with relatively few fairway hazards (barring a wild pig now and then). Facilities include a driving range, practice greens, club rental, and **Birdies** restaurant, in the clubhouse.

Kukuiolono Park, 854 Puu Rd., Kalaheo. ✆ **808/332-9151.** Greens fees $9 per day, optional cart rental $9; cash only. From Lihue, take Kaumualii Hwy. west into Kalaheo, turn left on Papalina Rd. and drive uphill for nearly a mile. Look for sign at right; the entrance has huge iron gates and stone pillars.

Poipu Bay Golf Course ★★   This 7,123-yard, par-72 course with a links-style layout was, for years, the home of the PGA Grand Slam of Golf. Designed by Robert Trent Jones, Jr., the challenging course features undulating greens and water hazards on 8 of the holes. The par-4 16th hole has the coastline weaving

along the entire left side. The most striking hole is the 201-yard par-3 on the 17th, which has an elevated tee next to an ancient *heiau* (place of worship) and a Hawaiian rock wall along the fairway. Facilities include a restaurant, lounge, locker room, pro shop, club and shoe rentals, and practice facilities (off grass).

2250 Ainako St. (off Poipu Rd., across from the Grand Hyatt Kauai), Poipu. www.poipubaygolf.com. © **808/742-8711.** Greens fees (includes $5 resort fee): $250 before noon ($180 for Grand Hyatt guests); $160 after noon; $125 after 2pm. Daily clinics $35.

Hiking

As beautiful as Kauai's drive-up beaches and waterfalls are, some of the island's most arresting sights aren't reachable by the road: You've got to hoof it. Highlights are listed below; for descriptions of the 34 trails in Kauai's state parks and forestry reserves, check out **Na Ala Hele Trail & Access System** (http:// hawaiitrails.ehawaii.gov; © **808/274-3433**).

Note: When heavy rains fall on Kauai, normally placid rivers and streams overflow, causing flash floods on some roads and trails. Check the weather forecast, especially November through March, and avoid dry streambeds, which flood quickly. Always bring more drinking water than you think you need, too. Stream water is unsafe to drink, due to the risk of leptospirosis.

Among the guides, Micco Godinez of **Kayak Kauai** (www.kayakkauai.com; © **888/596-3853** or 808/826-9844) is just as expert on land as he is at sea. He and his savvy guides lead regular trips (with shuttles from the Wailua River Marina) to Waipoo Falls through Kokee/Waimea Canyon ($126), Napali's Hanakapiai Beach ($126) and Hanakapiai Falls ($168), Kapaa's Sleeping Giant ($81) and Kuilau Ridge ($85), and the

Awaawapuhi/Nualolo loop trail ($231), an impressive 11-mile loop starting in Kokee and leading to dazzling overlooks of Napali. Departing from Poipu Beach Park, naturalists with **Kauai Nature Adventures** (www. kauainaturetours.com; ☎ **888/233-8365** or 808/742-8305) lead a similar variety of day hikes, focusing on Kauai's unique geology, environment, and culture; they're $135 to $165 adults and $100 to $135 for children 7 to 12, including lunch.

The Kauai chapter of the **Sierra Club** (http:// sierraclubkauai.org) offers four to seven different guided hikes around the island each month, varying from easy 2-milers to 7-mile-plus treks for serious hikers only; they may include service work such as beach cleanups and trail clearing. Listings on the online "Outings Calendar"

Hiking the Kalalau Trail.

include descriptions and local phone contacts; requested donation per hike is $5 adults and $1 for children under 18 and Sierra Club members.

EAST SIDE

The dappled green wooded ridges of the Lihue-Koloa and Nounou (Sleeping Giant) forest reserves provide the best hiking opportunities here. From Kuamoo Road (Hwy. 580) past Opaekaa Falls, you can park at the trailhead for the easy, 2-mile **Kuamoo Trail,** which connects with the steeper, 1.5-mile **Nounou West Trail;** both have picnic shelters. Stay on Kuamoo Road until just before the Keahua Arboretum to pick up the scenic, 2.1-mile **Kuilau Trail,** often used by horses, which can be linked with the more rugged, 2.5-mile **Moalepe Trail,** ending at the top of Olohena Road in Kapaa. In the arboretum, you'll find the

WATERFALL ADVENTURE: rappelling

Kauai's latest outdoor activity provides a unique perspective of two hidden waterfalls—by walking down them. Technically, you're rappelling on the 30- and 60-foot cataracts, with help from experienced guide Charlie Cobb-Adams of **Island Adventures** (www.island adventures.com; © **808/246-6333**). A Native Hawaiian nicknamed "Hawaiian Dundee," Cobb-Adams leads a practice session on a 25-foot wall before a 15-minute hike near the Huleia National Wildlife Refuge to the falls, which are otherwise off-limits. The 5½-hour tour ($180 adults, $158 children 6–17, including lunch) departs from Lihue at 8am Tuesday; tours with kayaking (same length and price) depart at 8am Monday, Wednesday, and Saturday.

trailhead for the challenging **Powerline Trail,** an unmaintained path that follows electric lines all the way to Princeville's Kapaka Street, on the *mauka* side of Kuhio Highway; avoid if it's been raining (the mud can suck your sneakers off, or worse). A steady climb, but worth the vista at the top, is the 2-mile **Nounou East Trail,** which takes you 960 feet up a mountain known as Sleeping Giant (which really does look like a giant resting on his back); the trail ends at a picnic shelter on his "chest," and connects with the west leg about 1.5 miles in. The east trailhead, which has parking, is on Kapaa's Haleilio Road; turn inland just past mile marker 6 on Kuhio Highway and head 1¼ miles uphill.

NORTH SHORE

Traversing Kauai's amazingly beautiful Napali Coast, the 11-mile (one-way) **Kalalau Trail** is the definition of breathtaking: Not only is the scenery magnificent, but even serious hikers will huff and puff over its extremely strenuous up-and-down route, made even trickier to negotiate by winter rains. It's on every serious hiker's bucket list, and a destination for seemingly every young backpacking bohemian on the island. That's one reason a camping permit ($20 per night; http://camping.ehawaii.gov) is required for those heading beyond the 2-mile mark of Hanakapiai Beach; the permits often sell out up to a year in advance (see "Camping & Cabins," p. 150).

People in good but not great physical shape can still tackle the 2-mile stretch from the trailhead at Kee Beach to Hanakapiai, which starts with a mile-long climb; the reward of Napali vistas starts about a half-mile in. You'll see the occasional barefoot local surfer on the first 2 miles, but wear sturdy shoes (preferably hiking boots) and a hat, and carry plenty of water. The trail can be very narrow and slippery in places; don't bring children who might need to be carried. At Hanakapiai Beach, sandy in summer and mostly rocks in winter, strong currents have swept more than 80 visitors to their deaths over the years; best just to admire the view. Those able to rock-hop can clamber another 2 miles inland to the 120-foot Hanakapiai Falls, but only when it has not been raining heavily. Allow 3 to 4 hours for the round-trip trek to the beach, and 7 to 8 hours with the falls added in.

Nearly as beautiful, but much less demanding and much less crowded, is the 2.5-mile **Okolehao Trail** in Hanalei, which climbs 1,232 feet to a ridge overlooking Hanalei Bay and the verdant valley. It starts at a marked parking area off Ohiki Road, heading inland from Kuhio Hwy.; take an immediate left just past the Hanalei Bridge and look for the parking lot on the left and the trailhead across a small bridge to the right. Be sure to brake for nene (geese).

If you don't mind paying for the privilege, **Princeville Ranch Adventures** (www.princeville ranch.com; © **808/826-7669**) leads guided hikes on private land along the five tiers of **Kalihiwai Falls.** The 4½-hour tour ($99) involves 3 hours of hiking, with swimming below an 80-foot cascade and an uphill climb to a point with sweeping North Shore views; it's open to ages 5 and up.

SOUTH SHORE

At the end of Shipwrecks (Keoneloa) Beach, in front of the Grand Hyatt Kauai, the limestone headland of Makawehi Point marks the start of the **Mahaulepu Heritage Trail** (www.hikemahaulepu.org), an easy coastal walk—after the first few minutes uphill—along lithified sand dunes, pinnacles, craggy coves, and ancient Hawaiian rock structures. Inland lie the green swath of Poipu Bay Golf Course and the Haupu summit. Keep a safe distance from the fragile edges of cliffs, and give the green sea turtles and endangered Hawaiian monk seals a wide berth, too. It's 1.5 miles to the overlook of Mahaulepu (Gillin's) Beach, but you can keep on another 2 miles to windy Haula Beach.

WEST SIDE

Some of Hawaii's best hikes are found among the 45 miles of maintained trails in **Kokee State Park** (p. 52), 4,345 acres of rainforest with striking views of the Napali Coast from up to 4,000 feet above, and the drier but no less dazzling **Waimea Canyon State Park** (p. 56). Pick up a trail map and tips at the **Kokee Museum** (www.kokee.org; © **808/335-9975**), which also describes a number of trails in the two parks on its website.

The best way to experience the bold colors and stark formations of Waimea Canyon is on the Canyon Trail, which starts after a .8-mile forested walk down and up unpaved Halemanu Road, off Kokee Road (Hwy. 550) between mile markers 14 and 15. From there it's another mile to a small waterfall pool, lined with yellow ginger, that lies above the main cascade of 800-foot **Waipoo Falls;** you won't be able to see the latter, but you can hear it, and gaze far across the canyon to try to spot the lookout points you passed on the way up. On the way back, check out the short spur called the **Cliff Trail** for more vistas. (**Note:** Families can hike this trail, but be mindful of the steep dropoffs.)

Two more challenging hikes beckon in dry conditions. The 6.2-mile round-trip **Awaawapuhi Trail** takes at least 3 hours—1 hour down, 2 hours coming back up, depending on your fitness level—but offers a jaw-dropping overlook for two Napali valleys, Awaawapuhi (named for the wild ginger blossom) and Nualolo. Usually well-maintained, it drops about 1,600 feet through native forests to a thin precipice with a guardrail at the overlook. (*Note:* The **Nualolo Cliff Trail,** which connects with the even more strenuous 8-mile **Nualolo Trail,** remained closed at press time due to significant erosion.) The trailhead is just past mile marker 17 on Kokee Road, at a clearing on the left.

Slippery mud can make the **Pihea Trail** impassable, but when the red clay is firm beneath your feet, it's another must-do for fit hikers. Starting at the end of the Puu O Kila Lookout at the end of Kokee Road (Hwy. 550), the trail provides fantastic views of Kalalau Valley and the distant ocean before turning into a boardwalk through a bog that connects with the **Alakai Swamp Trail,** which you'll want to follow to its end at the Kilohana Overlook; if it's not socked in with fog, you'll have an impressive view of Wainiha Valley and the North Shore. The Pihea-Alakai Swamp round-trip route is 8.6 miles; allow at least 4 hours, and be prepared for drizzle or rain.

Horseback Riding

Ride a horse across the wide-open pastures of a working ranch under volcanic peaks and rein up near a waterfall pool, or explore a pristine shoreline hidden by former sugarcane fields: You'll see parts of Kauai many have missed, while helping keep its treasured *paniolo* (cowboy) culture alive. Pack jeans or long pants and closed-toe shoes.

CJM Country Stables ★★ A trail ride through the rugged Mahaulepu region, passing through former plantation fields and natural landscape to the untrammeled sandy beaches under the shadow of Haupu Ridge, may well be the highlight of your trip. CJM's standard rides both include 2 hours of riding, but the Secret Beach Picnic Ride ($140) adds an hour for lunch and beach exploration; reserve early. Private rides, which allow paces faster than a walk, are also available. *Note:* CJM also hosts rodeos throughout the year that are open to the public (see www.princekuhio. net and www.koloaplantationdays.com for details).

Off Poipu Rd., Poipu. From Grand Hyatt Kauai, head 1½ miles east on unpaved Poipu Rd. and turn right at sign for stables. www.cjmstables.com. © **808/742-6096. 2-hr. Mahaulepu Beach Ride:** $110; Mon–Sat 9:30am and 2pm. **3-hr. Secret Beach Picnic Ride:** $140; Wed and Fri 1pm. Private rides from $140 per hour.

Princeville Ranch Adventures ★★ There's no nose-to-tail riding at this working North Shore ranch, owned by descendants of the area's first missionaries. Instead, horses amble across wide-open pastures with mountain and ocean views as you learn about Kauai's *paniolo* (cowboy) history and distinctive landscape. The "ride n' glide" option ($145) takes you to a secluded valley that you traverse via ziplines (see "Ziplining," p. 115), while the Waterfall Picnic Ride ($135) leads to a short (but steep) hike down to a trail to a swimming pool at the base of an 80-foot waterfall; after a picnic lunch, you'll climb out via a 10-foot rock wall. Both rides last 3 hours, with 90 minutes in the saddle. Less exertion is required on the 2-hour Paniolo Ride ($99) through

Seeing Kauai on horseback.

pastures and the occasional herd of cattle. *Note:* Tours go out rain or shine, just like the cowboys.

Check in makai side of Kuhio Hwy., just north of mile marker 27, Princeville. www.princevilleranch.com. © **888/955-7669** or 808/826-7669. Booking by phone required. **Ride N' Glide:** $145; Mon–Sat 1:30pm; ages 10 and older. Waterfall Picnic Ride: $135; Mon–Sat 9am, noon, and 1pm (8am June–Aug); ages 8 and older. **Paniolo Ride:** $99; Mon–Sat 10am; ages 8 and older. Rental shoes $5.

Silver Falls Ranch Stables ★★ The falls here are not as impressive as those on Princeville Ranch—they're wide but not tall—but the swimming hole is equally refreshing and the scenery just as stimulating. The 300-acre ranch in Kalihiwai Valley features an 80-acre tropical garden and close-up views of the 2,800-foot-tall Makaleha Range. The 2-hour Silver Falls Ride ($115) includes a barbecue picnic that's a cut above the usual sandwich fare on Kauai, plus a dip in the "refreshing" waterfall pool, while the 90-minute Hawaiian Discovery Ride ($99) follows flower-lined streams through the garden, home to more than 150 species of palms. Combine the two itineraries on the 3-hour Tropical Trail Adventure ($139). *Note:* **Esprit**

de Corps Riding Academy (www.kauaihorses.com; ℭ **808/822-4688**) also operates out of Silver Falls Ranch, with private rides for advanced riders.

Kamookoa Rd., Kilauea. From Lihue, take Kuhio Hwy. north past mile marker 24 to a left turn on Kahiliholo Rd. at Kalihiwai Ridge sign, follow 2¼ miles to a left on Kamookoa Rd. www.silverfallsranch.com. ℭ **808/828-6718. Discovery Ride:** $99. **Silver Falls Ride:** $119. **Tropical Trails:** $139. All rides offered 3 times daily 9am–3:30pm June–Aug, twice daily Sept–May.

Tennis

Public tennis courts are managed by the **Kauai County Parks and Recreation Department** (www. kauai.gov; click on "Government," then "Departments," then "Parks & Recreation" in the left column, and then "Parks Facilities"; ℭ **808/241-4460**). Its webpage lists the 24 public tennis courts around the island, 20 of which are lighted and all of which are free. Private courts that are open to the public include those of **Hanalei Bay Resort,** Princeville (www. hanaleibayresort.com; ℭ **808/821-8225**), which has eight courts available for $15 per person per day; the resort also offers private lessons, daily clinics, and a pro shop. Also in Princeville, the **Makai Club** (www. makaigolf.com; ℭ **808/826-1912**) charges the same per player on its four courts, with private lessons available.

The South Shore is brimming with courts on resorts—including **Sheraton Kauai, Grand Hyatt Kauai, Poipu Kai Resort, Nihi Kai Villas,** and **Kukuiula**—but they're restricted to overnight guests. Guests in **Kiahuna Plantation** units managed by Castle Resorts (see p. 139) and Poipu rentals of **Great**

ESPECIALLY FOR kids

Climbing the Wooden Jungle Gyms at Kamalani Playground (p. 36)   Located in Lydgate Park, Wailua, this unique playground has a maze of jungle gyms for kids of all ages, including an actual labyrinth. Spend an afternoon whipping down slides, exploring caves, hanging from bars, and climbing all over.

Exploring a Magical World (p. 44)   **Na Aina Kai Botanical Gardens** sits on some 240 acres, sprinkled with around 70 life-size (or larger-than-life-size) whimsical bronze statues, hidden off the beaten path of the North Shore. The tropical children's garden features a gecko hedge maze, a tropical jungle gym, a treehouse in a rubber tree, and a 16-foot-tall Jack-and-the-Beanstalk giant with a 33-foot wading pool below. It's open Tuesday through Friday only, so book before you leave home to avoid disappointment.

Riding an Open-Sided Train (p. 35)   The **Kauai Plantation Railway** at Kilohana Plantation is a trip back in time (albeit on new tracks and replica cars) to the sugarcane era, with younger kids exhilarated just by the ride. Parents can justify it as an informal botany class, since passengers learn about the orchards, gardens, and forests they pass along the 2½-mile journey. Children of all ages will enjoy the stop to feed goats, chickens, and wild pigs (as long as they watch their fingers)

Vacation Retreats (www.alohagvr.com; ⓒ 866/541-1033) have access to the otherwise members-only tennis courts and other facilities at the **Poipu Beach Athletic Club.** On the East Side, **Marriott's Kauai**

Lagoons–Kalanipuu and **Aston Aloha Beach Resort** are among those with courts only for overnight guests.

Ziplining

Kauai apparently has Costa Rica to thank for its profusion of ziplines, the metal cable-and-pulley systems that allow harness-wearing riders to "zip" over valleys, forests, and other beautiful but inaccessible areas. After reading a "National Geographic" article about Costa Rica's rainforest canopy tours, Outfitters Kauai co-founder Rick Haviland was inspired to build the Garden Isle's first zipline, on Kipu Ranch, in 2003. Others soon followed, with ever longer, higher, and faster options. It may seem like a splurge, but keep in mind that ziplines not only offer an exhilarating rush and breathtaking views, they also help keep the verdant landscape gloriously undeveloped.

Be sure to book ahead, especially for families or groups—because of the time spent on harness safety checks, tour sizes are limited—and read the fine print about height, age, and/or weight restrictions. Tours usually go out rain or shine, except in the most severe weather. Plan to tip your guides ($10–$20).

SOUTH SHORE Opened in 2012, **Koloa Zipline** (www.koloazipline.com; ✆ **877/707-7088** or 808/742-2894) has an eight-line course ($139) in Koloa that includes a 2,500-foot zip—Kauai's longest—over the Waita Reservoir. For just $10 more, the Flyin Kaua'ian harness option allows you to soar like a superhero over most of the lines on the 3½- to 4-hour tour. Check in at the office at 3477-A Weliweli Rd., Koloa, in the Kauai ATV office behind the Old Koloa Town shops. **Skyline Eco Adventures** (www.zipline.com;

© **888/864-6947** or 808/878-8400) opened its eight-line course above Poipu in 2013 and shares a different legend of Kauai for each of the progressively longer, faster lines on the 2½- to 3-hour tour. The cost is $140 for eight zips, $90 for five (with 50% off for one child or teen for each paid adult, and 10% online discount for everyone else); check in at the office at Shops at Kukuiula, 2829 Ala Kalanikaumaka St., Poipu.

EAST SIDE **Outfitters Kauai** (www.outfitterskauai. com; © **888/742-9887** or 808/742-9667) updated its original zipline course on 4,000-acre Kipu Ranch in 2012; the nine-line course includes suspension bridges, tandem lines, and a "zippel" (a zipline/rappelling combo) over picturesque streams and waterfalls. The full-length, 6-hour course, called Zipline Trek Nui Nui Loa, costs $163 for adults and $142 for children 7 to 14; the six-line, 4-hour Lele Eono option is $121 for adults and $111 for children 7 to 14. My favorite, the all-day Kipu Zipline Safari ($194 adults, $152 children 3 to 14), includes two of the course's longest ziplines and a water zipline over a swimming hole, plus kayaking the Huleia River, hiking, swimming, and lunch. Check in at the Poipu office, 2827 Poipu Rd., Poipu, across from the fire station, or at the Outfitters Kayak Shack in Nawiliwili Small Boat Harbor at Wilcox and Niumalu roads, Lihue.

Kauai Backcountry Adventures (www.kauai backcountry.com; © **888/270-0555** or 800/245-2506) is the only outfitter with excursions through 17,000 acres of former sugarcane plantation land above Lihue. In addition to its unique tubing ride (see "Tubing," p. 95), the company has a seven-line zip course leading from the lush mountainside to a bamboo grove, where you can take a dip in a swimming hole (book the 9am tour for the warmest swimming weather). The 3-hour tour costs $130, with check-in at the office at 3-4131 Kuhio Hwy., Hanamaulu, between Hanamaulu Road and Laulima Street.

The ecology-focused **Just Live! Zipline Tours** (www.ziplinetourskauai.com; ✆ **808/482-1295**) offers three tours ranging from 2½ to 4½ hours ($79–$125). All glide over forest canopy in multiple shades of green, and the longest includes a 60-foot rock-climbing wall and 100-foot rappelling tower. The online-only Early Bird Special offers $20 to $30 off tours with 7 and 7:45am check-ins, held at the office/outdoor gear store in Anchor Cove Shopping Center, 3416 Rice St., Lihue, between Kalapaki Beach and Nawiliwili Harbor.

NORTH SHORE   If you just want to zip nine lines over a verdant valley, then take the 3½-hour Zip Express Tour ($125) at **Princeville Ranch Adventures** (www.princevilleranch.com; ✆ **888/955-7669** or 808/826-7669). But it would be a shame, particularly in summer, to miss the chance to swim in a waterfall pool offered by the 4½-hour Zip N' Dip ($145, including picnic lunch). The company also pairs ziplines with its popular horseback rides and kayak/hike excursions (3 and 4½ hours, respectively; $145). *Note:* The latter Jungle Valley Adventure is unique in that it allows children as young as 5 and weighing as little as 50 pounds to zip on the two 400-foot-plus lines included on the tour ($99 ages 5–11).

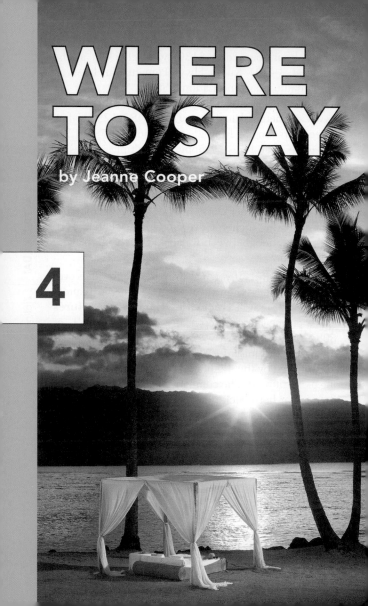

WHERE
TO STAY

by Jeanne Cooper

4

To avoid long drives, it pays to base your lodgings on the kind of vacation you envision, and consider dividing your time among locations. The island's East Side makes the most sense for those planning to divide their time equally among island sights; however, the best resorts for families and winter weather are on the South Shore. The most gorgeous scenery and best summertime ocean conditions are on the North Shore. If you're planning more than a day of hiking in Waimea Canyon or Kokee, or just want to experience the low-key island lifestyle, the West Side will definitely suit.

Taxes of 13.42% are added to all hotel bills. Parking is free, and pools are outdoors unless otherwise noted. Parking, Internet, and resort fees where applicable are charged daily; "cleaning" fees refer to one-time charges for cleaning after your stay, not daily housekeeping— the latter may be available for an additional fee for condos and other vacation rentals.

East Side

Convenient to all parts of the island (except during rush hour), Lihue and the Coconut Coast have the

hot-button **ISSUE: VACATION RENTALS & B&BS**

As on other Hawaiian Islands, vacation rentals and bed-and-breakfasts outside of areas zoned for tourism have become a hot-button issue for many on Kauai. Since 2008, owners of all such rentals and B&Bs have needed permits to operate, with special restrictions on agricultural land; the benefit for guests is knowing that your lodgings conform to planning and safety codes, the taxes you're paying are actually going to the county, and your stay won't be in jeopardy of a surprise shutdown. At press time, the county was not enforcing the rules for B&Bs as much as for vacation rentals, which among other requirements must display their permit number (often starting with "TVR" or "TVNC") on any online advertising, and post a sign on the premises listing that number, plus the name and phone number of an on-island emergency contact.

The Kauai Visitors Bureau also urges special caution when booking a vacation rental online from sources other than licensed agencies, such as those listed here. Some visitors, usually those who paid by check or money order, arrive on island only to discover their unit belongs to somebody else; they have no place to stay and no recourse to recover their payments.

When booking a condo, also keep in mind that companies that manage multiple properties in a complex may be able to find you another unit if you're dissatisfied with your view or problems arise during your stay—generally not the case for a unit booked on VRBO.com and other do-it-yourself rental sites. However, some management companies are eliminating daily maid service and other niceties to remain competitive; read the fine print before you arrive to know what to expect.

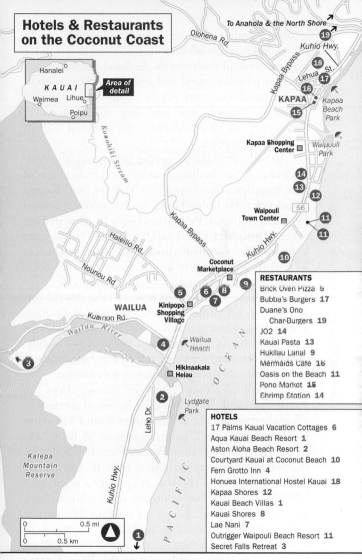

Hotels & Restaurants on the Coconut Coast

KAUAI
Hanalei
Waimea
Lihue
Poipu

Area of detail

To Anahola & the North Shore

Olohena Rd.
Kuhio Hwy.
Kapaa Bypass
Lehua St.

KAPAA

Kapaa Beach Park

Kapaa Shopping Center

Waipouli Park

Komohiki Stream

Waipouli Town Center

56

Haleilio Rd.

Nounou Rd.

Kapaa Bypass

Kuhio Hwy.

Coconut Marketplace

WAILUA

Kuamoo Rd.

Kinipopo Shopping Village

Wailua River

Wailua Beach

Hikinaakala Heiau

Lydgate Park

Leho Dr.

Kalepa Mountain Reserve

Kuhio Hwy.

PACIFIC OCEAN

0   0.5 mi
0   0.5 km

RESTAURANTS
Brick Oven Pizza **5**
Bubba's Burgers **17**
Duane's Ono Char-Burgers **19**
JO2 **14**
Kauai Pasta **13**
Hukilau Lanai **9**
Mermaids Cafe **16**
Oasis on the Beach **11**
Pono Market **16**
Shrimp Station **14**

HOTELS
17 Palms Kauai Vacation Cottages **6**
Aqua Kauai Beach Resort **1**
Aston Aloha Beach Resort **2**
Courtyard Kauai at Coconut Beach **10**
Fern Grotto Inn **4**
Honuea International Hostel Kauai **18**
Kapaa Shores **12**
Kauai Beach Villas **1**
Kauai Shores **8**
Lae Nani **7**
Outrigger Waipouli Beach Resort **11**
Secret Falls Retreat **3**

121

greatest number of budget motels, affordable beach-front condos, and moderately priced hotel rooms, along with a couple of posh resorts. Bed-and-breakfasts and vacation rentals in rural and residential areas such as Anahola and upcountry Kapaa are outside the official "visitor destination area" and may not be licensed, although many have paid taxes and operated without complaints for years.

In addition to the properties below, consider renting a one- or two-bedroom oceanfront condo at one of two complexes in Kapaa. At the 84-unit **Kapaa Shores ★**, 900 Kuhio Hwy., the 10 condos managed by Garden Island Properties (www.kauaiproperties.com; ✆ **800/801-0378** or 808/822-4871) run from $800 a week for a one-bedroom, one-bathroom unit to $1,050 for a two-bedroom, two-bathroom unit (plus $100–$130 cleaning and $25–$50 reservation fees). At the more upscale **Lae Nani ★★**, 410 Papaloa Rd. (off Kuhio Hwy.), Outrigger (www.outrigger.com/laenani; ✆ **866/956-4262** or 808/823-1401) manages about a quarter of the 83 spacious units ($159–$349 nightly; cleaning fees $135–$175); the beach here offers a rock-walled swimming area perfect for children.

If you prefer something more private, check out the two elegantly furnished (and licensed) cottages in a leafy setting known as **17 Palms Kauai Vacation Cottages ★** (www.17palmskauai.com; ✆ **888/725-6799**), a block away from Wailua's beaches. Rates for the one-bedroom, one-bathroom Hale Iki (sleeps two adults, plus a small child) start at $185 a night, plus $110 cleaning; the two-bedroom, one-bathroom Meli Meli (sleeps four adults, plus a small child) starts at $275, plus $145 cleaning. Tucked off Kapaa's busy Kuamoo Road, with easy access to the Wailua River, the pleasant compound known as the **Fern Grotto**

Inn ★ (www.ferngrottoinn.com; © **808/821-9836**) comprises five quaint cottages (most sleeping just two), for $140 to $200 a night, plus $75 to $100 cleaning, and one three-bedroom house (up to six adults) for $250 to $350 nightly and $225 cleaning.

EXPENSIVE

Kauai Marriott Resort ★★★ This 10-story, multi-wing hotel—the tallest on Kauai since opening in 1986—may be what prompted the local ordinance that no new structures be higher than a coconut tree, but it would be hard to imagine the Garden Island without it. Superlatives include Kauai's largest swimming pool, a sort of Greco-Roman fantasy that would fit in at Hearst Castle; its location on Kalapaki Beach, the best protected on the East Side for watersports; and one of the island's most popular restaurants, **Duke's Kauai** (p. 155), among other dining outlets. The long escalator to the central courtyard lagoon, the immense statuary, and handsome lobby sporting a koa outrigger canoe make you feel like you've arrived somewhere truly unique. Two shopping centers (Harbor Mall and Anchor Cove) with more restaurants are within a short walk; in the opposite direction lies the 18-hole championship course of the Kauai Lagoons Golf Club. Rooms tend to be on the smaller side but feel plush and look chic, with hues of taupe and burnt umber. Try to get at least a partial ocean view—the rugged green Haupu ridge, the bay, and Nawiliwili Harbor provide a mesmerizing backdrop.

Note: The "vacation ownership" **Marriott's Kauai Beach Club** (www.marriott.com/lihka; © **800/845-5279** or 808/245-5050), which offers attractive studio, one-bedroom/two-bathroom, and two-bedroom/two-bathroom "villas" with kitchenettes ($309–$599

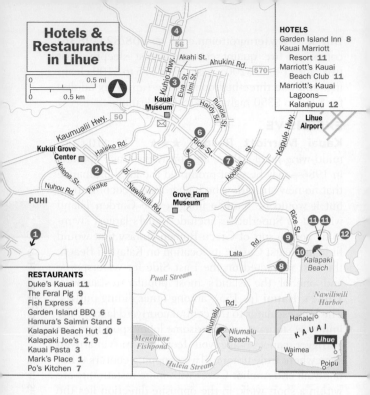

Hotels & Restaurants in Lihue

nightly), is on the same grounds and shares all the Kauai Marriott Resort's facilities. There's no resort fee or charge for Wi-Fi or rollaway beds, while self-parking costs $16; it often has limited availability, due to the popularity of Hawaii properties in timeshare exchange programs.

Marriott's Kauai Lagoons—Kalanipuu (www. marriott.com/lihkn; © **800/845-5279** or 808/632-8200), another timeshare with the possibility of nightly rentals, opened on the 800-acre resort in 2010. Overlooking the oceanfront Kauai Lagoons Golf Club, its roomier two-bedroom/two-bathroom and three-bedroom/three-bathroom villas have full kitchens ($379–$679, including Wi-Fi and self-parking), but guests do not have privileges to use the Kauai Marriott Resort's sprawling pool or its lounge chairs at Kalapaki Beach (reached by a hillside elevator or free shuttle). Details below apply only to Kauai Marriott Resort.

3610 Rice St. (at Kalapaki Beach), Lihue. www.marriott.com/lihhi. ⓒ **800/220-2925** or 808/245-5050. 356 units. $279–$484 double; check for online packages and discounts. Rollaway $25. $30 resort fee. $19 valet parking (self-parking included in resort fee). **Amenities:** 5 restaurants; 2 bars; free airport shuttle (on request); baby-sitting; children's program; concierge; fitness center; 5 Jacuzzis; pool; room service; watersports equipment rentals; Wi-Fi (included in resort fee).

Outrigger Waipouli Beach Resort ★★

Although its namesake beach is not good for swimming, kids and quite a number of adults are happy to spend all day in the heated fantasy pool here; it stretches across 2 acres with a lazily flowing river, sandy-bottomed hot tubs and children's pool, twin water slides, and waterfalls, amid lush landscaping. Inside the individually owned condos (mostly two-bedroom/three-bathroom units), adults will delight in the high-end kitchen appliances (SubZero fridge, Fisher & Paykel dishwasher drawers, Wolf glass cooktop) and luxurious finishes such as granite counters, Travertine stone tiles, and African mahogany cabinets. There's room for the whole family, too: Most of the two-bedroom units are 1,300 square feet, and a few corner penthouses run as large as 1,800 square feet. All units have washer-dryers and central air conditioning to boot. Opened in 2006, the $200-million complex covers 13 acres in Waipouli, between Wailua and Kapaa, conveniently across the street from Safeway and close to other shops and restaurants—but you'll want to avoid the cheaper units facing the parking lot and highway due to noise. Outrigger, which manages the most units here and operates the front desk, recently hiked its one-time cleaning fees by $30 to $80; you may want to compare resort rates with those of independently rented condos.

4–820 Kuhio Hwy., Kapaa. www.outrigger.com. © **877/418-0711** or 808/823-1401. 196 units. From $155 studio; $205–$385 1-bedroom/2-bathroom for 4; $295–$465 2-bedroom/3-bathroom for 6. Cleaning fee $105–$199. Resort fee $12. 2-night minimum. **Amenities:** Restaurant; business center; fitness center; pool; day spa; 3 outdoor whirlpools; Wi-Fi (included in resort fee).

MODERATE

Aqua Kauai Beach Resort ★★ Less than 5 minutes from the airport, but hidden from the highway by a long, palm-lined drive, this is the jewel in the crown of Aqua Hotels and Resorts' 15 moderately priced hotels in the islands, thanks to its extensive, beautifully sculpted pools—four in all, with adult and children's options, a 75-foot lava-tube water slide, whirlpools, waterfalls, and a sandy-bottomed beachfront lagoon. Decorated in a Balinese wood/Hawaiian plantation motif, rooms in the hotel itself are not particularly commodious, and some "mountain view" (odd-numbered rooms) units overlook parking lots, where wild chickens like to congregate. No matter: If you're not lingering by the pool, you can be walking for miles along the windswept beach (not recommended for swimming), which passes by the budget-friendly Wailua Golf Course, or indulging in a spa treatment.

Note: Aqua's hotel rates listed below reflect typical availability online; rack rates are higher. A number of hotel rooms are also individually owned "condos";

Aqua Kauai Beach Resort.

you'll find lower daily rates when booking through an owner, but you'll pay an extra $80 in resort/cleaning fees, with maid service upon request for $15 to $30 daily. The 25-acre resort is also home to the **Kauai Beach Villas,** spacious one- and two-bedroom condos operated as timeshares or privately owned rentals, all with access to the hotel's facilities; **Kauai Vacation Rentals** (www.kauaivacationrentals.com; ☎ **800/367-5025** or 808/245-8841) manages most of the non-timeshare units, with daily rates and cleaning fees starting at $165 and $110, respectively, plus a $35 reservation fee. Details below apply only to the Aqua Kauai Beach Resort hotel.

4331 Kauai Beach Dr., Lihue. From airport, drive 2½ miles northeast on Hwy. 51 to Kuhio Hwy. and turn right on Kauai Beach Dr. www.kauaibeachresorthawaii.com. ☎ **866/536-7976** or 808/245-1955. 350 units. $159–$319 double; $297–$540 suite. Check for online specials. Extra person $45. Rollaway $20. Resort fee $20 (includes parking and Internet access). **Amenities:** 2 restaurants; cafe; lounge; poolside bar; free airport/golf shuttle; babysitting; concierge; fitness center; 2 Jacuzzis; laundry facilities; 4 saltwater pools; rental cars; room service; Hawaiian Rainforest Spa & Salon; high-speed Internet.

Courtyard Kauai at Coconut Beach ★   Under Marriott management since 2010, this centrally located hotel wins the most raves for its oceanfront courtyard and pool, offering firepits, fountains, and a large whirlpool spa. A well-manicured lawn separates the hotel from golden-sand Makaiwa Beach, which is too reefy to do much swimming in, but just the ticket for long walks. Rooms, most of which are just 320 square feet, have lanais with cinnamon wood shutters to match the dark-veneered, Hawaiian-themed decor; two-thirds have at least partial ocean views. If you're looking for more space, book the executive oceanfront rooms, 528 square feet, where standard rates start at $209. The $20 resort fee is more comprehensive than most and includes self-parking (plus first night of valet parking), Wi-Fi, two complimentary mai tais, free meals for children 12 and under with paying adults at the **Voyager** restaurant, yoga classes, and beach-gear rentals, among other perks.

650 Aleka Loop, Kapaa. www.courtyardkauai.com. © **877/997-6667** or 808/822-3455. 311 units. $139–$239 double; from $249 suite. Check for online packages. Extra person $25. Children 17 and under stay free in parent's room. Resort fee $20. Valet parking $5 after 1st free night. **Amenities:** Restaurant; bar; business center; fitness center; Jacuzzi; pool; room service; spa; basketball/tennis court; Wi-Fi (included in resort fee).

INEXPENSIVE

In addition to the hotels listed below, young backpackers and adventurous adults on a shoestring budget should consider **Honuea International Hostel Kauai** (www.kauaihostel.com; © **808/823-6142**) in historic Kapaa. Bunks in the three, 10-bed single-sex and co-ed dorm rooms (each sharing just one bathroom) start at $30 per person, including taxes; the two deluxe private rooms, which share a bathroom, have the nicest setting, in the main house, for $70 a night (single or double occupancy, taxes included). There's a 10pm curfew, but there's also little reason to stay out that late on Kauai.

B&B fans who don't mind having breakfast only on the first morning should consider **Secret Falls Retreat** (www.secretfallsretreat.com; © **808/823-6398**), formerly the Mohala Ke Ola Bed and Breakfast. On a quiet side street just past Opaekaa Falls in Kapaa, the recently renovated inn offers five spacious rooms, all but one with private bathroom, for $99 to $180, with waterfall views and a large saltwater pool and hot tub adding to the serenity. The owner's two-bedroom, two-bathroom apartment (sleeps six) is also available for $289 (5-night minimum).

Aston Aloha Beach Resort ★ The location of this 10-acre beachfront property is great for families: next to the protected swimming/snorkeling ponds of Lydgate Beach, the fanciful Kamalani Playground, and

The pool area at the Aston Aloha Beach Resort.

historic Hawaiian sites by the Wailua River. With tropical decor that includes Hawaiian quilt–print comforters and pineapple lamps, the larger-than-average rooms became a little shabby around the edges in recent years—one reason the prices have been relatively low—but management has promised to complete "upgrades" by 2016. **Note:** All rooms have mini-fridges, while junior suites and cottages also have microwaves; cottages are the only units with lanais (patios) and are closest to Kamalani Playground.

3–5920 Kuhio Hwy., Kapaa. www.astonalohabeachhotel.com. © **877/997-6667** or 808/823-6000. 216 units. $89–$129 double; $145–$195 1-bedroom cottage; $150–$215 suite; check for online discounts and packages. Resort fee $18 daily (includes self-parking, Internet, DVD/Playstation rentals, fruit platter, and more). Extra person $30. Children 18 and under stay free in parent's room. **Amenities:** Restaurant; bar; business center; fitness room; Jacuzzi; coin laundry; 2 pools; tennis court; Wi-Fi (included in resort fee).

Garden Island Inn ★★ Thrifty travelers will love this cheerily renovated, well-maintained motel within a short walk of Kalapaki Beach, shops, and restaurants, while families will appreciate the large suites (with up to one king-size bed with three twin beds) and extra guest fees of just $10 per person. It's easy to make breakfast on the cheap, too, thanks to the mini-fridge, microwave, wet bar, and kitchenware, plus standard coffeemaker—grab free coffee and pie at the front desk, too. Other freebies include parking, Wi-Fi, and use of beach gear, not to mention happily given advice. Hanalei artist Camille Fontaine's bright, island-inspired murals and paintings make this a welcome antidote to neutral, cookie-cutter resort decor, while owners Lis and Steve Layne work tirelessly to improve their guests' comfort, even providing DVDs of movies made on Kauai to watch on flatscreen TVs. One caveat: Consider bringing earplugs to offset street noise. **Note:** The inn also manages two two-bedroom condos (sleep six) at the nearby hilltop Banyan Harbor complex ($174), which boasts a pool and tennis courts.

3445 Wilcox Rd. (across the street from Kalapaki Beach, near Nawiliwili Harbor), Lihue. www.gardenislandinn.com. © **800/648-0154** or 808/245-7227. 21 units. $113–$164 double. Extra person $10. **Amenities:** Free use of watersports equipment and beach gear; Wi-Fi (free).

Kauai Shores ★★ Formerly called Kauai Sands, this 6-acre beachfront bargain recently underwent a major overhaul of nearly all rooms and public areas under new ownership and management. The small but functional updated rooms feature modern, slightly quirky, Ikea-style furnishings (curvy mirrors, square lamps) with orange and lime accents, bright blue geometric-patterned rugs, and compact but tidy bathrooms, while the spruced-up, ocean-view pool especially inviting. A free continental breakfast (pastries, bananas, coffee/tea) is offered in the open-air lobby—at least until the Big Island's **Lava Lava Beach Club** opens its planned offshoot in the beachfront half of the building. Swimming isn't safe here, but the rock-walled pool in front of neighboring Lae Nani is good for children, and the Lydgate Beach ponds are just a short drive away; yoga fans can take a free class on the oceanfront lawn three mornings a week. **Note:** If you can carry your own bags, request a second-floor room for more privacy, and a location away from the parking lot (which fills up quickly).

420 Papaloa Rd. (off Kuhio Hwy.), Kapaa. www.kauaishores hotel.com. © **855/309-5483** or 808/822-4951. 206 rooms. $79–$219 double; studio suite with kitchenette $149–$299. Check for

online discounts. Extra person $25. $15 resort fee (includes Wi-Fi). **Amenities:** 2 pools; barbecue grills; business center; coin laundry; Wi-Fi (free).

North Shore

Despite this magical region's popularity with visitors, only Princeville is officially one of Kauai County's "visitor destination areas"; it's important to be aware that many rural bed-and-breakfasts and vacation rentals here are unlicensed. While the county may temporarily be leaving B&Bs alone, in 2014 the state abruptly shut down one longtime Hanalei B&B for building and operating in a conservation district, and unhappy neighbors of unlicensed rentals may report them to authorities. If you're not staying in one of the few hotels, I recommend booking through one of the following agencies, which manage only licensed properties and are known for their integrity.

Founded in 1978, **Kauai Vacation Rentals** (www.kauaivacationrentals.com; ✆ **800/367-5025** or 808/245-8841) manages well-maintained homes and condos across the island, with the majority—100 at press time—on the North Shore. Most have a 3- to 5-night minimum that expands to 1 week or 2 weeks from December 15 to January 6, when rates also rise. You can search online listings by location, size, view, and amenities such as air-conditioning (not so common where trade winds blow), swimming pool, and Internet access (increasingly more common); agents are happy to help you find the perfect match. In **Haena,** for example, the standard rate for a one-bedroom, one-bathroom garden-view cottage that's a short walk to Tunnels (Makua) Beach is $270 a night or $1,350 a week; for an ocean-view, two-bedroom, one-and-a-half-bathroom cottage right on **Anini Beach,** it's

$360 a night or $1,800 a week—a good deal if you're splitting the expenses with another couple. For all rentals, you'll also pay a $35 reservation fee and one-time cleaning fee, anywhere from $90 for a studio condo to as high as $565 for a five-bedroom house.

Parrish Collection Kauai (www.parrishkauai. com; ✆ **800/325-5701** or 808/742-2000), which has made a name for itself with high-quality Poipu vacation rentals (see "Finding a Perfect Place in Poipu," p. 138), also represents 14 homes and cottages from Kilauea to Haena and 53 properties (nearly all condos) in Princeville. Many of the latter are in the **Hanalei Bay Resort ★★**, which has spectacular views rivaling those of the St. Regis, air-conditioning in units, and a fantasy pool with waterfalls and slides; rates start at $125 a night (5-night minimum) for a garden-view studio. If you can forgo an ocean view, Parrish's best values are in the **Plantation at Princeville ★**, roomy two- and three-bedroom air-conditioned units in a complex built in 2004 with a pool, spa, barbecues, and fitness center; rates start at $130 for a two-bedroom, two-bathroom unit. Not included in the rates are the $50 "processing" fee per booking and cleaning fees, starting at $100 for a studio and increasing by size.

Coldwell Banker Bali Hai Realty (www.bali hai.com; ✆ **808/826-8000**) manages about 80 luxury vacation rentals, all of them licensed; expect a 7-night minimum June 1 to August 31 and December 15 to January 5; otherwise 4 to 5 nights. Its Princeville properties include 11 units at the desirable **Pali Ke Kua ★** and **Puu Poa ★★** complexes, less than a half-mile from one another on the bluff above Hideaways Beach. At Pali Ke Kua, nightly rates start as low as $130 for a two-bedroom, two-bathroom mountain-view unit, and $160 for an ocean-view one-bedroom unit with sleeper sofa that sleeps four. Its lowest rate at Puu Poa is $290 a night for a two-bedroom, two-bathroom ocean-view unit (ideal for couples to share). For condo bookings, Bali Hai charges a reservation fee of $25 to $50 and a cleaning fee of $150 to $180.

A frequent resource for Hollywood movie crews on the island, Mike Lyons of **Kauai Style Vacation Rentals** (www.kauaistyleconcierge.com; © **808/482-1572**) specializes in licensed properties on the North Shore; you won't find listings on his site because he prefers to work with clients individually. A passionate surfer, Lyons also enjoys escorting guests on ocean and trail adventures and can arrange private chefs and other services.

EXPENSIVE

Hanalei Colony Resort ★★ With two bedrooms (separated by louvered wooden doors), one-and-a-half to two bathrooms, full kitchens, and living rooms, these 48 individually owned, updated condos are perfect for families—or anyone who can appreciate being as little as 10 feet from the beach, in the shadow of green peaks near the end of the road. It has no TVs, phones, or entertainment systems, although free Wi-Fi means guests don't disconnect quite as much as they used to. The beach is generally not safe for swimming, but you're less than a mile from Tunnels (Makua) Beach, and the barbecue area by the small pool boasts lush landscaping and a koi pond. The resort runs a 13-passenger shuttle to Hanalei and beaches during the day, when it's free; in the evening, the shuttle takes guests to and from dining and entertainment destinations in Hanalei and Princeville for a $10 charge per unit. The independently run Ayurvedic-themed **Hanalei Day Spa** and the award-winning

A suite at the Hanelei Colony Resort.

Mediterranean Gourmet (p. 165) restaurant are also on site. Check online for romance and activity packages.

5–7130 Kuhio Hwy. (makai side), Haena, about 5mi west of Hanalei. www.hcr.com. © **800/628-3004** or 808/826-6235. 48 units. $299–$579 2-bedroom apt for 4. 2-night minimum; 7th night free. **Amenities:** Restaurant; coffee bar/art gallery; free weekly continental breakfast; babysitting; barbecues; concierge; Jacuzzi; coin laundry; pool; day spa; Wi-Fi (free).

St. Regis Princeville ★★ Hawaii's first and only St. Regis—a brand renowned for its opulence and service—opened in late 2009, following a multimillion-dollar transformation of the Princeville Hotel. The dramatic cliffside layout didn't change: You still enter on the ninth floor, with a dazzling panorama of Hanalei Bay and Makana (the "Bali Hai" mountain) across the airy lobby and an elevator to take you down to the narrow but pleasant sandy beach and handsome, 5,000-square-foot infinity pool. The spacious (540 sq. ft. and up) rooms also still feature extra-large bedroom windows as well as "magic" bathroom windows, which toggle between clear and opaque. A welcome sheen of sophisticated Hawaiiana has replaced the formerly palatial European decor, however, typified by the 11,000-square-foot **Halelea Spa,** which combines traditional Hawaiian healing practices and local botanicals with Western treatments and waterfall showers. Among the many lavish amenities are goose-down comforters, 42- and 52-inch flatscreen TVs, and, in junior suites on up, personal butler service.

5520 Ka Haku Rd., Princeville. www.stregisprinceville.com. ✆ **877/787-3447** or 808/826-9644. 252 units. $450–$1,100 double; $630–$1,010 jr. suite (820 sq. ft.); $1,885–$2,500 St. Regis suite (1,200 sq. ft.) Extra person $100. Children 17 and under stay free in parent's room. Parking (valet only) $32. **Amenities:** 3 restaurants; 3 bars; children's program; concierge; fitness center; golf; Jacuzzis; pool; room service; spa; watersports equipment rentals; Wi-Fi (free).

Westin Princeville Ocean Villas ★★★   A superb "vacation ownership" property that nonetheless offers nightly rentals, this 18½-acre bluffside resort is a winner with families and couples seeking condo-style units with resort furnishings and amenities. Besides Westin's justly famed "Heavenly Beds," the roomy studios and one-bedroom suites (which can be combined into two-bedroom units) have immaculate, well-stocked kitchens, washer-dryers, and huge bathrooms with separate glass showers and deep whirlpool tubs. Playful statuary and fountains mark the centrally located children's pool next to the main pool; adults will appreciate the quieter, bluff-side plunge pools. The indoor-outdoor **Nanea Restaurant and Bar,** one of the better hotel restaurants on Kauai, has substantial discounts for children 11 and younger, and the on-site deli has a tempting array of farm-fresh items. *Note:* The resort is near a steep, often muddy, unmaintained trail to Anini Beach, but most guests opt to take the free shuttle to the St. Regis Princeville, where they walk down nearly 200 steps to Puu Poa beach, or drive themselves to Anini or another nearby beach.

3838 Wyllie Rd., Princeville. www.westinprinceville.com. © **808/ 827-8700.** 346 units. From $276–$410 studio (sleeps 2); $383–$500 1-bedroom (sleeps 4); $655–$1,085 2-bedroom (sleeps 8). $13 parking. **Amenities:** 2 restaurants, bar, deli/store; barbecues; children's program; concierge; fitness room w/steam room and sauna, plus use of Makai Lap Pool and Fitness Center, 1 mile away; 4 pools; free resort shuttle; Wi-Fi (free).

MODERATE

The best values on the North Shore can be found among Princeville's many condo complexes, which vary widely in age and amenities; check the listings of the brokers mentioned above. I recommend either the dramatically perched **Hanalei Bay Resort** ★★ (www.hanaleibay resort.com; © 877/344-0688) or the residential-style **Cliffs at Princeville** ★★ (www.cliffsatprinceville. com; © 808/826-6129); both participate in time-share and vacation rental programs but also offer direct bookings; both recently underwent sizable renovations and have pools and hot tubs. Rates at the 22-acre Hanalei Bay Resort, just west of the St. Regis, start at $145 a night for a hotel-style unit with king-size bed, plus a $15 daily resort fee. At the posher, more tranquil Cliffs, on the northern edge of the Princeville bluff, one-bedroom, two-bathroom units (sleeping four) with full kitchen, living room, and two lanais start at $324 ($384 for loft units that sleep six) plus a weekly resort fee of $75. *Note:* The three-story Cliffs has no elevators or air conditioning; it does have two tennis courts, a playground, and a putting green.

FINDING A PERFECT PLACE
in poipu

The best way to find a high-quality, licensed vacation rental in Poipu is through **Parrish Collection Kauai** (www.parrishkauai.com; ☎ **800/325-5701** or 808/742-2000). Parrish manages more than 200 units for 20 different island-wide condo developments, plus dozens of vacation houses ranging from quaint cottages to elite resort homes; about three-quarters are in Poipu, in a wide range of prices. The company sets resort-like standards for decor and maintenance, classifying its lodgings into four categories ("premium plus" is the highest, for new or completely renovated units), sending linens out for professional laundering, and providing signature bathroom amenities. At Parrish's flagship **Waikomo Stream Villas** ★ and **Nihi Kai Villas** ★★ in Poipu, where the company manages about half the condos (75 in total), there's even concierge service—with no kickbacks for referrals, according to owner J. P. Parrish. "Our guides know the island really well and have no agenda; we only recommend what works and has good customer service," he notes.

Each well-equipped rental offers a full kitchen, washer/dryer, TV/DVD, phone, and free Wi-Fi; condo rates in the introductory Value Collection start as

South Shore

The most popular place to stay year-round, the resort area of Poipu Beach is definitely a "visitor destination area," with hundreds of rental condos, cottages, and houses vying with Kauai's best luxury resorts for families and a romantic boutique hotel. Upcountry Lawai and Kalaheo brim with more modest, not necessarily licensed, B&Bs and vacation homes.

low as $100 a night; you'll pay cleaning but not resort or parking fees. At Nihi Kai Villas, which has a heated pool (a rarity here) and large floor plans, off-peak nightly rates start at $167 for a two-bedroom condo (sleeps six), plus $153 cleaning; at Waikomo Stream Villas, a one-bedroom condo (sleeps four) starts at $115 a night, plus $125 cleaning.

Parrish, which also rents vacation cottages and sumptuous multimillion-dollar ocean estates, is the exclusive agent for the villas, cottages, and bungalows at heavenly **Kukuiula ★★★**;

renters gain access to Kukuiula's private, ultra-posh spa, golf course, and clubhouse dining (see www.stayatkukuiula.com for details.)

There's a 3- to 5-night minimum for condos, a 7-night minimum for houses, and no minimum at Kukuiula cottages, except during winter holidays. For 5-night or longer stays, inquire about the **Frommer's Preferred Guest Discount,** good for 5% to 10% off; if a better deal is available, agents will let you know. The company also offers a price-match guarantee.

EXPENSIVE

Besides the resorts below, the 35-acre, green-lawned **Kiahuna Plantation Resort ★★**, on the sandy beach next to the Sheraton, is also worth considering, although its 333 individually furnished, one- and two-bedroom condos vary widely in taste; they also rely on ceiling fans (and trade winds) for cooling, and there's no elevator in the three-story buildings. **Outrigger** (www.outrigger.com; © **808/742-6411**) manages more than half of the units, but only those rented from

Castle Resorts (www.castleresorts.com; ℂ **800/367-5004** or 808/545-5310) receive daily housekeeping and access to the tennis courts and resort-style pool of the Poipu Beach Athletic Club across the street. Outrigger's nightly one-bedroom rates start at $115 garden-view and $339 oceanfront, plus $135 cleaning, while Castle's equivalent units start at $224 to $374, plus $50 to $115 cleaning; both include free Wi-Fi and parking in their rates.

Grand Hyatt Kauai Resort & Spa ★★★   Kauai's largest hotel aims to have one of the smallest carbon footprints. Its 602 luxurious rooms feature not only a gold-and-green palette and new pillow-top beds, but also eco-friendly elements such as recycled-yarn carpets and plush robes made from recycled plastic bottles. Grass-covered roofs and solar panels reduce emissions, a new hydroponic garden grows produce for its dining outlets (such as the thatched-roof **Tidepools** restaurant), and used cooking oil becomes biodiesel fuel. But that's just green icing on the cake of this sprawling, family-embracing resort, where the elaborate, multi-tiered fantasy pool and saltwater lagoon more than compensate for the rough waters of Shipwrecks (Keoneloa) Beach; the 45,000-square-foot indoor/outdoor **Anara Spa** and adjacent **Poipu Bay Golf Course** offer excellent adult diversions, as do the new firepits overlooking the pool by **Dondero's** Italian restaurant. To feel even more virtuous about splurging on a stay, check out the hotel's volunteer programs with the National Tropical Botanical Garden and Kauai Humane Society, among others.

1571 Poipu Rd., Poipu. www.grandhyattkauai.com. ℂ **800/554-9288** or 808/742-1234. 602 units. $429–$589 double; from $599

Grand Club; from $779 suite. $25 resort fee includes self-parking, Wi-Fi, fitness classes, and more. Children 17 and under stay free in parent's room. Packages available. Valet parking $15. **Amenities:** 5 restaurants; 5 bars; babysitting; bike and car rentals; children's program; club lounge; concierge; fitness center; golf course and clubhouse; 3 Jacuzzis; 1½-acre saltwater swimming lagoon; luau; 2 non-chlorinated pools connected by river pool; room service; spa; 2 tennis courts; watersports equipment rentals; Wi-Fi (included in resort fee.)

Koa Kea Hotel & Resort ★★★

If everything seems to run like clockwork at this oceanfront jewel box, hidden between the sprawling Kiahuna Plantation Resort and the densely built Marriott Waiohai Beach Club, chalk it up to general manager Chris Steuri, whose Swiss family has been in the hotel business for generations. He oversaw the years-long, multimillion-dollar transformation of the old Poipu Beach Hotel (dormant since 1992's Hurricane Iniki) into a posh boutique inn boasting the island's best hotel restaurant, **Red Salt** (p. 172), as well as a small but expertly staffed spa. *Ko'a kea* means "white coral," which inspires the white and coral accents in the sleek, modern decor; all rooms feature lanais, many with views of the rocky coast (a short walk from sandy beaches). Steuri's European flair shows in the Nespresso espresso machines and L'Occitane bath products, but his staff resounds with pure Hawaiian aloha. *Note:* At prices this steep, the "garden view" will disappoint—best to spring for at least a partial ocean view, and sign up for the free Preferred Hotels & Resorts loyalty program to check for specials.

2251 Poipu Rd., Poipu. www.koakea.com. © **888/898-8958** or 808/828-8888. 121 units. $369–$900 double; from $1,625 suite. Packages available. $26 resort fee includes valet parking, Wi-Fi, fitness center, and more. **Amenities:** Restaurant; 2 bars; concierge; fitness room; Jacuzzi; pool; room service; spa; water-sports equipment rentals; Wi-Fi (included in resort fee).

Poipu Kapili Resort ★★

All of the 60 upscale, individually owned and furnished condos overlook the waves crashing on the rocky shoreline just across the little-traveled street. Floor plans start at 1,200 square feet for a one-bedroom unit with one-and-a-half to two bathrooms, all on the ground floor with pool and ocean views; the larger two-bedroom units come with either three bathrooms in two-level townhomes with ground-level entries, or with two bathrooms in third-floor penthouses accessed by elevator. The layouts are especially appealing to families, but couples will appreciate the high priority the management places on maintaining a tranquil atmosphere, especially around the central pool area; cooks should take note of the spacious kitchens and free herb garden. The online interactive map and detailed photos can help you pick the unit for you. Friday mornings there's a free social with juice, coffee, and pastries by the pool.

2221 Kapili Rd., Poipu. www.poipukapili.com. **©** **800/443-7714** or 808/742-6449. 60 units. $255–$320 1-bedroom (sleeps up to 4); $385–$550 2-bedroom (up to 6); $485–$525 2-bedroom penthouse. Check online for longer-stay discounts and specials. **Amenities:** Barbecue area; saltwater pool; 2 tennis courts (night-lit); coin laundry (washer-dryer in all 2-bedroom units, some 1 bedrooms); Wi-Fi (free).

Sheraton Kauai Resort ★★

Thanks to a $16-million remodel, this appealingly low-key resort is finally living up to its ideal beachfront location, where the western horizon sees a riot of color at sunset and rainbows arc over a rocky point after the occasional shower. The expanded oceanfront pool—with mini-slide, rock-lined whirlpool, and luxurious cabanas (for

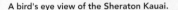

A bird's eye view of the Sheraton Kauai.

rent)—provides a much more inviting place for a dip, which conveniently makes the traditional pool in the garden wing a quieter oasis. Nights here are livelier, too, thanks to large firepits in the ocean-view courtyard and the tasty libations and wine-tasting social hours at **RumFire Poipu Beach,** the resort's ambitious, island-inspired restaurant/lounge with walls of glass. *Tip:* Ask for a room on the ocean side, even if garden view, to avoid frequent street crossings; oceanside rooms seem larger, too. Prices listed below can be found online.

2440 Hoonani Rd., Poipu. www.sheraton-kauai.com. © **866/ 716-8109** or 808/742-1661. 394 units. $239–$429 double (prepaid as low as $199–$259); $490–$699 suite. $31 resort fee includes self-parking (and 1st night valet parking), Wi-Fi, use of fitness center, bicycles, Poipu shuttle, bottled water, and more. Extra person $70. Valet parking $10. **Amenities:** 3 restaurants; bar; babysitting; concierge; free computer use; fitness room; Jacuzzi; beachfront luau; 2 pools; room service; spa services; 3 tennis courts (2 night-lit); watersports equipment rentals; Wi-Fi (included in resort fee).

MODERATE

Among other options outside of Poipu, **Kauai Banyan Inn** ★ (www.kauaibanyan.com; © **888/786-3855**) in rural Lawai offers six airy suites and a cottage, all with gleaming wood floors, Hawaiian quilts, and kitchenettes or full kitchens, for $155 to $230 per night plus $45 cleaning. Although the inn is not licensed, co-owners Lorna and John Hoff, who live on the 11-acre compound that they helped build and now run as a bed-and-breakfast, say it's not in an agricultural zone, and do forward accommodations taxes to the county.

Kauai Cove Cottage ★★ Honeymooners and other romance seekers find a serene oasis in the namesake cottage of this collection of studio, condo, and suite units. On a quiet lane just a few houses up from the snorkel spot of Koloa Landing and a short walk to a sandy cove known as Baby Beach, the bright cottage ($149–$229) provides a fourposter canopy queen-size bed under high vaulted ceilings, private bamboo-walled lanai with barbecue grill, flatscreen TV with DVD player, and a full kitchen. Since it can get hot in Poipu, the wall-unit air conditioning (plus ceiling fan) is a nice touch. Helpful owners E. J. and Diane Olsson live nearby in Poipu Kai, where they also rent out an attractive studio and one-bedroom suite ($115–$185) that include use of a pool and hot tub; another two-bedroom, two-bathroom condo ($205–$325) is available at the 12-unit, oceanfront Poipu Palms complex (cleaning fees listed below).

2672 Puuholo Rd., Poipu. www.kauaicove.com. © **800/624-9945** or 808/742-2562. 4 units. $149–$185 double, cleaning $50–$75; $205–$324 two-bedroom, cleaning $160. **Amenities:** Wi-Fi (free).

Poipu Plantation B&B Inn & Vacation Rentals ★★★ This ultra-tranquil compound almost defies description. It comprises four adults-only, bed-and-breakfast suites of various sizes in a lovingly restored 1938 plantation house; seven vacation rental units in three modern cottage-style wings behind the B&B; and a one-bedroom condo across the street at the 35-unit Sunset Kahili complex. The B&B suites, fully renovated in 2013, feature handsome hardwood floors, sturdy vintage furnishings, bright tropical art, and (thankfully) modern bathrooms; the 700-square-foot Alii Suite also includes a wet bar, two-person whirlpool tub, and private lanai. The one- and two-bedroom cottage units on the foliage-rich 1-acre lot have less character, but offer more space and full kitchens; some have ocean views across the rooftops of Sunset Kahili, where the neatly maintained ocean-view condos have use of a small pool (but no air conditioning). Innkeepers Chris and Javed Moore and their friendly staff delight in offering travel tips. *Note:* When comparing rates, consider that the units here have no cleaning, resort, parking, or Wi-Fi fees; plus, breakfasts for the B&B units include Kauai coffee, hot entrees, and fresh island fruit and juice.

1792 Pee Rd., Poipu. www.poipubeach.com. ✆ **800/643-0263** or 808/742-6757. 12 units. Rental units: $135–$210 1-bedroom (sleeps 2–3), $165–$235 2-bedroom (sleeps up to 5). Condo: $145–$200 (sleeps up to 3); additional person $20. Inn: $140–$220 (including breakfast and daily housekeeping); adults only (2 maximum); 3-night minimum (5 for winter holidays). **Amenities:** Use of beach gear; laundry facilities; Wi-Fi (free).

INEXPENSIVE

In pricey Poipu, staying anywhere for $150 a night—especially if fees and taxes are included—can be a real challenge. **Kauai Vacation Rentals** (www.kauai vacationrentals.com; ☏ **800/367-5025** or 808/245-8841) manages 10 garden- and ocean-view studios in the well-kept **Prince Kuhio** ★★ complex across from Lawai Beach that cost about $140 a night (5-night minimum), even with taxes, reservation and cleaning fees rolled in; it also has eight one-bedroom/one-bathroom units (some sleeping four) that, all told, cost about $175 a night. During spring and fall, **Suite Paradise** (www.suite-paradise.com; ☏ **800/367-8020**) frequently has garden-view one-bedroom/one-bathroom units in the **Kahala** ★ condominium on the 70-acre, verdant Poipu Kai resort for $145 to $155 a night, all inclusive.

Marjorie's Kauai Inn ★   In keeping with its hilltop pastoral setting in Lawai, this three-room bed-and-breakfast prides itself on green touches: energy-efficient appliances, eco-friendly cleaning products, and local organic produce (some of it grown on site). You're more likely to notice the sweeping valley views from your private lanais. All rooms have private entrances and kitchenettes. Sunset View, the largest, boasts its own hot tub in a gazebo and a fold-out couch for extra guests. Everyone can use the 50-foot-long main pool and hot tub, down a long flight of stairs (this isn't the best place for young children). Rooms include TV with cable and DVD player, but in the tradition of the original owner, Marjorie Ketcher, guests are encouraged to explore the island with a booklet of helpful suggestions and free use of bikes, a surfboard, a kayak, and beach gear.

Off Hailima Rd., Lawai. www.marjorieskauaiinn.com. ☏ **800/717-8838** or 808/332-8838. 3 units. $170–$225 double, including continental breakfast. Extra person $20. **Amenities:**

Barbecue; complimentary use of bikes, kayak, and beach gear; Jacuzzi; laundry facilities; pool; Wi-Fi (free).

West Side

EXPENSIVE

Waimea Plantation Cottages ★★ Serenity now: That's what you'll find at this 30-acre oceanfront enclave of restored vintage cottages, spread among large lawns dotted with coconut palms, banyan trees, and tropical flowers. The black-sand beach is not good for swimming (there's a small pool for that), but it offers intriguing driftwood for beachcombers and mesmerizing sunset views. The charmingly rustic cottages feature period-style furnishings, full kitchens, lanais, and modern perks such as Wi-Fi; they come in one- and two-bedroom units with one bathroom (594–726 sq. ft.) and three-bedroom, two-bathroom versions (1,088 sq. ft.). Owned by the heirs of Norwegian immigrant Hans Peter Faye, who ran a sugar plantation, and managed by Coast Hotels, the property also includes the four-bedroom, three-bathroom Jean Faye House and five-bedroom Manager's House, both oceanfront (1,250 and 4,240 sq. ft., respectively), and the five-bedroom, five-bathroom Kruse House (4,020 sq. ft.), which offers air conditioning in all the bedrooms and a kitchenette in the master suite. Opened in 2014, the on-site restaurant, **Kalapaki Joe's,** is also a popular sports bar. *Note:* Lower rates reflect garden-view units in non-peak periods—the prices for most stays definitely qualify for the "expensive" category.

9400 Kaumualii Hwy. (*makai* side, west of Huakai Rd.), Waimea. www.waimea-plantation.com. © **808/338-1625.** 56 units. $169–$339 1-bedroom double; $289–$379 2-bedroom (sleeps up to 4); $329–$569 3-bedroom (up to 5); from $515 4-bedroom (up to 8); from $633 5-bedroom (up to 10). $19 resort fee. Children 17 and under stay free in parent's room. Check for online specials. **Amenities:** Restaurant; bar; laundry; pool; volleyball; Wi-Fi (included in resort fee).

MODERATE

The West Inn ★   The closest thing the West Side has to a Holiday Inn Express, the West Inn opened in 2011, and its clean, neutral-toned rooms with bright accents and stone counters still look new. One two-story wing of medium-size rooms is just off the highway across from Waimea Theater; some second-story rooms have an ocean view over corrugated metal roofs from the long, shared lanai, and all units have refrigerators, microwaves, air conditioning, coffeemakers, and cable TV. Another wing of one- and two-bedroom suites, designed for longer stays with full kitchens and living rooms, is tucked off to the side, with a small barbecue area between the wings. *Note:* There's no elevator; call ahead to arrange check-ins after 6pm.

9690 Kaumualii Hwy. (*makai* side, at Pokole Rd.), Waimea. http://thewestinn.com. © **808/338-1107.** 20 units. $198 king or double; $229 king with kitchen; $243 1-bedroom suite (5-night minimum), $349 2-bedroom suite (sleeps up to 4; 5-night minimum). $30 extra person. **Amenities:** Barbecue grills, coin laundry, Wi-Fi (free).

INEXPENSIVE

Inn Waimea/West Kauai Lodging ★★   If you're looking for accommodations with both character and modern conveniences, check out the small lodge and four vacation rentals managed by West Kauai Lodging. A former parsonage that's also known as Halepule ("House of Prayer"), **Inn Waimea** is a Craftsman-style cottage in the center of quaint Waimea, with simple, tropical-tinged, plantation-era decor in its four wood-paneled suites, all but one with a separate living area. Updated in 2013 and under new management, the suites now offer flatscreen TVs, Wi-Fi, and (in summer) air-conditioning, as well as private bathrooms with pedestal sinks, coffeemakers, mini-fridges, and ceiling fans. Upstairs, the Banana Suite boasts a king-size bed separated from a large Jacuzzi tub by a banana leaf wrought-iron screen, while the Bamboo Suite has a partial ocean view. Bring eyeshades—most curtains are just sheers. West Kauai Lodging also manages three moderately priced two-bedroom cottages in Waimea (owned by the Faye family, which has deep roots on the island), plus the newly built three-bedroom **Hale La** beach house in Kekaha, all with full kitchens, laundry facilities, and summertime air-conditioning. The plantation-style **Beach Cottage,** which includes a claw-foot tub, bamboo furniture, and sunset views over the ocean and Waimea Pier, is closest to the inn; the homey, Craftsman-inspired **Ishihara Cottage,** which features exotic hardwoods and an eat-in kitchen, and the tree-shaded **Pali Cottage,** with vintage furnishings and an enclosed lanai, are above town, with sweeping views of ridges and the distant sea. Manager Patrick McLean, who owns Hale La, is a former Kauai bed-and-breakfast pro who loves to help visitors plan where to eat, when to take a boat tour, you name it.

4469 Halepule Rd. (off Hwy. 50), Waimea. www.westkauai lodging.com. ✆ **808/652-6852.** Inn (4 units) $120–$150 ($25 for 3rd person). 3 cottages (sleep 4–6) $179–$235, plus $125 cleaning fee. Hale La beach house (sleeps 8) $495, plus $250 cleaning. **Amenities:** Wi-Fi (free).

Camping & Cabins

Kauai offers tent camping in seven county-run beach parks and, for extremely hardy and self-sufficient types, several state-managed, backcountry areas of the **Napali Coast** and **Waimea Canyon.** Tents and simple cabins are also available in the cooler elevations of **Kokee State Park,** and minimal campgrounds at **Polihale State Park;** I can't recommend camping in the latter, due to its rugged conditions and potential for crime.

All camping requires permits, which must be purchased in advance, and camping in vehicles is not allowed.

County campsites, often busy with local families on weekends, close one day each week for maintenance. The most recommended for visitors, both for scenery and relative safety, are at **Haena, Hanalei Blackpot, Anini,** and **Lydgate** beach parks. Go to **www.kauai.gov**, click on "Visiting," and then "Camping Information," for schedules, downloadable mail-in permit applications, and hours and addresses for the neighborhood centers where permits are issued in person. Permits for nonresidents cost $3 per adult (free for children 17 and under, with adult), except for Lydgate, which is $25 per site.

For camping in state parks and forest reserves, **Hawaii's Department of Land and Natural Resources** (http://camping.ehawaii.gov; ✆ **808/274-3444**) prefers to issue online permits; its office in Lihue, 3060 Eiwa St., Suite 306, is also open 8am to 3:30pm weekdays. **Napali Coast State Wilderness Park** allows camping at two sites along the 11-mile Kalalau Trail—Hanakoa Valley, 6 miles in, and Kalalau

Valley, at trail's end—for a maximum of 5 nights (no more than 1 consecutive night at Hanakoa). Camping is also permitted at Milolii, for a maximum of 3 nights; it's reached only by kayak or authorized boats mid-May through early September. Although there's no drinking water, trash must be packed out, and composting toilets are not always in good repair, permits ($20 per night) often sell out a year in advance. (**Note:** Due to frequent overstays, rangers conduct periodic permit checks here, so make sure yours is handy.)

Permits for primitive campsites in eight backcountry areas of Waimea Canyon and nearby wilderness preserves cost $18 per night, with a 5-night maximum; see http://camping.ehawaii.gov for detailed descriptions.

In **Kokee State Park,** which gets quite chilly on winter nights, **Kokee Lodge** (www.thelodgeatkokee.net, ☎ **808/335-6061**) offers 12 rustic, often unkempt cabins ($74–$94 a night) that sleep up to six and should be reserved 3 to 6 months in advance; ask for a newer, two-bedroom unit, such as quiet No. 12. Kokee Lodge also manages the nearby state campgrounds ($18 per night; see above for permits). Less than a mile away, down a dirt road, the YWCA of Kauai's **Camp Sloggett** (www.campingkauai.com; ☎ **808/245-5959**) allows tent camping in its large forest clearing for $15 per tent per night, with toilets and hot showers available; there's also a four-person cottage ($120–$150). Groups may rent its bunkhouse ($160–$200) or lodge ($200–$225), both of which sleep up to 15.

If you need gear, **Just Live** (www.ziplinetours kauai.com; ☎ **808/482-1295**) sells and rents top brands of tents, camping stoves, sleep sacks, and more in the Anchor Cove Shopping Center, 3416 Rice St., Lihue. **Kayak Kauai** (www.kayakkauai.com; ✆ **888/596-3853** or 808/826-9844) offers rentals, supplies, and even car and bag storage at its Wailua River Marina shop, 3-5971 Kuhio Hwy., Kapaa. **Pedal 'n Paddle** (www.pedalnpaddle.com; ✆ **808/826-9069**) sells hiking boots, freeze-dried food, and other necessities and rents tents, backpacks, and sleeping bags; it's in Ching Young Village, 5-5190 Kuhio Hwy., Hanalei.

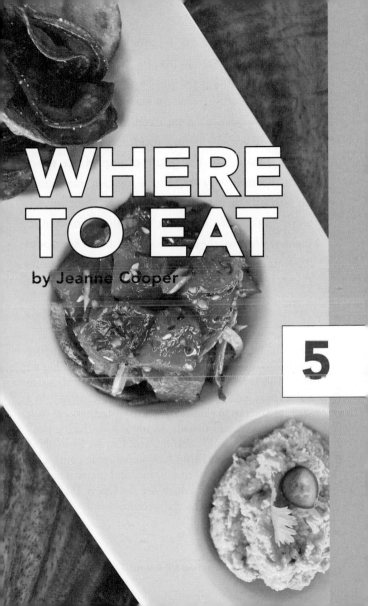

WHERE
TO EAT

by Jeanne Cooper

5

Thanks to a proliferation of hamburger joints, plate-lunch counters, and food trucks, you'll find affordable (by local standards) choices in every town; even in pricey Princeville, the shopping center food court offers a few tasty bargains. At the gourmet end of the spectrum, Kauai's very expensive restaurants—both on and off the resorts—provide excellent service along with more complex but reliably executed dishes. And nearly every establishment trumpets its Kauai-grown ingredients, which help keeps the Garden Island green as well as the flavors fresh.

5

Introduction

WHERE TO EAT

The challenge is finding exceptional quality in the moderate to expensive range. Costs are indeed higher here, and service is often slower; it's best not to arrive anywhere—even at one of the many food trucks—in a state of starvation. Patience and pleasantness on your part, however, will usually be rewarded. During peak holiday and summer seasons, avoid stress by booking online with **Open Table** (www.opentable.com), currently available for 30 restaurants and luaus. The listings below, not all of which are on Open Table, will note where reservations are recommended.

PREVIOUS PAGE: **Appetizers from Merrimans.**

For those with access to a kitchen (or just a mini-fridge), check out "Farmer's Markets & Fruit Stands" (p. 190) for fresh produce and more.

East Side

Note: You'll find the restaurants in this section on either the "Hotels & Restaurants on the Coconut Coast" map (p. 121) or the "Hotels & Restaurants in Lihue" map (p. 124).

EXPENSIVE

In addition to the options below, foodies will want to check out chef Jean-Marie Josselin's recent triumphant return to Kapaa, **JO2** (www.jotwo.com; © **808/212-1627**), 4-971 Kuhio. Hwy. Josselin, a Hawaii Regional Cuisine co-founder who gained renown in the 1990s with A Pacific Cafe in Kapaa before moving to Las Vegas, reestablished himself on Kauai in 2010 with Josselin's Tapas Bar & Grill in Poipu (p. 171). Now he has opened to acclaim JO2, an island-sourced, "natural cuisine" restaurant with Asian influences (main courses $21–$35), serving dinner 5 to 10pm daily.

Duke's Kauai ★ STEAK/SEAFOOD The view of Kalapaki Beach, an indoor waterfall and koi pond, and a lively beachfront bar have as much, if not more, to do with the popularity of Kauai's outpost of the California-Hawaii TS Restaurants chain as do the fresh seafood, vast salad bar, and belt-straining Hula Pie (a macadamia-nut-ice-cream confection built for sharing). The downstairs bar's lunch and dinner menu offers the best values, with burgers, hearty salads, and flatbread pizzas, but the dinner-only upstairs dining room shows local flair, with Hanalei taro cakes, seared ahi with papaya mustard sauce, and Kauai Kunana Dairy goat cheese atop grilled New York steak—among

Duke's Kauai.

other tasty but less ambitious dishes such as shrimp scampi and macnut-crusted mahimahi. All upstairs dinner entrees include a trip to Kauai's biggest salad bar ($18 as a stand-alone item).

At west end of Kauai Marriott Resort, 3610 Rice St., Lihue (valet parking at restaurant or self-parking in hotel lot). www.dukes kauai.com. © **808/246-9599.** Reservations recommended for dinner. Main courses $13–$20 lunch; dinner $23–$35 in dining room, $13–$20 in bar. "Taco Tuesdays" 4–6pm, with $3 fish or kalua pork tacos and $5 draft beer. Bar daily 11am–11pm; dining room daily 5–9:30pm.

Hukilau Lanai ★★ SEAFOOD/ISLAND FARM Although his restaurant is hidden inside the nondescript Kauai Coast Resort off the main highway in Kapaa, chef/owner Ron Miller has inspired residents and visitors to find their way here in droves since 2002. The lure: a hearty menu that's virtually all locally sourced—from Kauai whenever possible, and other islands when not—as well as expertly prepared and presented. Four to six seafood specials, incorporating local produce, are offered nightly; try the Kauai coffee-spiced candied ahi, or the hebi (short-billed spearfish) when available. The local mushroom meatloaf also packs a savory punch, thanks to grass-fed beef from Kauai's Sanchez Ranch and Big Island mushrooms. Value-conscious diners should order the special five-course tasting menu for $32 ($50 with wine pairings) offered from 5pm to 5:45pm. Reservations are strongly recommended, especially for ocean-view seating; the less-scenic lobby bar offers nightly music. **Note:** There's an extensive gluten-free menu.

In the Kauai Coast Resort, 520 Aleka Loop, Kapaa. www.hukilau kauai.com. © **808/822-0600.** Reservations recommended. Main courses $18–$32. Tues–Sun 5–9pm; happy hour daily 3–5pm.

MODERATE

The Feral Pig ★ GASTROPUB Let's dispense with the atmosphere first: There really isn't any. The self-proclaimed "pub and diner" is inside a mini-mall, with bare tables and just a few photos and chalkboards on the wall. At first glance, the menus are also not that impressive, emphasizing burgers, sandwiches, and fries at lunch and dinner, eggs at breakfast. But look closely, and you'll find an attention to Kauai ingredients—especially beef and pork—and a flair for German-inspired dishes, such as house-smoked pork loin with blue-cheese mashed potatoes and a vinegary coleslaw. The seafood and many of the vegetables are local, too, but as the name suggests, pig is preeminent. Meat lovers should try the off-the-menu Feral burger, a potent mix of ground Kauai beef and house-smoked pork shoulder, topped with pork belly, caramelized onions, and aioli. The former bar manager of Town in Honolulu, co-owner Dave Power has crafted a first-rate cocktail menu with a goodly number of specialty beers on tap. Service can be uneven; weekends can get loud (and crowded) with live music.

In Harbor Mall, 3501 Rice St., Lihue. www.theferalpigkauai. com. ⓒ **808/246-1100.** Main courses $9–$13 breakfast, $10–$15 lunch, $9–$20 dinner. Wed–Mon 7:30am–9pm. Reservations recommended Fri–Sat nights.

Kauai Pasta ★ ITALIAN   The owners' marital split has led to a breakup of the two Kauai Pasta locations, but fortunately you don't have to choose which one to remain loyal to. They've kept essentially the same menus, emphasizing homemade standards like chicken parm and fettuccine Alfredo, and meat specials such as osso buco or *sous-vide* pork. The larger Kapaa site also offers $10 lunch specials, a late-night lounge with its own menu (try the truffled prawn "ramen" with angel-hair pasta), and, at dinner, *pizzetta* choices such as rosemary grilled chicken with Gorgonzola. Try the butternut squash ravioli at either site if available. Portions are generous, but plan to order at least one of the tasty sides to share—I recommend the truffle parmesan fries with four dipping sauces. The *keiki* (kids') menus are a good deal too, from $5 pastas to $10 for grilled shrimp with mashed potatoes and vegetable. **Note:** Brown rice pasta can be substituted for most dishes at both locations.

4-939 Kuhio Hwy., Kapaa (mauka side, north of Taco Bell.) www. kauaipasta.com. ⓒ **808/822-7447.** Main courses $12–$24 lunch, $12–$33 dinner. Restaurant daily 11am–9pm; lounge Mon–Sat 11am–midnight, Sun 11am–10pm, happy hour daily 3–5pm. Dinner reservations recommended. Also: 3-3142 Kuhio Hwy., Lihue (btw. Poinciana and Hardy sts., in the Garden Island Publishing building). www.kplihue.com. ⓒ **808/245-2227.** 11am–9pm daily. Main courses lunch $13–$24, dinner $13–$30.

Oasis on the Beach ★★ SEAFOOD/ISLAND FARM Though not actually on the sand, the open-air, oceanfront setting at the Waipouli Beach Resort is still memorable, as are the daily fresh-catch (grilled or pan-seared) and curry specials, the grilled kale salad with whipped Brie, and soy-glazed short ribs with yummy truffle fried rice. Chef de cuisine Sean Smull proudly notes that 90% of the ingredients come from Kauai. Presentation wins points, too: Witness the pretty flower of blackberry syrup in the pineapple martini. Luckily, half portions of many dinner entrees make sharing a breeze; the handsome canoe bar and sounds of ocean surf also make the occasional wait worthwhile. Save room for the apple banana spring roll with salted caramel ice cream, or another seasonal gelato from Papalani, the island's premium ice cream. Wednesdays are an ideal time to discover this culinary oasis, with live music and a special "chef's choice" menu from 4 to 6pm. *Note:* Brunch entrees are tasty but petite by island standards.

In the Waipouli Beach Resort, 4-820 Kuhio Hwy., Kapaa (across from Safeway). www.oasiskauai.com. (✆ **808/822-9332.** Reservations recommended. Main courses $11–16 lunch, $16–$35 dinner, $11–$17 brunch. Mon–Sat 11:30am–3pm and 4–9pm; Sun brunch 10am–2pm; dinner 4–9pm.

INEXPENSIVE

Hamura's Saimin Stand ★★★ JAPANESE NOODLES Honored by the august James Beard Foundation in 2006 as one of "America's Classics," this hole in the wall has been satisfying local palates since 1951. Visitors have also now caught on to the appeal of saimin: large bowls of ramen noodles in salty broth with green onion, cabbage, and slices of fish cake, hard-boiled eggs, and pork, for starters. Here the

PLATE lunch, BENTO & POKE

A reflection of the appetites (huge) and ethnic palates (varied) of early-20th-century plantation workers, traditional plate lunches include two scoops of rice, potato or macaroni salad, and a beef, chicken, fish, or pork entree, often a cutlet served **katsu** style—breaded and fried—and slathered in a rich, salty gravy.

A Japanese creation, **bentos** are takeout trays offering smaller portions of more items, often with pickled vegetables, edamame (soybeans), and other nibbles. Bento and plate lunches usually range from $8 to $12. **Poke** (*poh-kay*), Hawaiian for "to slice," covers any number of diced, usually raw seafood dishes (sometimes made with tofu or vegetables), although the most common is ahi tuna, drizzled with *shoyu* (soy sauce) and sesame oil, and seasoned with green onions and crunchy *ogo* seaweed. Poke is usually sold by the pound ($12–$16).

EAST SIDE On the Coconut Coast, the indispensable **Pono Market,** 4–1300 Kuhio Hwy., Kapaa (✆ **808/822-4581**), has enticing counters of sashimi, poke, sushi, and a diverse assortment of takeout fare. The roast pork and the potato-macaroni salad are top sellers, but it's also known for plate lunches.

In Lihue, **Po's Kitchen,** 4100 Rice St. (✆ **808/246-8617**), packs a lot of goodies in its deluxe bentos, including shrimp tempura, chicken katsu, chow fun noodles, spaghetti mac salad, hot dog, ham, and rice balls. It's hidden behind Ace Hardware. One block away, **Garden Island BBQ,** 4252-A Rice St. (www.garden islandbbq.com; ✆ **808/245-8868**), is the place for Chinese plate lunches. Off the main highway across from Wal-Mart, **Fish Express,** 3343 Kuhio Hwy. (✆ **808/245-9918**), draws crowds for its wide assortment of poke (the ahi with spicy crab in a light mayo sauce is a favorite), pork laulau, Spam musubi, bentos, and plate lunches. The downside: no seating (but you can ask for directions to nearby Isenberg Park).

Mark's Place, in Puhi Industrial Park at 1610 Haleukana St., Lihue (www. marksplacekauai.com;

(© 808/245-2722), fashions daily salad and entree specials with a California-healthy bent. But it also serves island standards such as Korean-style chicken, beef stew, and chicken katsu.

NORTH SHORE Everything is pricier on the North Shore, and ahi poke and plate lunches are no exception at **Kilauea Fish Market,** 4270 Kilauea Rd. (enter from Keneke St., across the street from Kong Lung Market), Kilauea (© 808/828-6244). At $29 a pound, skip the poke and opt for Korean BBQ or grilled teri chicken plates ($11–$12). Locals head to **Village Snack Shop & Bakery,** across from Puka Dog inside Hanalei's Ching Young Village, 5-5190 Kuhio Hwy. (© 808/826-6841), for loco moco (eggs, meat, and gravy on rice) at breakfast and chili pepper chicken at lunch. Near the end of the road in Wainiha, **Sushigirl Kauai,** 5-6607 Kuhio Hwy. (www.sushigirlkauai.fish; © 808/827-8171), offers gluten-free takeout, from ahi poke bowls with rice, local organic greens, or quinoa

($12) to huge seafood and veggie sushi rolls ($12–$15).

SOUTH SHORE The **Koloa Fish Market,** 5482 Koloa Rd. (© 808/742-6199), in Old Town Koloa, is a tiny corner store with two stools on the veranda. Grab some excellent fresh poke, plate lunches, or seared ahi to go. You can also pick up raw seafood to grill. Down the road is **Sueoka's Snack Shop** (© 808/742-1112), the cash-only window counter of Sueoka grocery store, 5392 Koloa Rd. (www.sueokastore.com; © 808/742-1611). It offers a wide selection of meat-based lunch plates, such as shoyu chicken or kalua pork for just $6.25.

WEST SIDE **Ishihara Market,** 9894 Kaumualii Hwy., Waimea (© 808/338-1751), a block past the bridge, is well worth a stop heading to or from Waimea Canyon. A local favorite founded in 1934, the family-run Ishihara's stocks an impressive variety of fresh poke (including hamachi, baby octopus, salmon, and cooked lobster). It also has a grill making plate lunches.

housemade noodles are served al dente, and sometimes brusquely: Figure out what you're going to order before seating yourself at one of the U-shape counters. The "special regular" includes wontons and diced ham; top off any dish with a barbecued chicken skewer. If your appetite isn't large, order a to-go slice of the ultra-fluffy *lilikoi* (passionfruit) chiffon pie, just as renowned as Hamura's saimin; the topping may be Cool Whip, but the filling is delectable. Shave ice is also delicious, but its separate counter isn't always open. ***Note:*** There's often a line inside and out; it moves fast, so keep track of your place in it.

2956 Kress St., Lihue (1 block west of Rice St., in small blue building on left; park farther down the street). © **808/245-3271.** All items under $10. No credit cards. Mon–Thurs 10am–10:30pm; Fri–Sat 10am–midnight; Sun 10am–9:30pm.

Mermaids Cafe ★ PAN-ASIAN There are just a couple of picnic tables on a deck outside the kitchen window of this cheerily bohemian spot in Old Kapaa Town, so plan on ordering your food to go. The laid-back Kapaa hippie vibe means waits are sometimes long, and the kitchen can be inconsistent, but when the stars align, it's a wonderfully Kauaian experience. The signature dish is the ahi nori wrap, a massive sushi burrito in a green tortilla: seared tuna with rice, cucumber, nori, wasabi cream sauce, pickled ginger, and soy sauce. Tofu and chicken are the only other proteins on the limited, mostly organic menu, which includes a mild yellow coconut curry with island vegetables and satay plates with peanut sauce. The hibiscus iced tea and lemonade are especially refreshing on a hot day.

4-1384 Kuhio Hwy., Kapaa (north of Kukui St., next to Java Kai). www.mermaidskauai.com. © **808/821-2026.** Main courses $10–$13. No credit cards. Daily 11am–9pm.

North Shore

Note: You'll find the restaurants in this section on the "Hotels & Restaurants on Kauai's North Shore" map (p. 164).

EXPENSIVE

Bar Acuda ★★★ TAPAS   Named one of "Food & Wine" magazine's "Top 10 New American Chefs" in 1996, when he was still working in San Francisco, chef/owner Jim Moffatt later decided to embrace a low-key lifestyle in Hanalei. But he hasn't relaxed his standards for expertly prepared food, in this case tapas—small plates inspired by several Mediterranean cuisines—enjoyed here on the torch-lit veranda or in the sleek, warm-toned dining room. Given Bar Acuda's deliciously warm, crusty bread, ordering one hearty and one light dish per person, plus a starter of spiced olives or Marcona almonds per couple, should suffice. But ask the server for help in ordering the right amount—some dishes, such as the delicious seared single scallop on mashed potatoes, aren't really suitable for sharing. The menu changes to reflect seasonal tastes and availability but usually includes a seared local fish and grilled beef skewers. An excellent finish is a wedge of North Shore honeycomb with Kauai Kunana Farms goat cheese and a slice of crisp apple. **Note:** Reservations are strongly recommended, and you'll find patrons more smartly dressed here than anywhere else in Hanalei, including diners at the handsome teak bar.

In Hanalei Center, 5-5161 Kuhio Hwy., Hanalei. www.restaurant baracuda.com. ✆ **808/826-7081.** Reservations recommended. Hearty tapas $9–$16. Daily 5:30–9pm.

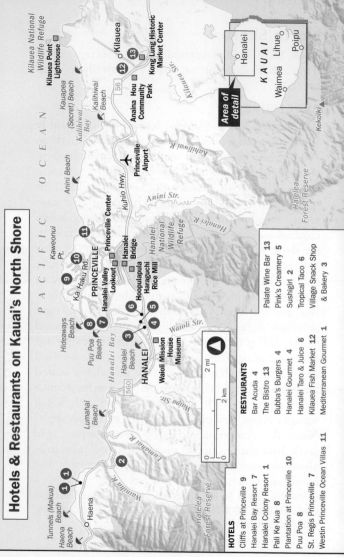

Hotels & Restaurants on Kauai's North Shore

PACIFIC OCEAN

Kilauea National Wildlife Refuge

Kilauea Point Lighthouse

Kauapea (Secret) Beach

Kalihiwai Bay

Kalihiwai Beach

Kilauea ○ **13**

12 Kong Lung Historic Market Center

Anaina Hou Community Park

Anini Beach

56

Princeville Airport

Kuhio Hwy.

Kahiliwai R.

Kaweonui Pt.

11

10

9

Ka Haku Rd.

8

Hideaways Beach

Puu Poa Beach

PRINCEVILLE

Princeville Center

Hanalei Valley Lookout

7

Anini Str.

Hanalei Bridge

Hanalei National Wildlife Refuge

Hanalei R.

Hoopulapula Haraguchi Rice Mill

6

5

4

3

Waioli Str.

HANALEI

Hanalei Bay

Hanalei Beach

Waioli Mission House Museum

Puu Poa Beach

Tunnels (Makua) Beach

1 **1**

Haena Beach

○ Haena

Lumahai Beach

Wainiha R.

Wainiha Str.

560

Waipa Str.

2

Halelea Forest Reserve

Kahiliwai R.

Hanalei R.

Hanalei Forest Reserve

Kekoiki ▲

Area of detail

K A U A I

Hanalei ○

○ Lihue

Waimea ○   ○ Poipu

N

2 mi

2 km

HOTELS

Cliffs at Princeville **9**
Hanalei Bay Resort **7**
Hanalei Colony Resort **1**
Pali Ke Kua **8**
Plantation at Princeville **10**
Puu Poa **8**
St. Regis Princeville **7**
Westin Princeville Ocean Villas **11**

RESTAURANTS

Bar Acuda **4**
The Bistro **13**
Bubba's Burgers **4**
Hanalei Gourmet **4**
Hanalei Taro & Juice **6**
Kilauea Fish Market **12**
Mediterranean Gourmet **1**

Palate Wine Bar **13**
Pink's Creamery **5**
Sushigirl **2**
Tropical Taco **6**
Village Snack Shop
& Bakery **3**

Mediterranean Gourmet ★★ MEDITERRA-
NEAN Imad and Yarrow Beydoun's unlikely but
delightful oasis between Hanalei and the end of the
road provides a welcome respite from the usual macnut-crusted mahimahi. At lunch, add fresh grilled fish
to one of several generous salads featuring Kauai-
grown kale or mixed greens, or the tabbouleh made
with quinoa instead of the usual bulgur wheat. Meat-
and-potato lovers can chow down on the well-spiced
beef and lamb gyros wrapped in fluffy pita. At dinner,
seafood paella or rosemary rack of lamb for two can
make a special occasion that much more special,
although the classic chicken shish-kabobs are no
slouch. Imad, the Lebanese-born chef, and his wife,
Yarrow, a Hanalei native, draw from traditions of both
regions for evening entertainment, with belly dancing
Thursday, a family-style luau (with Hawaiian buffet)
Tuesday, and Hawaiian music and hula Sunday; more
live music is offered the rest of the week. The dining
room could use some updating, and the exceptional
ocean view is better when windows are open—you're
so close that sea salt peppers the glass. Reserve early
to enjoy a sunset dinner.

Hanalei Colony Resort, 5–7132 Kuhio Hwy., Haena. www.kauai
medgourmet.com. 📞 **808/826-9875.** Dinner reservations
recommended. Main courses $13–$32 lunch, $24–$37 dinner,
$14–$17 lounge menu. Lunch Mon–Sat 11am–3pm, Sun 10am–
3pm (brunch 10am–1:30pm). Dinner Wed–Mon 4:30–8pm.
Lounge menu Wed–Mon noon–8pm, Tues noon–3pm. Happy
hour (50% off lounge menu) daily 3 to 6pm. Luau Tues 6pm.

MODERATE

The Bistro ★★★ CONTEMPORARY AMERICAN/
ISLAND FARM John-Paul Gordon is yet another
Kauai chef taking inspiration from the bounty of local
fields and fishing grounds, with an admirably inventive

palate and a well-practiced eye for presentation. Although his menu is largely seasonal, the "fish rockets" starter of seared ahi in lumpia wrappers with wasabi aioli is a signature dish; rich cuts of grass-fed beef from Kauai's Medeiros Farms are another standard, complemented by dill aioli, Gorgonzola cream sauce, or compound butter. If you crave something lighter, order the curly kale salad with local goat cheese and macadamia nuts, or the grilled fresh catch with white bean, arugula, and tomato ragu. Lunch includes simpler but satisfying options such as a Kauai beef burger and barbecued pork sandwich. The wine list is reasonably priced; ask about the $5 daily special. Part of the Kong Long Historic Market Center, the airy Bistro hosts live music Thursday to Saturday. In 2015, its owners opened **Palate Wine Bar** (www.palatewinebar.net; © **808/212-1974**) a few doors down in the former Kilauea Town Market (2474 Keneke St.); the wine bar serves panini ($9–$14) and tapas ($5–$15) from 4 to 10pm daily, with quality wine and beer starting at $8 a glass.

In Kong Lung Historic Market Center, 2484 Keneke St., Kilauea. http://lighthousebistro.com © **808/828-0480.** Reservations recommended for parties of 6 or more. Lunch $10–$17; dinner main courses $15–$26. Daily noon–2:30pm and 5:30–9pm. Bar noon–9pm.

Hanalei Gourmet ★ AMERICAN   Located in a former Hanalei schoolhouse that's now a quaint shopping center, this casual, decidedly non-gourmet spot offers the best values at lunch, with a variety of burgers and ample sandwiches on freshly baked bread starting at $8 (order the latter to go from the deli). The market-priced beer-battered fish and chips, accompanied by a suitably tart Asian slaw and soy wasabi sauce, is also notable. (If you want a half papaya, though, skip

CHEESEBURGERS in paradise

Delicious as Hawaii's fresh seafood is, sometimes what you're really looking for—in the words of Jimmy Buffett—is a cheeseburger in paradise. Luckily, Kauai boasts several inexpensive burger joints that are bound to satisfy.

The first thing to know about **Duane's Ono Char-Burger,** 4-4350 Kuhio Hwy., ocean side, Anahola (℃ **808/822-9181**), is that its burgers ($5–$8) are not made of the fish called ono (wahoo); they're just 'ono ("delicious" in Hawaiian.) The second thing to know is that waits can be long at this red roadside stand, opened in 1973, where wild chickens, cats, and birds are ready to share your meal with you. Duane's is open Monday to Saturday 10am to 6pm and Sunday 11am to 6pm. The founders of Duane's also run **Kalapaki Beach Hut,** 3474 Rice St., Lihue, near the west end of Kalapaki Beach (www.kalapakibeachhut.com; ℃ **808/246-6330**). The two-story ocean-view "hut" offers grass-fed Kauai beef burgers ($6–$10), a unique taro burger ($7) made from organic taro grown nearby, and a shave-ice stand.

Famed for its sassy slogans ("We Cheat Tourists, Drunks & Attorneys," among them) as much as for its Kauai beef burgers ($4–$7), **Bubba's** (www.bubbaburger.com) claims to have been around since 1936. It's certainly had time to develop a loyal following even while charging $1 for lettuce and tomato. Hearty appetites will want to try the Coors-spiked chili that comes on the open-face Slopper ($6) and with the Hubba Bubba ($7), in which it's poured over rice, a burger patty, and a grilled hot dog. The oldest Bubba's is in **Kapaa** (4-1421 Kuhio Hwy.; ℃ **808/823-0069**), where the deck has a view of the ocean across Kapaa Beach Park. Bubba's other two locations are in **Hanalei** (5-5161 Kuhio Hwy., in Hanalei Center; ℃ **808/826-7839**) and in **Poipu,** at the Shops at Kukuiula (2829 Ala Kalanikamauka, Poipu; (℃ **808/742-6900**). All three are open daily from 10:30am to 8pm, although the Kukuiula closing time may vary depending on business.

the $7 version here and walk a few steps to Harvest Market or across the street to the Big Save grocery.) Dinner has rather higher aspirations, not always met, as well as prices, but you can still order from much of the lunch menu. The atmosphere tends to be lively if not downright noisy, thanks to wooden floors, the popular bar, TV, and occasional live music, which draws an enthusiastic local crowd. Service is laidback but friendly.

In Hanalei Center, 5–5161 Kuhio Hwy., Hanalei. www.hanalei gourmet.com. © **808/826-2524.** Main courses $8–$13 lunch, $10–$29 dinner. Daily deli 8am–10:30pm; restaurant 11am–9:30pm; bar 11am–10:30pm.

INEXPENSIVE

Beside plate lunches (see above), the best bargains in North Shore dining usually come from food trucks, often found at Anini, Hanalei, and Haena beach parks, but with fickle hours. **Hanalei Taro & Juice** (© **808/826-1059;** www.hanaleitaro.com), *makai* side of Kuhio Hwy. a mile west of the Hanalei Bridge, has reliable hours and shaded seating. It's open Monday to Saturday from 11am to 3pm, with most items under $10; don't miss the banana-bread-like taro butter mochi. Nearby, the tiny storefront **Pink's Creamery,** 4489 Aku Rd., is justifiably renowned for its grilled cheese sandwiches on sweet bread with pineapple and optional kalua pork ($9, including chips) not to mention delicious tropical ice creams and housemade frozen yogurt and ices; it's open daily 11am to 9pm.

Tropical Taco ★ MEXICAN-SEAFOOD Roger Kennedy operated a North Shore taco wagon for 20-odd years before taking up residence over a decade ago in this cottage-style building with a pleasant porch; dishes still come on paper plates. While the menu has local/sustainable touches—the fresh seafood comes from North Shore fishermen, the lettuce mix is organic, and the fish and chips come with taro fries—the focus here is on satisfying hefty appetites. You might opt for the grilled fish special in soft corn tacos or as a crispy tostada rather than the gut-busting, deep-fried Fat Jack beef or veggie burrito, and be aware that any extras (cheese, sour cream, avocado) drive up prices quickly. *Note:* Hanalei has few places that are open for breakfast, so it's worth the occasional wait for your choice of one of four scrambled-egg burritos (try the taro and cheese).

5–5088 Kuhio Hwy. (*makai* side, parking in rear), Hanalei. http://tropicaltaco.com. © **808/827-8226.** Most items $12–$15, breakfast $6–$7. No credit cards. Mon–Fri 8am–8pm; Sat–Sun 11am–5pm.

South Shore

Note: You'll find the restaurants in this section on the "Hotels & Restaurants on Kauai's South Shore" map (p. 170).

EXPENSIVE

At press time, fans of Hawaii Regional Cuisine co-founder Roy Yamaguchi were eagerly awaiting the opening of his new, plantation-era restaurant concept, **Eating House 1849** (www.eatinghouse1849.com) in Poipu's Shops at Kukuiula—especially since he was simultaneously closing the 20-year-old Roy's in Poipu Shopping Village. The closure of Princeville Golf Course also forced Yamaguchi to shutter the Tavern at Princeville in late 2014.

The Beach House ★★★ HAWAII REGIONAL Call it dinner and a show: As sunset approaches, diners at this beloved oceanfront restaurant start leaping

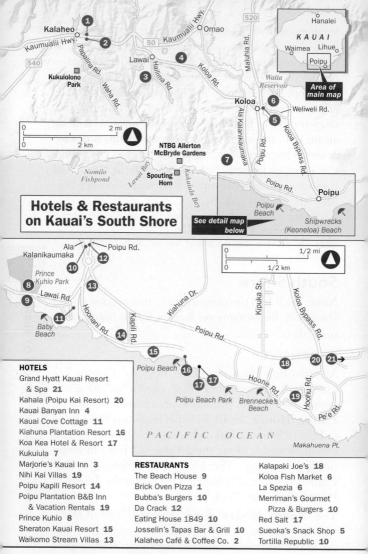

Hotels & Restaurants on Kauai's South Shore

See detail map below

Poipu Beach

Shipwrecks (Keoneloa) Beach

KAUAI
Hanalei
Waimea · Lihue
Poipu

Area of main map

NTBG Allerton McBryde Gardens

Spouting Horn

Nomilo Fishpond

Ala Kalanikaumaka — Poipu Rd.

Prince Kuhio Park

Lawai Rd.

Baby Beach

Kiahuna Dr.

Poipu Rd.

Kipuka St.

Koloa Bypass Rd.

Hoonani Rd.

Kapili Rd.

Poipu Beach

Poipu Beach Park

Brennecke's Beach

Hoone Rd.

Hoohu Rd.

Pe'e Rd.

PACIFIC   OCEAN

Makahuena Pt.

HOTELS
Grand Hyatt Kauai Resort
  & Spa **21**
Kahala (Poipu Kai Resort) **20**
Kauai Banyan Inn **4**
Kauai Cove Cottage **11**
Kiahuna Plantation Resort **16**
Koa Kea Hotel & Resort **17**
Kukuiula **7**
Marjorie's Kauai Inn **3**
Nihi Kai Villas **19**
Poipu Kapili Resort **14**
Poipu Plantation B&B Inn
  & Vacation Rentals **19**
Prince Kuhio **8**
Sheraton Kauai Resort **15**
Waikomo Stream Villas **13**

RESTAURANTS
The Beach House **9**
Brick Oven Pizza **1**
Bubba's Burgers **10**
Da Crack **12**
Eating House 1849 **10**
Josselin's Tapas Bar & Grill **10**
Kalaheo Café & Coffee Co. **2**

Kalapaki Joe's **18**
Koloa Fish Market **6**
La Spezia **6**
Merriman's Gourmet
  Pizza & Burgers **10**
Red Salt **17**
Sueoka's Snack Shop **5**
Tortilla Republic **10**

from their tables to pose for pictures on the grass-covered promontory, while nearby surfers try to catch one last wave. The genial waiters are as used to cameras being thrust upon them as they are reciting specials featuring local ingredients—a staple here long before "farm to table" became a culinary catchphrase. But there are plenty of other good reasons to dine at the Beach House, whether you're splurging on dinner or sampling the more affordable lunch. Among them: the sherry-finished corn chowder, brimming with rock crab and fresh fish; the house ceviche of fish, prawns, and scallops in a citrus-lilikoi marinade, attractively served in a half coconut; the Kauai-grown beet salad with Gorgonzola; and any of the grilled fresh-catch dishes, such as black Thai rice, local green papaya salad, and red coconut curry sauce. (The sautéed preparations tend to be on the sweet and rich side.) Desserts are less memorable than the well-crafted cocktails and wine list. *Note:* Vegan and gluten-free diners have ample menu options.

5022 Lawai Rd., Koloa. www.the-beach-house.com. © **808/742-1424.** Reservations recommended. Main courses $9–$19 lunch, $20–$48 dinner. Lunch daily 11am–3pm; light fare daily 3-5:30pm; dinner daily 5:30–10pm mid-Sept to mid-Mar (6–10pm mid-Mar to mid-Sept); lounge daily 11am–10pm.

Josselin's Tapas Bar & Grill ★★ TAPAS Other than Bar Acuda in Hanalei, this casual-chic bistro has the most New York/San Francisco urban vibe on Kauai. Chef Jean Marie Josselin, who closed his long-revered A Pacific Café in Kapaa in 2000 for a stint in Vegas, returned in 2010 with a radically different, rustic Asian-Mediterranean tapas concept in a lively (and sometimes very loud) atmosphere, on the second story of the upscale Shops at Kukuiula. When the sangria cart stops by your table, try the white lychee version—not too sweet—or, for nondrinkers, the strawberry pepper lemonade, while you persuse the eclectic menu. The "deconstructed ahi roll" may be a fancy way of saying poke on rice, but it's delicious, as are the unctuous slow-cooked butterfish and seared diver scallops. The wood-burning oven's use of *kiawe* (mesquite) adds smoky complexity to roasted cauliflower. The tapas are designed for sharing, but ask one of the friendly waiters about portion sizes so you don't run up an even higher tab.

The Shops at Kukuiula, 2829 Ala Kalanikaumaka St., Poipu. www.josselinstapas.com. ✆ **808/742-7117.** Reservations recommended. Tapas $11–$36. Daily 5–9pm (bar until 11pm Fri–Sat). Happy hour ($5 sangria/wine, $6–$10 tapas) 5–6:30pm daily, 9:30-11pm Fri–Sat. Live flamenco music Wed.

Red Salt ★★★ HAWAII REGIONAL The best hotel restaurant on Kauai may also be one of the smallest and hardest to find, tucked inside the discreetly located **Koa Kea Hotel & Resort** (p. 141). Although rivals offer arguably more dramatic ocean views in plusher settings, Red Salt consistently executes elegantly presented dishes from an intriguing menu designed by El Bulli–trained chef Ronnie Sanchez. Executive chef Adam Watten continues to showcase tender, moist fish with specials such as

Red Salt Restaurant.

onaga (snapper) with giant snow peas and hearts of palm in a citrus curry or steamed *hapuupuu* (grouper) in a lemongrass shrimp broth with kabocha and Molokai sweet potatoes. The richer pan-roasted chicken and lobster saffron ravioli on the regular menu are equally compelling. A cloud of candlelit cotton candy (in varying flavors) makes a dramatic if sugary finish. **Note:** On most nights the adjacent lounge serves exquisite sashimi and sushi, along with small plates such as kalua pork potstickers and crab cakes.

In Koa Kea Hotel & Resort, 2251 Poipu Rd., Poipu. www.koakea.com. © **808/828-8888.** Dinner reservations recommended. Valet parking. Main courses $14–$17 breakfast, $10–$21 lunch, $25–$69 dinner (most $33–$39). Daily breakfast 6:30–11am, lunch (poolside) 11am–6pm, dinner 6–10pm; sushi lounge Tues–Sat 5:30–9pm.

MODERATE

La Spezia ★★★ ITALIAN The definition of charming, this much-needed stylish but cozy bistro in Old Koloa Town, opened in 2013, doesn't accept reservations for parties of fewer than six—reason enough to make a few friends at the pool to join you for dinner. Still, walk-ins will find it worth the possible wait for a table, handmade from wine crates by co-owner Dan Seltzer (formerly of Casablanca and Dali Deli); don't hesitate to take a seat at the small but handsome bar, either. Stalwarts on the seasonal, home-style menu include spicy veggie arrabbiata, rib-sticking lasagne Bolognese, pan-roasted chicken, seared pork tenderloin with capers, and hanger steak with Gorgonzola polenta. At breakfast or the expanded Sunday brunch, French toast made with Hawaiian sweet bread, Brie, bacon, and raspberry jam provides the ultimate guilty pleasure, balanced by the Caprese-style egg-white frittata.

Note: The gluten-free zucchini noodles are a great alternative no matter what your dietary requirements. 5492 Koloa Rd., Koloa (across from Koloa Post Office). www.laspeziakauai.com. *©* **808/742-8824.** Reservations accepted for parties of 6 or more. Main courses $9–$14 breakfast, $15–$23 dinner, $12 Sun brunch. Breakfast Tues and Thurs–Sat 8am–11am, Wed 8:30am–11am; dinner 5–10pm Tues–Sun; brunch Sun 8am–1pm.

Merriman's Gourmet Pizza & Burgers ★★ AMERICAN/ISLAND FARM A pioneer in Hawaii Regional Cuisine, Maui-based chef Peter Merriman first expanded onto Kauai with his gourmet restaurant upstairs, **Merriman's Fish House** ★★ (main courses $24–$59). While it's well worth a visit, you're more likely to make repeat trips to this downstairs, much more casual spot. The thin-crust organic wheat pizzas ($1 more for gluten-free) are topped with such Hawaii-grown ingredients as roasted Hamakua mushrooms, kalua pork with grilled pineapple, or ahi with wasabi aioli (in lieu of cheese); the vegan version has a surprisingly decadent kale pesto and hearty roasted vegetables. (Don't worry, you can still get pepperoni and sausage.) The innovative burgers feature local grass-fed beef and lamb, although the turkey option, with Asian pear, white cheddar, and arugula, may be the most popular. Fries are extra but worth it (if you're not on a first date, order them with garlic and cilantro). In the Shops at Kukuiula, 2829 Ala Kalanikaumaka St., Poipu. www.merrimanshawaii.com. *©* **808/742-8385.** Main courses $13–$18. Daily 11am–10pm. Live music Wed and Fri.

Tortilla Republic ★★ GOURMET MEXICAN A smash with visitors and locals since opening in 2012, this vibrant, bi-level restaurant offers two ways to

Flautas at Tortilla Republic.

experience its modern, sophisticated take on Mexican cuisine: the upstairs **Grill** and the downstairs **TR Taqueria & Margarita Bar,** each with menus based on natural, organic, and local ingredients where possible. Open for dinner and Sunday brunch on the upstairs veranda (book for sunset), the Grill specializes in exotic-for-Kauai seasonings: Sautéed black tiger shrimp are served with a sauce of *pipián rojo* (red squash seeds), while the day's fresh catch comes rubbed in ancho chili and a serrano cilantro citrus sauce. Service is congenial but sometimes slow; order the table made guacamole ($16) for sheer entertainment value. The indoor/outdoor Taqueria & Margarita Bar offer simpler but still outstanding dishes, including a trio of guajillo-rubbed grilled fish tacos, but at press time owners were mulling a new concept (and name) for this space.

In the Shops at Kukuiula, 2829 Ala Kalanikaumaka St., Poipu. http://tortillarepublic.com. © **808/742-8884.** Dinner/brunch reservations recommended. Grill main courses $18–$32 dinner, $10–$20 Sun brunch. Taqueria main courses $10–$15 breakfast, $11–$15 lunch and dinner. Grill: Mon–Sat 5:30–9pm; Sun 9am–2pm. Taqueria/bar: Mon–Sat 7:30am–5pm; daily 5–9pm. Happy hour daily 3–5pm.

IN EXPENSIVE

Brick Oven Pizza ★ PIZZA There's nothing particularly gourmet about these pizzas, made with a hand-tossed, medium-thin, chewy crust (white with garlic butter, wheat, or, for $4 more, gluten-free) and the usual toppings, plus Portuguese sausage. Still, this local favorite is relatively easy on the budget—the large, 12-slice pizzas are genuinely large, and there's a bountiful, all-you-can-eat buffet from 5 to 9pm Monday and Thursday ($17 adults, $13 children 4–12). Pastas, subs, and salads are fairly basic, but well-priced. For island flavors, order the kimchee tofu or guava-glazed smoked pork appetizers at the bar, which has a surprisingly broad beer list. *Note:* Order takeout from here or the Kapaa location through **Delivery Kauai** (www.deliverykauai.com; © **808/755-5377**).

2–2555 Kaumualii Hwy., Kalaheo (mauka side, across the street from Brick Oven Pizza). www.brickovenpizzahi.com. © **808/332-8561.** Kapaa: 4-4361 Kuhio Hwy. (mauka side, across from Kinipopo Shopping Village). © **808/823-8561.** Sandwiches $10–$11; medium (10-slice) pizzas $17–$25. Daily 11am–9pm.

Da Crack ★ MEXICAN Now *this* is a hole in the wall—hence the local nickname for a long-lived Mexican takeout window here, which the Kauai-reared Mexican-American chef Daniel Hurtado officially adopted in 2011. Portions are huge but ingredients are fresh, including housemade chips and guacamole. It's also relatively healthful: Beans are vegan and the rice is brown. Wasabi cream on the fresh fish taco (recommended) is about the only local twist; wash it down with a Mexican Coke or pop into neighboring Kukuiula Market for a smoothie at **Aloha Aina Juice Bar** (open until 4pm weekdays, 3pm weekends). *Note:* Delivery is available from **Delivery Kauai** (www.deliverykauai.com; ✆ **808/ 755-5377**).

Next to Kukuiula Market, 2827 Poipu Rd., Koloa (north of the roundabout). www.dacrack.com. ✆ **808/742-9505.** Most items under $10. Mon–Sat 11am–8pm; Sun 11am–4pm.

Kalaheo Café & Coffee Co. ★★ BAKERY CAFE/ ISLAND FARM Whether you just grab a freshly baked cookie and cup of Kauai coffee to go or make a full meal of it, you'll quickly discover why visitors and locals jockey for parking spots at this casual restaurant and bakery. Early hours and hearty breakfasts (including wraps to go) make it a popular stop for folks on the way to snorkel cruises or Waimea Canyon. About a 15-minute drive from Poipu, the plantation-style cafe also offers a great alternative to high-priced resort dining. Greens grown nearby dominate the extensive salad list, while the rustic housemade buns pair nicely with grass-fed Kauai beef, veggie, or turkey burgers. Dinner is on the pricier side, but fresh seafood and produce shine, with such island-style accompaniments as stir-fried long beans and pohole ferns (similar to fiddleheads) and purple sweet potatoes.

2–2560 Kaumualii Hwy., Kalaheo (*makai* side, across the street from Brick Oven Pizza). www.kalaheo.com. ✆ **808/332-5858.** Breakfast $5–$13; lunch $7–$13; dinner main courses $13–$29. Breakfast Mon–Sat 6:30–11:30am; Sun 6:30am–2pm. Lunch Mon–Sat 11am–2:30pm; Sun 11am–2pm. Dinner Tues–Thurs 5–8:30pm; Fri–Sat 5–9pm.

West Side

With fewer visitor lodgings and residents who can afford pricey dining, the West Side offers rather unassuming food options, with most restaurants inconsistent at best. This explains why many visitors just stop in Waimea for shave ice—try **Jo-Jo's Shave Ice** at

9734 Kaumualii Hwy., *makai* side, across from the high school (© **808/635-7615**)—or for luscious Roselani ice cream and tropical shakes at **Super Duper,** 9889 Waimea Rd. (© **808/338-1590**). **Ishihara Market** (see "Plate Lunch, Bento & Poke," p. 161) can also provide picnic fare.

MODERATE

Kauai Island Brewery & Grill ★★ BREWPUB

The owners and brewmaster of the former Waimea Brewing Company opened this snazzier (but still sensibly priced) industrial/loft-style microbrewery and restaurant in Port Allen in 2012. The house lilikoi ale flavors the batter on fish and chips, but I prefer the excellent ahi poke with seaweed salad and the unique taro goat cheese spinach dip, which uses taro leaves (rather than the purple corm) with a dash of cayenne for seasoning. If the ample appetizers don't fill you up, the burgers, wraps, sandwiches, and beef and seafood platters certainly will. Up to 10 house beers are on tap, along with draft and bottled specials. The open-air mezzanine provides an angled view of sunset over the nearby harbor—and it can be mobbed when snorkel boats return mid-afternoon. Five 55-inch flatscreen TVs draw crowds for sports broadcasts.

Kauai Island Brewery & Grill.

Note: The kitchen closes around 9:30pm, but the bar often stays open past 10pm.

4350 Waialo Rd., Port Allen. www.kauaiislandbrewing.com. ℂ **808/335-0006.** Main courses $12–$25. Daily 11am–10pm.

Kalapaki Joe's ★ AMERICAN/LOCAL   Opened in 2014 in Waimea Plantation Cottages' compound of vintage wood-framed buildings, the third of the four Kalapaki Joe's sports bar/restaurants boasts not only the best location but also the most beers on tap (24). The list of burgers, sandwiches, meal-size salads, and Mexican items—tacos, quesadillas, enchiladas—is even more extensive; you can fill up just as easily from the appetizer menu. It's typical Mainland pub grub, but you can also order dishes with a local twist, such as kalua pork and seared cabbage with warm flour tortillas, the fresh ahi and avocado poke, or the fish of the day, grilled with a guava jelly glaze and topped with roasted macadamia nuts. Deep discounts at happy hour ($3 fish tacos, $1 shrimp tempura, and 25¢ chicken wings) and a convenient location (it's the first pit stop heading back from Waimea Canyon) mean it's often packed in late afternoons, as well as when any major sporting event is broadcast.

9400 Kaumualii Hwy., Waimea. www.kalapakijoes.com. ℂ **808/ 338-1666.** Also 1941 Poipu Rd., Poipu. (ℂ **808/742-6366**), 3501 Rice St., Lihue (in Harbor Mall; ℂ **808/245-6266**); 3-2600 Kaumualii Hwy. (in Kukui Grove mall; ℂ **808/245-6366**). Main courses $10–$20. Daily 11am–10pm. Happy hour 3–6pm. Poipu location also serves breakfast on weekends 7–11am ($8–$14).

INEXPENSIVE

Kokee Lodge ★★ AMERICAN/LOCAL   It would be inexcusable to drive all the way up to Waimea Canyon or Kokee State Park and not schedule a meal here— at least if you order one of its hearty, local-fave specialties.

The go-to entrees are Portuguese bean soup (add a giant hunk of cornbread for an extra $3.50), kalua pork (served with rice or on a sesame-seed bun), and loco moco (hamburger patty, two eggs over rice, and brown gravy). Vegetarians can opt for the broccoli-spinach quiche or a simple peanut butter and guava jelly sandwich (served with fruit, for under $4). Sadly, the limited hours don't benefit all-day hikers, so it's worth having at least one person circle back early to place a to-go order, especially for a generous slice of *lilikoi* chiffon pie or the warm, chocolate-bottomed coconut pie. With wooden tables and chairs, the dining room occupies the front half of a long cabin with picture windows overlooking the meadow next to the Kokee Museum; the rear gift shop is fun to browse while waiting for food to arrive. Service is no-frills: Everything comes on paper plates, drinks and chips are self-serve, and you pay at the cashier.

9400 Kaumualii Hwy., Waimea. www.thelodgeatkokee.net. ℂ **808/335-6061.** Main courses $7–$8 breakfast, $3–$8 lunch. Daily 9am–2:30pm (takeout until 3pm, bar service until 4pm.)

Shrimp Station ★ SHRIMP   The name explains it all at this popular roadside stop on the way to or from Waimea Canyon and Polihale, with another branch in Kapaa. Shrimp plates—most featuring about 10 juicy shrimp in savory sauces with fries or two scoops of white rice—are the top draw, but you can also order chopped shrimp on large flour tacos or a fried shrimp burger. Order the latter, or the lightly battered fried coconut shrimp plate (including a zesty papaya ginger tartar sauce), if you don't want to get your hands messy from peeling shrimp, although the sweet chili and garlic sauces are indeed finger-licking good. The covered open-air picnic tables and trash cans can attract flies, so consider making yours a to-go order to eat at one of the nearby parks along the highway or on the beach. *Note:* The Kapaa location has a nicer dine-in area, though it still serves on paper plates.

9652 Kaumualii Hwy., Waimea (*makai* side, at Makeke Rd.). © **808/338-1242.** Also 4-985 Kuhio Hwy., Kapaa (*mauka* side, at Keaka Rd.). © **808/821-0192.** Shrimp platters $13. Daily 11am–5pm.

6

SHOPPING & NIGHTLIFE

by Jeanne Cooper

Kauai has more than a dozen open-air shopping centers and historic districts well-suited to browsing, so souvenir and gift hunters are unlikely to leave the island empty-handed—though often it's with items made elsewhere. To find something unique to the Garden Isle, just look for the purple KAUAI MADE logo. The image of a *ho'okupu*, the ti-leaf wrapping for special presents, means the county certifies that these handicrafts and food items are made on the island using local materials where possible, and in relatively small batches. Some producers have their own storefronts, while other retailers post the logo to indicate they carry one or more Kauai Made lines; search the website, **http://kauaimade.net,** by type of product and region.

The similar but privately run **Kauai Grown** program, **www.kauaigrown.org**, showcases fresh and processed farm products (including cheese, chocolate, and soaps) containing at least 51% locally grown ingredients. Many of those items are available at local farmer's markets; see p. 190 for listings. Below are some of the island's more distinctive boutiques and shopping enclaves.

FACING PAGE: **Shopping on Lawai Road in Koloa.**

Open-air shops in Kauai.

East Side

LIHUE

The well-curated gift shop at the **Kauai Museum,** 4428 Rice St. (www.kauaimuseum.org; © **808/245-6931**), carries the best selection of books about Kauai, plus exquisite artwork and handicrafts by local and other Hawaii artisans, from Niihau-shell lei to block-print fabrics.

The island's largest mall, **Kukui Grove Shopping Center, Kaumualii** Highway, makai side at Nawiliwili Road (www.kukuigrovecenter.com) attracts locals with department stores such as **Macy's** and **Sears;** visitors on a tight schedule or budget should browse the competitively priced, locally made food-stuffs (coffees, jams, cookies, and the like) at **Longs Drugs** (© **808/245-7785**). The mall's family-run **Déjà Vu Surf Hawaii** (www.dejavusurf.com; © **808/245-2174**) has a large selection of local and national brands.

Anchor Cove (3416 Rice St.) and **Harbor Mall** (3501 Rice St.), two small shopping centers near Nawiliwili Harbor, mostly offer typical T-shirts, aloha wear, and souvenirs. One exception is Harbor Mall's **Beachrail of Kauai** (✆ 808/245-6732), which sells toys, kites, Kala ukuleles, miniature trains—even Hawaiian-themed metal soldiers. Fans of tropical-print fabrics, batiks, and Hawaiian quilts will want to seek out **Kapaia Stitchery,** 3-3351 Kuhio Hwy., mauka side at Laukini Road (www.kapaia-stitchery. com; ✆ 808/245-2281), which also offers ready-made aloha wear.

The 1930s mansion at **Kilohana Plantation,** 3-2087 Kaumualii Hwy. mauka side next to Kauai Community College, is a handsome setting for a half-dozen boutiques selling locally made, Hawaiian-inspired artwork and jewelry, as well as vintage Hawaiiana (www. kilohanakauai.com). The stand-alone **Koloa Rum Co.** (www.koloarum.com; ✆ 808/246-8900) carries locally made rum, logowear, and rum-spiked goodies.

WAILUA & KAPAA

Parts of **Coconut MarketPlace,** 4-484 Kuhio Hwy. (*makai* side at Aleka Loop; www.coconutmarketplace. com), remained under renovation at press time, but it's still a haven for lower-cost souvenirs. **Auntie Lynda's Treasures** (www.hawaiianjewelryandgift.com; ✆ 808/821-1780) sells native woodcarvings, jewelry, and island-themed tchotchkes—the staff is happy to chat, too. **Pagoda,** 4-369 Kuhio Hwy. (*makai* side, across from Kintaro; ✆ 808/821-2172), offers Chinese antiques and curios, Hawaiiana, Asian-inspired decor, candles, soaps, and other gifts.

The historic (and hippie) district of Kapaa offers an intriguing mix of shops, cafes, and galleries. **Hula**

Girl, 4-1340 Kuhio Hwy. (makai side, at Kauwila St.; www.ilovehulagirl.com; © 808/822-1950), not only sells women's resort wear (much of it made in Hawaii), but also aloha shirts, board shorts, and other menswear, plus tiki-style barware, island-made soaps, and accessories. Natural fibers rule the day at **Island Hemp & Cotton,** 4–1373 Kuhio Hwy. (mauka side, at Huluili St.; © 808/821-0225), where the stylish men's and women's clothing lines also include linen, silk, and bamboo creations and boho accessories.

North Shore

KILAUEA

On the way to Kauapea (Secret) Beach and the lighthouse, **Kong Lung Historic Market Center,** at the corner of Keneke Street and Kilauea Road (http://konglungkauai.com), deserves its own slot on the itinerary, with a bakery, bistro, and a half-dozen chic shops in vintage buildings with historical markers. Of the stores, the flagship **Kong Lung Trading** (www.konglung.com; © 808/828-1822) is an attractive showcase for Asian-themed ceramics, jewelry, stationery, books, and home accessories, including sake sets and hand-turned Hawaiian wood bowls. Souvenir seekers can find less pricey options at the factory store of **Island Soap & Candle Works** (www.islandsoap.com; © 808/828-1955), renowned for its Surfer's Salve, tropical soaps, and soy candles in coconut shells.

PRINCEVILLE

Island Soap also has a small store in **Princeville Center,** off Kuhio Highway just past the main Princeville entrance (www.princevillecenter.com).

Although the two-level center is mostly known for its inexpensive dining options and local businesses, the **Hawaiian Music Store** kiosk (no phone) outside Foodland grocery has good deals on CDs, while **Magic Dragon Toy & Art Supply** (© 808/826-9144) provides a wide array of rainy-day entertainment for kids.

HANALEI

As you enter Hanalei, look for **Ola's Hanalei,** 5016 Kuhio Hwy. (*makai* side, next to Dolphin restaurant; © 808/826-6937). Opened in 1982 by award-winning artist Doug Britt and wife, Sharon, this compact gallery features Doug's whimsical paintings, wooden toy boats, and furniture made from *objets trouvés,* plus engaging jewelry, glassware, koa boxes, and other works by Hawaii and Mainland artisans.

The center of town reveals more of Hanalei's bohemian side, with two eclectic shopping and dining complexes in historic buildings facing each other on Kuhio Highway. In the two-story rabbit warren of **Ching Young Village Shopping Center** (www.chingyoungvillage.com), **Divine Planet** (www.divineplanet.com; © 808/826-8970) brims with beads, star-shape lanterns, silver jewelry from Thailand and India, and Balinese quilts. **On the Road to Hanalei** (© 808/826-7360) also stocks unique gifts, from colorful pareos and clever figurines of Kauai roosters to Japanese pottery and African masks.

Across the street, the old Hanalei Schoolhouse is now the **Hanalei Center,** with two true gems tucked out of view: **Yellowfish Trading Company** (© 808/826-1227) and **Havaiki Oceanic and Tribal Art** (www.havaikiart.com; © 808/826-7606). At Yellowfish, retro hula girl lamps, vintage textiles and pottery, and collectible Hawaiiana mingle with reproduction signs, painted guitars, and other beach-shack musts, with ever-changing inventory. The owners of Havaiki have helpfully posted a "National Geographic" map of Oceania outside their gallery, all the better to appreciate the literal lengths they've gone to obtain the museum-quality collection of gleaming wood bowls and fishhooks, exotic masks, shell jewelry, and intricately carved weapons and paddles; they also sell music CDs, handmade cards, and other tasteful gifts.

WAINIHA

Roughly halfway between Hanalei and the end of the road, the **7 Artists Gallery**, 5-6607 Kuhio Hwy. (*©* **808/826-0044**), always has at least one of the local artists in residence. Look for Suzy Staulz's bold acrylics of local scenes, Lauren Johnson's garnet necklaces, and Alia DeVille's photographs of Kauai "sunrise" shells and other ocean treasures. It's makai side, next to the **Wainiha General Store** (good for a cold drink).

South Shore
KOLOA

Between the tree tunnel road and beaches of Poipu, **Old Koloa Town** (www.oldkoloa.com) has the usual tourist tees and trinkets, but also two sources of well-made local items and the island's best wine shop. The factory store of **Island Soap and Candle Works** (www.islandsoap.com; *©* **808/742-1945**) is similar to the one in Kilauea (see above), while the **Koa Store** (www.thekoastore.com; *©* **808/742-1214**) showcases boxes, frames, and other small pieces by local woodworkers using native wood. In addition to wine,

the Wine Shop (www.thewineshopkauai.com; © 808/742-7305) sells high-quality, locally made treats such as Monkeypod Jam's tropical curds and Hula Baby biscotti.

POIPU

Poipu Shopping Village, 2360 Kiahuna Plantation Dr. (www.poipushoppingvillage.com), is home to a couple of independent clothing boutiques as well as local branches of Hawaii resort and surfwear chains. But the newer **Shops at Kukuiula,** just off the Poipu Road roundabout (www.kukuiula.com), has even more intriguing (often expensive) options spread among plantation-style cottages, flowering hibiscus, and greenery. **Palm Palm** (www.palmpalmkauai.com; © 808/742-1131) prides itself on exclusive, limited-edition collections of items such as vintage fabric handbags and glassware etched with tropical images, as well as women's designer clothing, jewelry, and other gifts. The airy boutique of **Malie Organics** (www.malie.com; © 808/322-6220) offers its signature line of bath and beauty products, which use special distillations of island plants, including Kauai's native *maile* vine (not to be confused with *malie,* which means "calm" or "serene"). Amid all the high-end chic, laidback surfers will feel right at home in **Poipu Surf** (www.poipusurf.com; © 808/742-8797) and **Quiksilver** (run by local Déjà Vu Surf Hawaii; www.dejavusurf.com; © 808/742-8088).

KALAHEO

Flavored with guava, Kona coffee, macadamia nuts, and other tropical ingredients, the crisp butter cookies of the **Kauai Kookie Kompany** are ubiquitous in Hawaii, but even better than a trip to the factory store

FARMER'S MARKETS & fruit stands

Even if you're not staying in a place with a kitchen, a trip to one of the county-sponsored **Sunshine Markets** is a fun glimpse into island life, with shoppers queued up before the official start—listen for a yell or car honk—to buy fresh produce at rock-bottom prices. Markets end in 2 hours at the latest; arrive in time for the start, especially in Koloa and Kapaa. The best Sunshine Markets for visitors include:

o **Monday:** Noon, **Koloa Ball Park,** off Maluhia Rd., on the left heading toward Old Town Koloa.

o **Tuesday:** 3pm, **Kalaheo Neighborhood Center,** Papalina Rd. off Kaumualii Hwy. (makai side).

o **Wednesday:** 3pm, **Kapaa New Town Park,** Kahau St. at Olohena Rd.

o **Thursday:** 4:30pm, **Kilauea Neighborhood Center,** Keneke St. off Kilauea (Lighthouse) Rd.

o **Friday:** 3pm, **Vidinha Stadium parking lot,**

Hoolako Rd. (off Hwy. 51), Lihue.

For the best selection of organic produce, visit North Shore farmer's markets. In **Kilauea,** that includes the **Sunshine Market** and the **Namahana Farmers Market** (www.anainahou.org; © **808/828-2118**) at Anaina Hou Community Park in Kilauea (mauka side of Kuhio Hwy., Sat 9am–1pm and Mon 4pm–dusk). Next to Anaina Hou, **Banana Joe's Fruit Stand** (www.bananajoekauai.com; © **808/828-1092**). Its prices are higher, but it's conveniently open

in Hanapepe (1-3529 Kaumualii Hwy., *makai* side) is a stop at the **Kauai Kookie Bakery & Kitchen** complex in Kalaheo, 2-2436 Kaumualii Hwy., *makai* side (© **808/332-0821**). One storefront is a small cafe

Monday to Saturday 9am to 5:30pm, with a great selection of exotic fruits, macadamia nuts, and locally made snacks.

In Hanalei, the popular **Waipa Farmers Market** (www.waipafoundation.org; 📞 **808/826-9969**) takes place on Tuesday at 2pm just west of Hanalei, mauka side of Kuhio Hwy., between the Waioli and Waipa one-lane bridges. Some vendors also sell baked goods and crafts, as they do from 9.30am to noon Saturday in the ballpark at Hanalei community center **Hale Halawai** (www.halehalawai.org; 📞 **808/826-1011**), Kuhio Hwy., makai side at Mahimahi Rd., next to the green church.

FRESH SLICED
PAPAYA & MANGO

selling specialty baked goods as well as a wide variety of "kookies"; the other is a vast space with rows of local products, souvenirs, and even more fresh treats to eat on the spot or buy as *omiyage* (food gifts).

West Side
HANAPEPE

Known for its Friday-night festival (see "Kauai Nightlife," p. 193), the historic town center of Hanapepe and its dozen-plus art galleries are just as pleasant to peruse by day, especially the cheery paintings at the **Bright Side Gallery,** 3890 Hanapepe Rd. (www.thebrightsidegallery.com; © **808/634-8671**), and the playful tiles and other ceramics of **Banana Patch Studio,** 3865 Hanapepe Rd. (www.bananapatch studio.com; © **808/335-5944**). The courtyard passage next to Little Fish Coffee leads to **MoonBow Magic Gift Gallery,** 3900 Hanapepe Rd. (www. moonbowmagic.com; © **808/335-5890**), which stocks an amazing potpourri of colorful gifts and baubles (such as beaded geckos and Kauai chickens), Niihau shells, and other jewelry.

If the door is open, the store is open at tiny **Taro Ko Chips Factory,** 3940 Hanapepe Rd. (© **808/335-5586**), where dry-land taro farmer Dale Nagamine slices and fries his harvest—along with potatoes, purple sweet potatoes, and breadfruit—into delectable chips, for $5 a bag (cash only). The wares of **Aloha Spice Company,** 3857 Hanapepe Rd. (www.aloha spice.com; © **808/335-5960**), include grill-ready seasonings with a base of Hawaiian sea salt, and Hawaiian cane sugar infused with hibiscus, vanilla, or lilikoi.

PORT ALLEN

Chocolate fiends need to try the luscious handmade truffles, fudge, and *"opihi"* (chocolate-covered shortbread, caramel, and macadamia nuts in the shape of a shell) at **Kauai Chocolate Company** in nearby Port

Allen, 4341 Waialo Rd. (www.kauaichocolate.us; ✆ **808/335-0448**).

WAIMEA

You have to plan ahead for a trip to the aptly named **Collectibles and Fine Junque,** 9821 Kaumualii Hwy., *mauka* side, next to the fire station (✆ **808/338-9855**), since Rose Schweitzer only sells her vintage Hawaiiana and other finds from 11am to 4pm Monday to Thursday. Like Kauai Kookies, the passionfruit (*lilikoi*) products of **Aunty Lilikoi**—including jelly, butter, wasabi mustard, and salad dressing—are increasingly found around the state, but the factory store at 9875 Waimea Rd., across from the Captain Cook statue (www.auntylilikoi.com; ✆ **808/338-1296**), offers shipping and in store-only baked goods such as scones, bars, and cookies.

When you head upcountry, leave time to pop into the gift shops of the **Kokee Museum** (www.kokee. org; ✆ **808/335-9975**) and **Kokee Lodge** (www.the-lodgeatkokee.net; ✆ **808/335-6061**), the former for an assortment of Kauai- and nature-themed books, maps, and DVDs, and the latter for an array of souvenirs, island foods, and locally made crafts.

KAUAI NIGHTLIFE

Kauai's nightlife is more suited to moonlight strolls than late-night partying, but if you're simply searching for live Hawaiian music, you're in luck. Most nights virtually every hotel restaurant or lounge presents a slack key guitarist singing traditional and contemporary Hawaiian music, with many off-resort restaurants hosting live Hawaiian music and other genres Thursday to Saturday. Search the **Kauai Music Scene** (www.kauaimusicscene.com) calendar by date, type of music, and venue.

Of the resort nightspots, **Duke's Barefoot Bar** (www.dukeskauai.com; © **808/246-9599**), inside the Kauai Marriott Resort, has long drawn a crowd of visitors and locals, especially at pau hana (end of work) on Friday. The downstairs bar features live Hawaiian music Wednesday through Monday from 4 to 6pm, and again Thursday through Saturday from 8:30 to 10:30pm.

The view isn't as memorable, but the pupu are tastier and the music more varied in the lounge of **Hukilau Lanai** (www.hukilaukauai.com; © **808/822-0600**) at the Kauai Coast Resort, 520 Aleka Loop, Kapaa; top musicians play Hawaiian, jazz, country, and blues Monday through Saturday 6 to 9pm. The **Grand Hyatt Kauai** (www.grandhyattkauai.com; © **808/741-1234**) has nightly live music at **Stevenson's Library,** a book-lined lounge and sushi bar; the Hyatt's **Seaview Terrace** has nightly Hawaiian music (6–9pm), plus gorgeous sunset views.

You'll meet more locals—and pay a good deal less for your drinks—by leaving the resorts. Here are highlights from around the island:

EAST SIDE A combination sports bar, sushi bar, family restaurant, and nightclub, **Rob's Good Times Grill,** in the Rice Shopping Center, 4303 Rice St., Lihue (www.kauaisportsbarandgrill.com; © **808/246-0311**), bustles with live music, karaoke, swing and salsa dancing, and DJs; check schedule online. **Mahiko Lounge,** the swankily remodeled living room of the Kilohana Plantation mansion, *mauka* side of Kaumualii Hwy. in Lihue (www.kilohanakauai.com; © **808/245-5608**), offers cocktails made with freshly crushed sugarcane, live music, and terrific happy-hour specials (Mon–Sat 4–6:30pm) from Gaylord's restaurant. **Old Kapaa Town** (www.facebook.com/OldKapaaTown) throws a party the first Saturday of the month with an **Art Walk** that includes live entertainment, sidewalk vendors, and extended shopping hours (5–9pm).

NORTH SHORE **Tiki Iniki** (www.tikiiniki.com; © 808/431-4242), tucked behind Ace Hardware in the Princeville Center, is a cheeky tiki bar/restaurant opened by Michele Rundgren and her rock-musician husband, Todd, in late 2013. Nightly cocktail specials and frequent theme nights have made it a big hit; table reservations are recommended. Opened in 1963, **Tahiti Nui,** 5-5134 Kuhio Hwy., Hanalei (www.thenui.com; © 808/826-6277), is pretty much as it appears in "The Descendants": a down-home, family-friendly restaurant with live Hawaiian music nightly. Live music cranks up at **Hanalei Gourmet,** in the Old Hanalei Schoolhouse, 5–5161 Kuhio Hwy. (© 808/826-2524), at 6pm Sunday and 8pm Wednesday.

SOUTH SHORE **Keoki's Paradise,** in the Poipu Shopping Village (www.keokisparadise.com; © 808/742-7534), offers live music in its tropical bar most nights, with more dance-oriented music Thursday to Saturday. The leafy courtyard of **The Shops at Kukuiula** (http://theshopsatkukuiula.com) hosts a *kani kapila* (jam) at 6:30pm every Friday, with more live music and sidewalk vendors at the monthly **Kukuiula Art Walk** (second Sat of the month; 6–9pm).

WEST SIDE **Kauai Island Brewery & Grill,** 4350 Waialo Rd., Port Allen (www.kauaiislandbrewing.com; © 808/335-0006), often hosts late-night live music

Tahiti Nui.

and DJ "aftah" parties, starting at 10pm, and serves as a sports bar with five huge, high-definition TVs.

The tutu kane (granddaddy) of local art events is **Hanapepe Friday Night Festival and Art Walk** (www.hanapepe.org), every Friday from 6 to 9pm along Hanapepe Road, featuring food trucks, live music, and brightly lit shops and galleries. *Tip:* Drive cautiously when leaving—Hanapepe Road near the eastern highway turnoff can be very dark.

HAWAII IN CONTEXT

by Shannon Wianecki

Since the Polynesians ventured across the Pacific to the Hawaiian Islands 1,000 years ago, these floating jewels have continued to call visitors from around the globe.

Located in one of the most remote and isolated places on the planet, the islands bask in the warm waters of the Pacific, where they are blessed by a tropical sun and cooled by gentle year-round trade winds—creating what might be the most ideal climate imaginable. Mother Nature has carved out verdant valleys, hung brilliant rainbows in the sky, and trimmed the islands with sandy beaches in a spectrum of colors. The indigenous Hawaiian culture embodies the "spirit of aloha," an easy-going generosity that takes the shape of flower leis freely given, monumental feasts shared with friends and family, and hypnotic Hawaiian melodies played late into the tropical night.

Visitors are drawn to Hawaii not only for its incredible beauty, but also for its opportunities for adventure. Go on, gaze into that fiery volcano, swim in a sea of rainbow-colored fish, tee off on a championship golf course, hike through a rainforest to hidden waterfalls, and kayak into the deep end of the ocean, where whales leap out of the water for reasons still mysterious. Looking for rest and relaxation? You'll discover that life moves at an unhurried pace here. Extra doses of sun and sea allow both body and mind to recharge.

Hawaii is a sensory experience that will remain with you, locked in your memory, long after your tan fades. Years later, a sweet fragrance, the sun's warmth on your face, or the sound of the ocean breeze will deliver you back to the time you spent in the Hawaiian Islands.

THE FIRST HAWAIIANS

Throughout the Middle Ages, while Western sailors clung to the edges of continents for fear of falling off the earth's edge, Polynesian voyagers crisscrossed the planet's largest ocean. The first people to colonize Hawaii were unsurpassed navigators. Using the stars, birds, and currents as guides, they sailed double-hulled canoes across thousands of miles, zeroing in on tiny islands in the center of the Pacific. They packed their vessels with food, plants, medicine, tools, and animals: everything necessary for building a new life on a distant shore. Over a span of 800 years, the great Polynesian migration connected a vast triangle of islands stretching from New Zealand to Hawaii to Easter Island and encompassing the many diverse archipelagos in between. Archaeologists surmise that Hawaii's first wave of settlers came via the Marquesas Islands sometime after A.D. 1000, though oral histories suggest a much earlier date.

Over the ensuing centuries, a distinctly Hawaiian culture arose. Sailors became farmers and fishermen. These early Hawaiians were as skilled on land as they had been at sea; they built highly productive fish ponds, aqueducts to irrigate terraced *kalo loi* (taro patches), and 3-acre *heiau* (temples) with 50-foot-high rock walls. Farmers cultivated more than 400 varieties of *kalo,* their staple food; 300 types of sweet potato; and 40 different bananas. Each variety served a different need—some were drought resistant, others medicinal, and others good for babies. Hawaiian women fashioned intricately patterned *kapa* (bark-cloth)—some of the finest in all of Polynesia. Each of the Hawaiian Islands was its own kingdom, governed by *alii* (high-ranking chiefs) who drew their authority from an established caste system and *kapu* (taboos). Those who broke the *kapu* could be sacrificed.

The ancient Hawaiian creation chant, the *Kumu-lipo,* depicts a universe that began when heat and light emerged out of darkness, followed by the first life form: a coral polyp. The 2,000-line epic poem is a grand genealogy, describing how all species are inter-related, from gently waving seaweeds to mighty human warriors. It is the basis for the Hawaiian concept of *kuleana,* a word that simultaneously refers to privilege and responsibility. To this day, Native Hawaiians view the care of their natural resources as a filial duty and honor.

WESTERN CONTACT
Cook's Ill-Fated Voyage

In the dawn hours of January 18, 1778, Captain James Cook of the HMS *Resolution* spotted an unfamiliar set of islands, which he later named for his benefactor, the Earl of Sandwich. The 50-year-old sea captain was already famous in Britain for "discovering" much of the South Pacific. Now on his third great voyage of exploration, Cook had set sail from Tahiti northward across uncharted waters. He was searching for the mythical Northwest Passage that was said to link the

Pacific and Atlantic oceans. On his way, he stumbled upon Hawaii (aka the Sandwich Isles) quite by chance.

With the arrival of the *Resolution*, Stone Age Hawaii entered the age of iron. Sailors swapped nails and munitions for fresh water, pigs, and the affections of Hawaiian women. Tragically, the foreigners brought with them a terrible cargo: syphilis, measles, and other diseases that decimated the Hawaiian people. Captain Cook estimated the native population at 400,000 in 1778. (Later historians claim it could have been as high as 900,000.) By the time Christian missionaries arrived 40 years later, the number of Native Hawaiians had plummeted to just 150,000.

In a skirmish over a stolen boat, Cook was killed by a blow to the head. His British countrymen sailed home, leaving Hawaii forever altered. The islands were now on the sea charts, and traders on the fur route between Canada and China stopped here to get fresh water. More trade—and more disastrous liaisons—ensued.

Two more sea captains left indelible marks on the Islands. The first was American John Kendrick, who in 1791 filled his ship with fragrant Hawaiian sandalwood and sailed to China. By 1825, Hawaii's sandalwood groves were gone. The second was Englishman George Vancouver, who in 1793 left behind cows and sheep, which ventured out to graze in the islands' native forest and hastened the spread of invasive species. King Kamehameha I sent for cowboys from Mexico and Spain to round up the wild livestock, thus beginning the islands' *paniolo* (cowboy) tradition.

King Kamehameha I was an ambitious *alii* who used western guns to unite the islands under single rule. After his death in 1819, the tightly woven Hawaiian

King Kamehameha I.

King David Kalakaua.

society began to unravel. One of his successors, Queen Kaahumanu, abolished the *kapu* system, opening the door for religion of another form.

Staying to Do Well

In April 1820, missionaries bent on converting Hawaiians arrived from New England. The newcomers clothed the natives, banned them from dancing the hula, and nearly dismantled the ancient culture. The churchgoers tried to keep sailors and whalers out of the bawdy houses, where whiskey flowed and the virtue of native women was never safe. To their credit, the missionaries created a 12-letter alphabet for the Hawaiian language, taught reading and writing, started a printing press, and began recording the islands' history, which until that time had been preserved solely in memorized chants.

IS EVERYONE hawaiian IN HAWAII?

Only *kanaka maoli* (Native Hawaiians) are truly Hawaiian. The sugar and pineapple plantations brought so many different people to Hawaii that the state is now a remarkable potpourri of ethnic groups: Native Hawaiians were joined by **Caucasians, Japanese, Chinese, Filipinos, Koreans, Portuguese, Puerto Ricans, Samoans, Tongans, Tahitians,** and other **Asian and Pacific Islanders.** Add to that a sprinkling of **Vietnamese, Canadians, African Americans, American Indians, South Americans,** and **Europeans** of every stripe. Many people retain an element of the traditions of their homeland. Some Japanese Americans in Hawaii, generations removed from the homeland, are more traditional than the Japanese of Tokyo. The same is true of many Chinese, Koreans, and Filipinos, making Hawaii a kind of living museum of Asian and Pacific cultures.

Children of the missionaries became business leaders and politicians. They married Hawaiians and stayed on in the islands, causing one wag to remark that the missionaries "came to do good and stayed to do well." In 1848, King Kamehameha III enacted the Great Mahele (division). Intended to guarantee Native Hawaiians rights to their land, it ultimately enabled foreigners to take ownership of vast tracts of land. Within two generations, more than 80% of all private land was in *haole* (foreign) hands. Businessmen planted acre after acre in sugarcane and imported waves of immigrants to work the fields: Chinese starting in 1852, Japanese in 1885, and Portuguese in 1878.

King David Kalakaua was elected to the throne in 1874. This popular "Merrie Monarch" built Iolani Palace in 1882, threw extravagant parties, and lifted the prohibitions on the hula and other native arts. For this, he was much loved. He proclaimed that "hula is the language of the heart and, therefore, the heartbeat of the Hawaiian people." He also gave Pearl Harbor to the United States; it became the westernmost bastion of the U.S. Navy. While visiting chilly San Francisco in 1891, King Kalakaua caught a cold and died in the royal suite of the Sheraton Palace. His sister, Queen Liliuokalani, assumed the throne.

The Overthrow

For years, a group of American sugar plantation owners and missionary descendants had been machinating against the monarchy. On January 17, 1893, with the support of the U.S. minister to Hawaii and the Marines, the conspirators imprisoned Queen Liliuokalani in her own palace. To avoid bloodshed, she abdicated the throne, trusting that the United States government would right the wrong. As the Queen waited in vain, she penned the sorrowful lyric "Aloha Oe," Hawaii's song of farewell.

U.S. President Grover Cleveland's attempt to restore the monarchy was thwarted by congress. Sanford Dole, a powerful sugar plantation owner, appointed himself president of the newly declared Republic of Hawaii. His fellow sugarcane planters, known as the Big Five, controlled banking, shipping, hardware, and every other facet of economic life on the islands. In 1898, through annexation, Hawaii became an American territory ruled by Dole.

Oahu's central Ewa Plain soon filled with row crops. The Dole family planted pineapple on its sprawling acreage. Planters imported more contract laborers from Puerto Rico (1900), Korea (1903), and the Philippines (1907–31). Many of the new immigrants stayed on to establish families and become a part of the islands. Meanwhile, Native Hawaiians became a landless minority. Their language was banned in schools and their cultural practices devalued, forced into hiding.

For nearly a century in Hawaii, sugar was king, generously subsidized by the U.S. government. Sugar is a thirsty crop, and plantation owners oversaw the construction of flumes and aqueducts that channeled mountain streams down to parched plains, where waving fields of cane soon grew. The waters that once fed taro patches dried up. The sugar planters dominated the territory's economy, shaped its social fabric, and kept the islands in a colonial plantation era with bosses and field hands. But the workers eventually went on strike for higher wages and improved working conditions, and the planters found themselves unable to compete with cheap third-world labor costs.

Tourism Takes Hold

Tourism in Hawaii began in the 1860s. Kilauea volcano was one of the world's prime attractions for adventure travelers. In 1865, a grass Volcano House was built on the rim of Halemaumau Crater to shelter visitors; it was Hawaii's first hotel. The visitor industry blossomed as the plantation era peaked and waned.

In 1901, W. C. Peacock built the elegant Beaux Arts Moana Hotel on Waikiki Beach, and W. C. Weedon convinced Honolulu businessmen to bankroll his plan to advertise Hawaii in San Francisco. Armed with a stereopticon and tinted photos of Waikiki, Weedon sailed off in 1902 for 6 months of lecture tours to introduce "those remarkable people and the beautiful lands of Hawaii." He drew packed houses. A tourism

The original Volcano House, Hawaii's first hotel.

promotion bureau was formed in 1903, and about 2,000 visitors came to Hawaii that year.

The steamship was Hawaii's tourism lifeline. It took 4½ days to sail from San Francisco to Honolulu. Streamers, leis, and pomp welcomed each Matson liner at downtown's Aloha Tower. Well-heeled visitors brought trunks, servants, and Rolls-Royces and stayed for months. Hawaiians amused visitors with personal tours, floral parades, and hula shows.

Beginning in 1935 and running for the next 40 years, Webley Edwards's weekly live radio show, "Hawaii Calls," planted the sounds of Waikiki—surf, sliding steel guitar, sweet Hawaiian harmonies, drumbeats—in the hearts of millions of listeners in the United States, Australia, and Canada.

By 1936, visitors could fly to Honolulu from San Francisco on the *Hawaii Clipper,* a seven-passenger Pan American Martin M-130 flying boat, for $360 one-way. The flight took 21 hours, 33 minutes. Modern tourism was born, with five flying boats providing daily service. The 1941 visitor count was a brisk 31,846 through December 6.

SPEAKING hawaiian

Most everyone in Hawaii speaks English. But many folks now also speak *olelo Hawaii*, the native language of these Islands. You will regularly hear *aloha* and *mahalo* (thank you). If you've just arrived, you're a *malihini*. Someone who's been here a long time is a *kamaaina*. When you finish a job or your meal, you are *pau* (finished). On Friday, it's *pau hana*, work finished. You eat *pupu* (Hawaii's version of hors d'oeuvres) when you go *pau hana*.

The Hawaiian alphabet, created by the New England missionaries, has only 12 letters: the five regular vowels (*a, e, i, o,* and *u*) and seven consonants (*h, k, l, m, n, p,* and *w*). The vowels are pronounced in the Roman fashion: that is, *ah, ay, ee, oh,* and *oo* (as in "too")—not *ay, ee, eye, oh,* and *you,* as in English. For example, *huhu* is pronounced *who-who*. Most vowels are sounded separately, though some are pronounced together, as in Kalakaua: "kah-lah-cow-ah."

World War II & Statehood

On December 7, 1941, Japanese Zeros came out of the rising sun to bomb American warships based at Pearl Harbor. This was the "day of infamy" that plunged the United States into World War II.

The attack brought immediate changes to the Islands. Martial law was declared, stripping the Big Five cartel of its absolute power in a single day. German and Japanese Americans were interned. Hawaii was "blacked out" at night, Waikiki Beach was strung with barbed wire, and Aloha Tower was painted in camouflage. Only young men bound for the Pacific came to Hawaii during the war years. Many came back to graves in a cemetery called Punchbowl.

The postwar years saw the beginnings of Hawaii's faux culture. The authentic traditions had long been suppressed, and into the void flowed a consumable brand of aloha. Harry Yee invented the Blue Hawaii cocktail and dropped in a tiny Japanese parasol. Vic Bergeron created the mai tai, a drink made of rum and fresh lime juice, and opened Trader Vic's, America's first themed restaurant that featured the art, decor, and food of Polynesia. Arthur Godfrey picked up a ukulele and began singing *hapa-haole* tunes on early TV shows. In 1955, Henry J. Kaiser built the Hilton Hawaiian Village, and the 11-story high-rise Princess Kaiulani Hotel opened on a site where the real princess once played. Hawaii greeted 109,000 visitors that year.

In 1959, Hawaii became the 50th state of the United States. That year also saw the arrival of the first jet airliners, which brought 250,000 tourists to the state. By the 1980s, Hawaii's visitor count surpassed 6 million. Fantasy megaresorts bloomed on the neighbor islands like giant artificial flowers, swelling the luxury market with ever-swanker accommodations. Hawaii's tourist industry—the bastion of the state's economy—has survived worldwide recessions, airline industry hiccups, and increased competition from overseas. Year after year, the Hawaiian Islands continue to be ranked among the top visitor destinations in the world.

HAWAII TODAY
A Cultural Renaissance

Despite the ever-increasing influx of foreign people and customs, the Native Hawaiian culture is experiencing a rebirth. It began in earnest in 1976, when members of the Polynesian Voyaging Society launched *Hokulea,* a double-hulled canoe of the sort that hadn't

Hula girls.

been seen on these shores in centuries. The *Hokulea*'s daring crew sailed her 2,500 miles to Tahiti without using modern instruments, relying instead on ancient navigational techniques. Most historians at that time discounted Polynesian wayfinding methods as rudimentary; the prevailing theory was that Pacific Islanders had discovered Hawaii by accident, not intention. The *Hokulea*'s successful voyage sparked a fire in the hearts of indigenous islanders across the Pacific, who reclaimed their identity as a sophisticated, powerful people with unique wisdom to offer the world.

The Hawaiian language found new life, too. In 1984, a group of educators and parents recognized that, with fewer than 50 children fluent in Hawaiian, the language was dangerously close to extinction. They started a preschool where *keiki* (children) learned lessons purely in Hawaiian. They overcame numerous bureaucratic obstacles (including a law still on the books forbidding instruction in Hawaiian) to establish

Hawaiian-language-immersion programs across the state that run from preschool through post-graduate education.

Hula—which never fully disappeared despite the missionaries' best efforts—is thriving. At the annual Merrie Monarch festival commemorating King Kalakaua, hula *halau* (troupes) from Hawaii and beyond gather to demonstrate their skill and artistry. Fans of the ancient dance form are glued to the live broadcast of what is known as the Olympics of hula. *Kumu hula* (hula teachers) have safeguarded many Hawaiian cultural practices as part of their art: the making of *kapa,* the collection and cultivation of native herbs, and the observation of *kuleana,* an individual's responsibility to the community.

In that same spirit, in May 2014, the traditional voyaging canoe *Hokulea* embarked on her most ambitious adventure yet: an international peace delegation. During the canoe's 3-year circumnavigation of the globe, the crew's mission is "to weave a lei around the world" and chart a new course toward a healthier and more sustainable horizon for all of humankind. The sailors hope to collaborate with political leaders, scientists, educators, and schoolchildren in each of the ports they visit.

The history of Hawaii has come full circle: the ancient Polynesians traveled the seas to discover these Islands. Today, their descendants set sail to share Hawaii with the world.

DINING IN HAWAII

In the early days of Hawaii's tourism industry, the food wasn't anything to write home about. Continental cuisine ruled fine-dining kitchens. Meats and produce

Ahi poke.

arrived much the same way visitors did: jet-lagged after a long journey from a far-off land. Island chefs struggled to revive limp iceberg lettuce and frozen cocktail shrimp—often letting outstanding ocean views make up for uninspired dishes. In 1991, 12 chefs staged a revolt. They partnered with local farmers, ditched the dictatorship of imported foods, and brought sun-ripened mango, crisp organic greens, and freshly caught *uku* (snapper) to the table. Coining the name "Hawaii Regional Cuisine," they gave the world a taste of what happens when passionate, classically trained cooks have their way with ripe Pacific flavors.

Two decades later, the movement to unite local farms and kitchens is still bearing fruit. The HRC heavyweights continue to keep things hot in island kitchens. But they aren't, by any means, the sole source of good eats in Hawaii.

Shave ice.

Haute cuisine is alive and well in Hawaii, but equally important in the culinary pageant are good-value plate lunches, shave ice, and food trucks.

The **plate lunch,** which is ubiquitous throughout the islands, can be ordered from a lunch wagon or a restaurant and usually consists of some protein—fried mahimahi, say, or teriyaki beef, shoyu chicken, or chicken or pork cutlets served katsu style: breaded and fried and slathered in a rich gravy—"two scoops rice," macaroni salad, and a few leaves of green, typically julienned cabbage. Chili water and soy sauce are the condiments of choice. Like **saimin**—the local version of noodles in broth topped with scrambled eggs, green onions, and sometimes pork—the plate lunch is Hawaii's version of comfort food.

Because this is Hawaii, at least a few fingerfuls of **poi**—steamed, pounded taro (the traditional Hawaiian staple crop)—are a must. Mix it with salty *kalua* pork (pork cooked in a Polynesian underground oven known as an *imu*) or *lomi* salmon (salted salmon with tomatoes and green onions). Other tasty Hawaiian foods include **poke** (pronounced *"po-kay,"* this popular appetizer is made of cubed raw fish seasoned with onions, seaweed, and roasted *kukui* nuts), **laulau** (pork, chicken, or fish steamed in *ti* leaves), **squid luau** (cooked in coconut milk and taro tops), **haupia** (creamy coconut pudding), and **kulolo** (a steamed pudding of coconut, brown sugar, and taro).

For a sweet snack, the prevailing choice is **shave ice.** Particularly on hot, humid days, long lines of shave-ice lovers gather for heaps of finely shaved ice topped with sweet tropical syrups. Sweet-sour *li hing mui* is a favorite, and new gourmet flavors include calamansi lime and red velvet cupcake. Aficionados order shave ice with ice cream and sweetened adzuki beans on the bottom or sweetened condensed milk on top.

WHEN TO GO

Most visitors come to Hawaii when the weather is lousy most everywhere else. Thus, the **high season**—when prices are up and resorts are often booked to capacity—is generally from mid-December to March or mid-April. The last 2 weeks of December, in particular, are prime time for travel to Hawaii. Spring break is also jam-packed with families taking advantage of the school holiday. If you're planning a trip during peak season, make your hotel and rental car reservations as early as possible, expect crowds, and prepare to pay top dollar.

The **off season,** when the best rates are available and the islands are less crowded, is late spring (mid-Apr to early June) and fall (Sept to mid-Dec).

If you plan to travel in **summer** (June–Aug), don't expect to see the fantastic bargains of spring and fall—this is prime time for family travel. But you'll still find much better deals on packages, airfare, and accommodations in summer than in the winter months.

Climate

Because Hawaii lies at the edge of the tropical zone, it technically has only two seasons, both of them warm. There's a dry season that corresponds to **summer** (Apr–Oct) and a rainy season in **winter** (Nov–Mar). It rains every day somewhere in the islands at any time of the year, but the rainy season can bring enough gray weather to spoil your tanning opportunities. Fortunately, it seldom rains in one spot for more than 3 days straight.

The **year-round temperature** doesn't vary much. At the beach, the average daytime high in summer is 85°F (29°C), while the average daytime high in winter is 78°F (26°C); nighttime lows are usually about 10° cooler. But how warm it is on any given day really depends on *where* you are on the island.

Each island has a **leeward** side (the side sheltered from the wind) and a **windward** side (the side that gets the wind's full force). The leeward sides (the west and south) are usually hot and dry, while the windward sides (east and north) are generally cooler and moist. When you want arid, sunbaked, desert-like weather, go leeward. When you want lush, wet, jungle-like weather, go windward.

Hawaii also has a wide range of **microclimates,** thanks to interior valleys, coastal plains, and mountain peaks. Kauai's Mount Waialeale is one of the wettest spots on earth, yet Waimea Canyon, just a few miles away, is almost a desert. At Puako, only 60 miles away, it rains less than 6 inches a year. The locals say if you don't like the weather, just drive a few miles down the road—it's sure to be different!

Average Temperature & Number of Rainy Days in Hanalei, Kauai

	JAN	FEB	MAR	APR	MAY	JUNE
HIGH (°F/°C)	79/26	80/27	80/27	82/28	84/29	86/30
LOW (°F/°C)	61/17	61/16	62/17	63/17	65/18	66/19
	JULY	AUG	SEPT	OCT	NOV	DEC
HIGH (°F/°C)	88/31	88/31	87/31	86/30	83/28	80/27
LOW (°F/°C)	66/19	67/19	68/20	67/19	65/18	62/17
	JAN	FEB	MAR	APR	MAY	JUNE
RAINY DAYS	8	5	6	3	3	2
	JULY	AUG	SEPT	OCT	NOV	DEC
	8	2	3	3	4	7

Holidays

When Hawaii observes holidays (especially those over a long weekend), travel between the islands increases, interisland airline seats are fully booked, rental cars are at a premium, and hotels and restaurants are busier.

Federal, state, and county government offices are closed on all federal holidays. Federal holidays in 2016 include New Year's Day (Jan 1); Martin Luther King, Jr., Day (Jan 18); Washington's birthday (Feb 16); Memorial Day (May 30); Independence Day (July 4); Labor Day (Sept 5); Columbus Day (Oct 12); Veterans Day (Nov 11); Thanksgiving Day (Nov 24); and Christmas (Dec 25).

State and county offices are also closed on local holidays, including Prince Kuhio Day (Mar 25), honoring the birthday of Hawaii's first delegate to the U.S. Congress; King Kamehameha Day (June 11), a

Hey, No Smoking in Hawaii

Well, not *totally* no smoking, but Hawaii has one of the toughest laws against smoking in the U.S. The Hawaii Smoke-Free Law prohibits smoking in public buildings, including airports, shopping malls, grocery stores, retail shops, buses, movie theaters, banks, convention facilities, and all government buildings and facilities. There is no smoking in restaurants, bars, and nightclubs. Most bed-and-breakfasts prohibit smoking indoors, and more and more hotels and resorts are becoming smoke-free even in public areas. Also, there is no smoking within 20 feet of a doorway, window, or ventilation intake (so no hanging around outside a bar to smoke—you must go 20 ft. away). Even some beaches have no-smoking policies.

statewide holiday commemorating Kamehameha the Great, who united the islands and ruled from 1795 to 1819; and Admission Day (third Fri in Aug), which honors the admittance of Hawaii as the 50th state on August 21, 1959.

Kauai Calendar of Events

Please note that, as with any schedule of upcoming events, the following information is subject to change; always confirm the details before you plan your trip around an event.

FEBRUARY

Waimea Town Celebration, Waimea, Kauai. This annual 2-day party on Kauai's west side celebrates the Hawaiian and multiethnic history of the town where Captain Cook first landed. This is the island's biggest event, drawing some 10,000 people. Top Hawaiian entertainers, sporting events, rodeo, and hat lei contests are just some of the draws of this weekend celebration. Details at www.waimeatowncelebration.com

or © **808/645-0996.** Weekend after Presidents' Day weekend.

Chinese New Year, most islands. In 2015, lion dancers will be snaking their way around the state on February 19, the start of the Chinese Year of the Sheep. Visit www.chinesechamber.com or call © **808/533-3181.** Also in Wailuku; call © **808/244-3888** for location.

Prince Kuhio Day Celebrations, all islands. On this state holiday, various festivals throughout Hawaii celebrate the birth of Jonah Kuhio Kalanianaole, who was born on March 26, 1871, and elected to Congress in 1902. Kauai, his birthplace, stages a huge celebration in Lihue; call © **808/240-6369** for details.

MAY

Outrigger Canoe Season, all islands. From May to September, canoe paddlers across the state participate in outrigger canoe races nearly every weekend. Go to www.ocpaddler.com for this year's schedule of events.

JUNE

Obon Season, all islands. This colorful Buddhist ceremony honoring the souls of the dead kicks off in June. Synchronized dancers circle a tower where Taiko drummers play, and food booths sell Japanese treats late into the night. Each weekend, a different Buddhist temple hosts the Bon Dance. Go to www.gohawaii.com for a statewide schedule.

AUGUST

Admission Day, all islands. Hawaii became the 50th state on August 21, 1959. On the third Friday in August, the state takes a holiday (all state-related facilities are closed).

SEPTEMBER

Aloha Festivals, various locations on all islands. Parades and other events celebrate Hawaiian culture and friendliness throughout the state. Go to www.alohafestivals.com or call © **808/ 923-2030.**

OCTOBER

Emalani Festival, Kokee State Park, Kauai. This festival honors Her Majesty Queen Emma, an inveterate gardener and Hawaii's first environmental queen, who made a forest trek to Kokee with 100 friends in 1871. Go to www.kokee.org or call © **808/335-9975.** Second Saturday in October.

NOVEMBER

Hawaiian Slack Key Guitar Festival, Kauai Beach Resort, Lihue, Kauai. The best of Hawaii's folk music (slack key guitar) performed by the best musicians in Hawaii. It's 6 hours long and free. Go to www.slackkeyfestival.com or call © **808/226-2697.** Mid-November.

Hawaii International Film Festival, various locations throughout the state. This cinema festival with a cross-cultural spin features filmmakers from Asia, the Pacific Islands, and the United States. Go to www.hiff.org or call © **808/792-1577.** Mid-October to early November.

DECEMBER

Festival of Lights, all islands. On Oahu, the mayor throws the switch to light up the 40-foot-tall Norfolk pine and other trees in front of Honolulu Hale, while on Maui, kids can play in a "snow zone" and make holiday crafts beneath the Lahaina Banyan tree, glowing with thousands of twinkle lights. Molokai celebrates with a host of activities in Kaunakakai; on Kauai, the lighting ceremony takes place in front of the former county building on Rice Street, in Lihue. Call © **808/768-6622** on Oahu; © **808/667-9175** on Maui; © **808/553-4482** on Molokai; or © **808/639-6571** on Kauai. Early December.

8

PLANNING

by Shannon Wianecki

Hawaii is rich in natural and cultural wonders, and that's especially true for Kauai, the oldest and most lushly tropical of the Hawaiian isles. Here we've compiled everything you need to know before escaping to the Islands.

Our biggest tip is to **fly directly to the island of your choice;** doing so can save you a 2-hour layover in Honolulu and another plane ride. Oahu, the Big Island, Maui, and Kauai now all receive direct flights from the Mainland.

So let's get on with the process of planning your trip. For pertinent facts and on-the-ground resources in Hawaii, turn to "Fast Facts: Hawaii," at the end of this chapter on p. 228.

GETTING THERE
By Plane

Most major U.S. and many international carriers fly to **Honolulu International Airport** (HNL), on Oahu. Some also offer direct flights to **Kahului Airport** (OGG), on Maui; **Lihue Airport** (LIH), on Kauai; and **Kona International Airport** (KOA) and **Hilo Airport** (ITO), on the Big Island. If you can fly directly to the island of your choice, you'll be spared a 2-hour layover in Honolulu and another plane ride. If you're heading to Molokai (MKK) or Lanai (LNY), you'll have the easiest connections if you fly into Honolulu. See island chapters for detailed information on direct flights to each island.

Hawaiian Airlines offers flights from more mainland U.S. gateways than any other airline. Hawaiian's easy-to-navigate website makes finding the cheapest fares a cinch. Its closest competitor, price-wise, is **Alaska Airlines,** which offers daily nonstop flights from West Coast cities including Anchorage, Seattle, Portland, and Oakland. From points farther east, **United, American, Continental,** and **Delta** all fly to Hawaii with nonstop service to Honolulu and most neighbor islands. If you're having difficulty finding an affordable fare, try routing your flight through Las Vegas. It's a huge hub for traffic to and from the Islands.

For travel from beyond the U.S. mainland, check these airlines: Air Canada, Air New Zealand, Qantas Airways, Japan Air Lines, All Nippon Airways (ANA), the Taiwan-based China Airlines, Korean Air, and Philippine Airlines. Hawaiian Airlines also flies nonstop to Australia, American Samoa, Philippines, Tahiti, South Korea, and Japan.

ARRIVING AT THE AIRPORT

IMMIGRATION & CUSTOMS CLEARANCE International visitors arriving by air should cultivate patience and resignation before setting foot on U.S. soil. U.S. airports have considerable security practices in place. Clearing Customs and Immigration can take as long as 2 hours.

AGRICULTURAL SCREENING AT AIRPORTS At Honolulu International and the neighbor-island airports, baggage and passengers bound for the Mainland must

be screened by agriculture officials. Officials will con-
fiscate local produce like fresh avocados, bananas, and
mangoes, in the name of fruit-fly control. Pineapples,
coconuts, and papayas inspected and certified for
export; boxed flowers; leis without seeds; and processed foods (macadamia nuts, coffee, jams, dried
fruit, and the like) will pass.

GETTING AROUND HAWAII

Here are all the ways to see the sights once you hit
Kauai.

Interisland Flights

The major interisland carriers have cut way back on
the number of interisland flights. The airlines warn
you to show up at least 90 minutes before your flight
and, believe me, with all the security inspections, you
will need all 90 minutes to catch your flight.

Hawaii has one major interisland carrier, **Hawaiian Airlines** (www.hawaiianair.com; © **800/367-
5320**), and two commuter airlines, **Island Air** (www.
islandair.com; © **800/323-3345**) and **Mokulele Airlines** (www.mokuleleairlines.com; © **866/260-7070**).
The commuter flights service the neighbor islands'
more remote airports and tend to be on small planes;
you'll board from the tarmac and weight restrictions
apply.

By Car

Bottom line: You will likely need a car to get around
Kauai, especially if you plan to explore outside your

A Weeklong Cruise Through the Islands

If you're looking for a taste of several islands in 7 days, consider **Norwegian Cruise Line** (www.ncl.com; © 866/234-7350), the only cruise line that operates year-round in Hawaii. NCL's 2,240-passenger ship *Pride of America* circles Hawaii, stopping on four islands: the Big Island, Maui, Kauai, and Oahu.

resort—and you absolutely should. Public transit in Kauai is spotty. So plan to rent a car.

That said, Hawaii has some of the priciest car-rental rates in the country. Keep in mind, too, that rental cars are often at a premium on Kauai, and may be sold out on any island over holiday weekends, so be sure to book well ahead. In fact, we recommend reserving your car as soon as you book your airfare.

To rent a car in Hawaii, you must be at least 25 years of age and have a valid driver's license and credit card. **Note:** If you're visiting from abroad and plan to rent a car in the United States, keep in mind that foreign driver's licenses are usually recognized in the U.S., but you should get an international one if your home license is not in English.

At Honolulu International Airport and most neighbor-island airports, you'll find many major car-rental agencies, including **Alamo, Avis, Budget, Dollar, Enterprise, Hertz, National,** and **Thrifty.** It's almost always cheaper to rent a car in Waikiki, or anywhere but at the airport, where you will pay a daily fee for the convenience of renting at the airport.

GASOLINE Gas prices in Hawaii, always much higher than on the U.S. mainland, vary from island to island. Expect to pay around $4 a gallon. Check www.gasbuddy.com to find the cheapest gas in your area.

INSURANCE   Hawaii is a no-fault state, which means that if you don't have collision-damage insurance, you are required to pay for all damages before you leave the state, whether or not the accident was your fault. Your personal car insurance may provide rental-car coverage; check before you leave home. Bring your insurance identification card if you decline the optional insurance, which usually costs from $9 to $45 a day. Obtain the name of your company's local claim representative before you go. Some credit card companies also provide collision-damage insurance for their customers; check with yours before you rent.

DRIVING RULES   Hawaii state law mandates that all car passengers must wear a **seat belt** and all infants must be strapped into a car seat. You'll pay a $92 fine if you don't buckle up. **Pedestrians** always have the right of way, even if they're not in the crosswalk. You can turn **right on red** after a full and complete stop, unless otherwise posted.

Stay off the Cellphone

Talking on a cellphone while driving in Hawaii is a big no-no. Fines range from $100 to $200 and double in school or construction zones. An Oahu woman was even ticketed for talking on her cellphone while parked on the side of the road! Save yourself the money; don't use a cell while you are driving.

ROAD MAPS   The best and most detailed maps for activities are published by **Franko Maps** (www.frankosmaps.com); these feature a host of island maps, plus a terrific "Hawaiian Reef Creatures Guide" for snorkelers curious about those fish they spot underwater. Free road maps are published by **"This Week Magazine,"** a visitor publication available on Oahu, the Big Island, Maui, and Kauai.

Another good source is the **University of Hawaii Press maps,** which include a detailed network of island roads, large-scale insets of towns, historical and contemporary points of interest, parks, beaches, and hiking trails. If you can't find them in a bookstore near you, contact **University of Hawaii Press,** 2840 Kolowalu St., Honolulu, HI 96822 (www.uhpress.hawaii.edu; © **888/UH-PRESS [847-7377]**). For topographic maps of the islands, go to the **U.S. Geological Survey** site (www.pubs.usgs.gov).

SPECIAL-INTEREST TRIPS & TOURS

This section presents an overview of special-interest trips and tours and outdoor excursions in Hawaii. We also list references for spotting birds, plants, and sea life. Always use the resources available to inquire about weather, trail, or surf conditions; water availability; and other conditions before you take off on your adventure.

Air Tours

Nothing beats getting a bird's-eye view of Hawaii. Some of the islands' most stunning scenery can't be seen any other way. You'll have your choice of aircraft here: **helicopter or small fixed wing plane.** For wide, open spaces such as the lava fields of Hawaii Volcanoes National Park, a fixed-wing plane is the safest and most affordable option. For exploring tight canyons and valleys, helicopters have an advantage: They can hover. Only a helicopter can bring you face to face with waterfalls in remote places like Mount Waialeale.

Today's pilots are part Hawaiian historian, part DJ, part amusement-ride operator, and part tour guide, sharing anecdotes about Hawaii's flora, fauna, history, and culture. Top trips include: **Na Pali Coast,** Kauai, where you soar over the painted landscape of Waimea Canyon, known as the "Grand Canyon of the Pacific," and visit the cascading falls of Mount Waialeale, one of the wettest spots on Earth.

Volunteer Vacations & Ecotourism

If you're looking to swap sunbathing for something more memorable on your next trip to Hawaii, consider volunteering while on vacation. Rewards include new friends and access to spectacular wilderness areas that are otherwise off-limits.

To participate in beach and reef cleanups, or monitor nesting sea turtles, contact the **University of Hawaii Sea Grant College Program** (© 808/956-7031) or the **Hawaii Wildlife Fund** (www.wildhawaii.org; © 808/280-8124). For land-based adventures, **Malama Hawaii** (www.malamahawaii.org/get_involved/volunteer.php) is a statewide organization dedicated to malama (taking care) of the culture and environment of Hawaii. The website lists a range of opportunities, such as weeding and potting plants in botanical gardens, restoring taro patches, cleaning up mountain streams, bird-watching, and even hanging out at Waikiki Beach to help with a reef project.

Check out the **Hawaii Ecotourism Association** (www.hawaiiecotourism.org; ⓒ **808/235-5431**), a comprehensive site that lists ecotourism volunteer opportunities, such as seabird habitat restoration. Local ecotourism opportunities are also discussed in the individual island chapters.

A great alternative to hiring a private guide is taking a trip with the **Nature Conservancy** or the **Sierra Club.** Both organizations offer guided hikes in preserves and special areas during the year, as well as day- to week-long volunteer work trips to restore habitats and trails and root out invasive plants. It's a chance to see the "real" Hawaii—including wilderness areas that are ordinarily off-limits.

All Nature Conservancy hikes and work trips are free (donations appreciated). However, you must reserve a spot, and a deposit is required for guided hikes to ensure that you'll show up; your deposit is refunded when you do. For all islands, call the Oahu office for reservations. Contact the **Nature Conservancy of Hawaii** (www.nature.org/ourinitiatives/regions; ⓒ **808/246-0543** on Kauai)

The Sierra Club offers half- or all-day hikes on Kauai. Hikes are led by certified Sierra Club volunteers and classified as easy, moderate, or strenuous. Donations of $1 for Sierra Club members and $5 for nonmembers (bring exact change) are recommended. Contact the **Hawaii Chapter of the Sierra Club** (www.sierraclubhawaii.com; ⓒ **808/538-6616** on Oahu).

[FastFACTS] HAWAII

Area Codes   Hawaii's area code is 808; it applies to all islands. There is a long-distance charge when calling from one island to another.

Customs   For details regarding U.S. Customs and Border Protection, consult your nearest U.S. embassy or consulate, or U.S. Customs (www.cbp.gov). You cannot take home fresh fruit, plants, or seeds (including some leis) unless they are sealed. You cannot seal and pack them yourself. For information on what you're allowed to bring home, contact one of the following agencies:

U.S. Citizens: U.S. Customs & Border Protection (CBP), 1300 Pennsylvania Ave., NW, Washington, DC 20229 (www.cbp.gov; ✆ 877/CBP-5511).

Canadian Citizens: Canada Border Services Agency (www.cbsa-asfc.gc.ca; ✆ 800/461-9999 in Canada, or 204/983-3500).

U.K. Citizens: HM Customs & Excise (www.hmce.gov.uk; ✆ 0845/010-9000 in the U.K., or 020/8929-0152).

Australian Citizens: Australian Customs Service (www.customs.gov.au; ✆ 1300/363-263).

New Zealand Citizens: New Zealand Customs, The Customhouse, 17–21 Whitmore St., Box 2218, Wellington (www.customs.govt.nz; ✆ 64/9-927-8036 outside of NZ, or 0800/428-786).

Electricity   Like Canada, the United States uses 110 to 120 volts AC (60 cycles), compared to 220 to 240 volts AC (50 cycles) in most of Europe, Australia, and New Zealand. Downward converters that change 220–240 volts to 110–120 volts are hard to find in the U.S., so bring one with you if you're traveling to Hawaii from abroad.

Embassies & Consulates   All embassies are in the nation's capital, Washington, D.C. Some consulates are in major U.S. cities, and most nations have a mission to the United Nations in New York City. If your country isn't listed below, check **www.embassy.org/embassies** or call for directory information in Washington, D.C. (✆ **202/555-1212**).

The embassy of **Australia** is at 1601 Massachusetts Ave. NW, Washington, DC 20036 (www.usa.embassy.gov.au; ✆ **202/797-**

3000). Consulates are in New York, Honolulu, Houston, Los Angeles, Denver, Atlanta, Chicago, and San Francisco.

The embassy of **Canada** is at 501 Pennsylvania Ave. NW, Washington, DC 20001 (www.canadainternational.gc.ca/washington; ✆ **202/682-1740**). Other Canadian consulates are in Chicago, Detroit, and San Diego.

The embassy of **Ireland** is at 2234 Massachusetts Ave. NW, Washington, DC 20008 (www.embassyofireland.org; ✆ **202/462-3939**). Irish consulates are in Boston, Chicago, New York, San Francisco, and other cities. See website for complete listing.

The embassy of **New Zealand** is at 37 Observatory Circle NW, Washington, DC 20008 (www.nzembassy.com; ✆ **202/328-4800**). New Zealand consulates are in Los Angeles, Salt Lake City, San Francisco, and Seattle.

The embassy of the **United Kingdom** is at 3100 Massachusetts Ave. NW, Washington, DC 20008 (http://ukinusa.fco.gov.uk; ✆ **202/588-6500**). Other British consulates are in Atlanta, Boston, Chicago, Cleveland, Houston, Los Angeles, New York, San Francisco, and Seattle.

Family Travel With beaches to build castles on, water to splash in, and amazing sights to see, Hawaii is paradise for children.

The larger hotels and resorts offer supervised programs for children and can refer you to qualified babysitters. By state law, hotels can accept only children ages 5 to 12 in supervised activities programs, but can often accommodate younger kids by hiring babysitters to watch over them. Contact **People Attentive to Children (PATCH)** for referrals to babysitters who have taken a training course in childcare. On Kauai, call ✆ **808/246-0622;** or visit www.patchhawaii.org.

For a list of more family-friendly travel resources, turn to the experts at www.frommers.com.

Gay & Lesbian Travelers   Hawaii welcomes all people with aloha. The number of gay- or lesbian-specific accommodations on the islands is limited, but most properties welcome gays and lesbians as they would any traveler. Since 1990, the state's capital has hosted the **Honolulu Pride Parade and Celebration.** Register to participate at www.honolulupride.org.

Gay Hawaii (www.gayhawaii.com) and **Pride Guide Hawaii** (www.gogayhawaii.com) are websites with gay and lesbian news, blogs, business recommendations, and other information for the entire state. Also check out the website for **Out in Hawaii** (www.outinhawaii.com), which calls itself "Queer Resources and Information for the State of Hawaii," with vacation ideas, a calendar of events, information on Hawaii, and even a chat room.

For more gay and lesbian travel resources, visit www.frommers.com.

Health **Mosquitoes, Centipedes & Scorpions** While insects can get a little close for comfort in Hawaii (expect to see ants, cockroaches, and other critters indoors, even in posh hotels) few cause serious trouble. Mosquitoes do not carry disease here (barring an isolated outbreak of dengue fever in 2001). Giant centipedes—as long as 8 inches—are occasionally seen; scorpions are rare. If you're stung or bitten by an insect and experience extreme pain, swelling, nausea, or any other severe reaction, seek medical help immediately.

Hiking Safety Before you set out on a hike, let someone know where you're heading and when you plan to return; too many hikers spend cold nights in the wilderness because they don't take this simple precaution. It's always a good idea to hike with a pal. Select your route based on your own fitness level. Check weather conditions with the **National Weather Service** (www.prh.noaa.gov/hnl; on Oahu), even if it looks sunny: The weather here ranges from blistering hot to freezing cold and can change in a matter of hours or miles. Do *not* hike if rain or a storm is predicted; flash floods are common in Hawaii and have resulted in many preventable deaths. Plan to finish your hike at least an hour before sunset; because Hawaii is so close to the equator, it does not have a twilight period, and thus it gets dark quickly after the sun sets. Wear sturdy shoes, a hat, clothes to protect you from the sun and from getting scratches, and high-SPF sunscreen on all exposed areas. Take plenty of water, basic first aid, a snack, and a bag to pack out what you pack in. Watch your step. Loose lava rocks are famous for twisting ankles. Don't rely on cellphones; service isn't available in many remote places.

Ocean Safety   The range of watersports available here is astounding—this is a prime water playground with conditions for every age and ability. But the ocean is also an untamed wilderness; don't expect a calm swimming pool. Many people who visit Hawaii underestimate the power of the ocean. With just a few precautions, your Pacific experience can be a safe and happy one. Before jumping in, familiarize yourself with your equipment. If you're snorkeling, make sure you feel at ease breathing and clearing water from the snorkel. Take a moment to watch where others are swimming. Observe weather conditions, swells, and possible riptides. If you get caught in big surf, dive underneath each wave until the swell subsides. Never turn your back to the ocean; rogue waves catch even experienced water folk unaware. Be realistic about your fitness—more than one visitor has ended his or her vacation with a heart attack in the water. Don't go out alone, or during a storm.

Note that sharks are not a big problem in Hawaii; in fact, local divers look forward to seeing them. Only 2 of the 40 shark species present in Hawaiian waters are known to bite humans, and then usually it's by accident. But here are the general rules for avoiding sharks: Don't swim at dusk or in murky water—sharks may mistake you for one of their usual meals. It should be obvious not to swim where there are bloody fish in the water, as sharks become aggressive around blood.

Seasickness   The waters in Hawaii can range from calm as glass (off the Kona Coast on the Big Island) to downright turbulent (in storm conditions); they usually fall somewhere in between. In general, expect rougher conditions in winter than in summer and on windward coastlines versus calm, leeward coastlines. If you've never been out on a boat, or if you've been seasick in the past, you might want to heed the following suggestions:

- The day before you go out on the boat, avoid alcohol, caffeine, citrus and other acidic juices, and greasy, spicy, or hard-to-digest foods.

- Get a good night's sleep the night before.

- Take or use whatever seasickness prevention works best for you—medication, an acupressure wristband, ginger tea or capsules, or any combination. But do it **before you board;** once you set sail, it's generally too late.

o While you're on the boat, stay as low and as near the center of the boat as possible. Avoid the fumes (especially if it's a diesel boat); stay out in the fresh air and watch the horizon. Do not read.

o If you start to feel queasy, drink clear fluids like water, and eat something bland, such as a soda cracker.

Stings   The most common stings in Hawaii come from jellyfish, particularly **Portuguese man-of-war** and box jellyfish. Since the poisons they inject are very different, you'll need to treat each type of sting differently.

A bluish-purple floating bubble with a long tail, the Portuguese man-of-war is responsible for some 6,500 stings a year on Oahu alone. These stings, although painful and a nuisance, are rarely harmful; fewer than 1 in 1,000 requires medical treatment. The best prevention is to watch for these floating bubbles as you snorkel (look for the hanging tentacles below the surface). Get out of the water if anyone near you spots these jellyfish. Reactions to stings range from mild burning and reddening to severe welts and blisters. Most jellyfish stings disappear by themselves within 15 to 20 minutes if you do nothing at all to treat them. "All Stings Considered: First Aid and Medical Treatment of Hawaii's Marine Injuries," by Craig Thomas and Susan Scott (University of Hawaii Press, 1997), recommends the following treatment: First, pick off any visible tentacles with a gloved hand or a stick; then, rinse the sting with salt- or fresh water, and apply ice to prevent swelling. Avoid applying vinegar, baking soda, or urine to the wound, which may actually cause further damage. See a doctor if pain persists or a rash or other symptoms develop.

Transparent, square-shaped **box jellyfish** are nearly impossible to see in the water. Fortunately, they seem to follow a monthly cycle: 8 to 10 days after the full moon, they appear in the waters on the leeward side of each island and hang around for about 3 days. Also, they seem to sting more in the morning, when they're on or near the surface. The stings from a box jellyfish can cause hive-like welts, blisters, and pain lasting from 10 minutes to 8 hours. "All

Stings Considered" recommends the following treatment: First, pour regular household vinegar on the sting; this will stop additional burning. Do not rub the area. Pick off any vinegar-soaked tentacles with a stick and apply an ice pack. Seek medical treatment if you experience shortness of breath, weakness, palpitations, or any other severe symptoms.

Punctures　Most sea-related punctures come from stepping on or brushing against the needle-like spines of sea urchins (known locally as *wana*). Be careful when you're in the water; don't put your foot down (even if you are wearing booties or fins) if you can't clearly see the bottom. Waves can push you into *wana* in a surge zone in shallow water. The spines can even puncture a wet suit. A sea urchin puncture can result in burning, aching, swelling, and discoloration (black or purple) around the area where the spines entered your skin. The best thing to do is to pull out any protruding spines. The body will absorb the spines within 24 hours to 3 weeks, or the remainder of the spines will work themselves out. Again, contrary to popular thought, urinating or pouring vinegar on the embedded spines will not help.

Cuts　Stay out of the ocean if you have an open cut, wound, or new tattoo. The high level of bacteria present in the water means that even small wounds can become infected. Staphylococcus, or "staph," infections start out as swollen, pinkish skin tissue around the wound that spreads and grows rather than dries and heals. Scrub any cuts well with fresh water and avoid the ocean until they heal. Consult a doctor if your wound shows signs of infection.

Internet & Wi-Fi　On every island, branches of the **Hawaii State Public Library System** have free computers with Internet access. To find your closest library, check **www.librarieshawaii. org/sitemap.htm**. There is no charge for use of the computers, but you must have a Hawaii library card, which is free to Hawaii residents and members of the military. Visitors can visit any branch to purchase a $10 visitor card that is good for 3 months.

If you have your own laptop, every **Starbucks** in Hawaii has Wi-Fi. For a list of locations, go to **www.starbucks.com/retail/ find/default.aspx**. Many, if not most, **hotel lobbies** have free Wi-Fi.

Most interisland airports have **Internet kiosks** that provide basic Web access for a per-minute fee that's usually higher than cybercafe prices. The **Honolulu International Airport** (http://hawaii.gov/hnl) provides **Wi-Fi access** for a fee through Shaka Net. Check out copy shops like FedEx Office, which offers computer stations with fully loaded software (as well as Wi-Fi).

Mail   At press time, domestic postage rates were 35¢ for a postcard and 49¢ for a letter. For international mail, a first-class postcard or letter up to 1 ounce costs $1.15. For more information go to **www.usps.com**.

If you aren't sure what your address will be in the United States, mail can be sent to you, in your name, c/o General Delivery at the main post office of the city or region where you expect to be. (Call ℰ **800/275-8777** for information on the nearest post office.) The addressee must pick up mail in person and must produce proof of identity (driver's license, passport, and the like). Most post offices will hold mail for up to 1 month, and are open Monday to Friday from 9am to 4pm, and Saturday from 9am to noon.

Always include zip codes when mailing items in the U.S. If you don't know your zip code, visit www.usps.com/zip4.

Medical Requirements   Unless you're arriving from an area known to be suffering from an epidemic (particularly cholera or yellow fever), inoculations or vaccinations are not required for entry into the United States.

Mobile Phones   Cellphone coverage is decent throughout Hawaii, but tends to be inconsistent in the more remote and mountainous regions of the Islands.

If you're not from the U.S., you'll be appalled at the poor reach of our **GSM (Global System for Mobile Communications) wireless network,** which is used by much of the rest of the world. You may or may not be able to send SMS (text messaging) home.

Do *not* use your cellphone while you are driving. Strict laws and heavy fines ($97–$150) are diligently enforced.

Money & Costs   Frommer's lists exact prices in the local currency. The currency conversions quoted below were correct at press time. However, rates fluctuate, so before departing consult a currency exchange website such as www.oanda.com or www.xe.com/ucc/convert/classic to check up-to-the-minute rates.

THE VALUE OF US$ VS. OTHER POPULAR CURRENCIES

US$	Can$	UK£	Euro (€)	Aus$	NZ$
1	C$1.09	£.59	€.72	A$.992	NZ$1.15

ATMs (cashpoints) are everywhere in Hawaii—at banks, supermarkets, Longs Drugs, and Honolulu International Airport, and in some resorts and shopping centers. The **Cirrus** (www.mastercard.com; ℂ **800/424-7787**) and **PLUS** (www.visa.com; ℂ **800/843-7587**) networks span the country; you can find them even in remote regions. Go to your bankcard's website to find ATM locations at your destination. Be sure you know your daily withdrawal limit before you depart.

Note: Many banks impose a fee every time you use a card at another bank's ATM, and that fee is often higher for international transactions (up to $5 or more) than for domestic ones (rarely more than $2.50). In addition, the bank from which you withdraw cash is likely to charge its own fee. Visitors from outside the U.S. should also find out whether their bank assesses a 1 to 3% fee on charges incurred abroad.

Credit cards are accepted everywhere except, most taxicabs (all islands), and some small restaurants and B&B accommodations.

Packing Tips Hawaii is very informal. Shorts, T-shirts, and sandals will get you by at most restaurants and attractions; a casual dress or a polo shirt and long pants are fine even in the most expensive places. Aloha wear is acceptable everywhere, so you may want to plan on buying an aloha shirt or a Hawaiian-style dress while you're in the islands. If you plan on hiking, horseback riding, or ziplining, bring close-toed shoes; they're required.

The tropical sun poses the greatest threat to anyone who ventures into the great outdoors, so pack **sun protection:** a good pair of sunglasses, strong sunscreen, a light hat, and a water bottle. Dehydration is common in the tropics.

One last thing: **It can get really cold in Hawaii.** If you plan to see the sunrise from the top of Maui's Haleakala Crater, venture into

WHAT THINGS COST IN HAWAII	US$
Hamburger	6.00–19.00
Movie ticket (adult/child)	11.00/7.50
20-ounce soft drink at convenience store	2.50
16-ounce apple juice	3.50
Cup of coffee	3.00
Moderately priced three-course dinner without alcohol	60.00

the Big Island's Hawaii Volcanoes National Park, or spend time in Kokee State Park on Kauai, bring a warm jacket. Temperatures "upcountry" (higher up the mountain) can sink to 40°F (4°C), even in summer when it's 80°F (27°C) at the beach. Bring a windbreaker, sweater, or light jacket. And if you'll be in Hawaii between November and March, toss some **rain gear** into your suitcase, too.

Passports   Virtually every air traveler entering the U.S. is required to show a passport. All persons, including U.S. citizens, traveling by air between the United States and Canada, Mexico, Central and South America, the Caribbean, and Bermuda are required to present a valid passport. *Note:* U.S. and Canadian citizens entering the U. S. at land and sea ports of entry from within the western hemisphere must now also present a passport or other documents compliant with the Western Hemisphere Travel Initiative (WHTI; check www.getyouhome.gov for details). Children 15 and under may continue entering with only a U.S. birth certificate, or other proof of U.S. citizenship.

Australia   Australian Passport Information Service (www.passports. gov.au; © **131-232** in Australia).

Canada   Passport Office, Department of Foreign Affairs and International Trade, Ottawa, ON K1A 0G3 (www.ppt.gc.ca; © **800/567-6868**).

Ireland   Passport Office, Setanta Centre, Molesworth Street, Dublin 2 (www.foreignaffairs.gov.ie; © **01/671-1633**).

New Zealand **Passports Office,** Department of Internal Affairs, 47 Boulcott St., Wellington, 6011 (www.passports.govt.nz; ☎ **0800/225-050** in New Zealand or 04/474-8100).

United Kingdom Visit your nearest passport office, major post office, or travel agency, or contact the **Identity and Passport Service (IPS),** 89 Eccleston Sq., London, SW1V 1PN (www.ips.gov.uk; ☎ **0300/222-0000**).

United States To find your regional passport office, check the U.S. State Department website (http://travel.state.gov) or call the **National Passport Information Center** (☎ **877/487-2778**) for automated ivnformation.

Safety Although tourist areas are generally safe, visitors should always stay alert, even in laidback Hawaii. It's wise to ask the island tourist office if you're in doubt about which neighborhoods are safe. Avoid deserted areas, especially at night. Don't go into any city park at night unless there's an event that attracts crowds. Generally speaking, you can feel safe in areas where there are many people and open establishments.

Avoid carrying valuables with you on the street, and don't display expensive cameras or electronic equipment. Hold on to your purse, and place your billfold in an inside pocket. In theaters, restaurants, and other public places, keep your possessions in sight. The Honolulu police department advises women to carry purses on the shoulder away from the street or, better yet, to wear the strap across the chest instead of on one shoulder. Women with clutch bags should hold them close to their chest.

Remember also that hotels are open to the public and that security may not be able to screen everyone entering, particularly in large properties. Always lock your room door—don't assume that once inside your hotel you're automatically safe.

Burglaries of tourists' rental cars in hotel parking structures and at beach parking lots have become more common. Park in well-lighted and well-traveled areas, if possible. Never leave any packages or valuables visible in the car. If someone attempts to rob you or steal your car, do not try to resist the thief or carjacker—report the incident to the police department immediately. Ask your rental agency about personal safety, and get written directions or a map with the route to your destination clearly marked.

Generally, Hawaii has the same laws as the mainland United States. Nudity is illegal in Hawaii. There are no legal nude beaches (we don't care what you have read). If you are nude on a beach (or anywhere) in Hawaii, you can be arrested.

Smoking marijuana also is illegal; if you attempt to buy it or light up, you can be arrested.

Senior Travel Discounts for seniors are available at almost all of Hawaii's major attractions and occasionally at hotels and restaurants. The Outrigger hotel chain, for instance, offers travelers ages 50 and older a 20% discount on regular published rates—and an additional 5% off for members of AARP. Always ask when making hotel reservations or buying tickets. And always carry identification with proof of your age—it can really pay off.

Smoking It's against the law to smoke in public buildings, including airports, shopping malls, grocery stores, retail shops, buses, movie theaters, banks, convention facilities, and all government buildings and facilities. There is no smoking in restaurants, bars, and nightclubs. Most B&Bs prohibit smoking indoors, and more and more hotels and resorts are becoming nonsmoking even in public areas. Also, there is no smoking within 20 feet of a doorway, window, or ventilation intake (so no hanging around outside a bar to smoke—you must go 20 ft. away).

Taxes The United States has no value-added tax (VAT) or other indirect tax at the national level. Every state, county, and city may levy its own local tax on all purchases, including hotel and restaurant checks and airline tickets. These taxes will not appear on price tags.

Hawaii state general excise tax is 4.166%, which applies to all items purchased (including hotel rooms). On top of that, the state's transient Accommodation Tax (TAT) is 9.25%. These taxes, combined with various resort fees, can add up to 17% to 18% of your room rate. Budget accordingly.

Telephones All calls on-island are local calls; calls from one island to another via a landline are long distance and you must dial 1, then the Hawaii area code (808), and then the phone number. Many convenience groceries and packaging services sell **prepaid calling cards** in denominations up to $50. Many public pay phones at airports now accept American Express, MasterCard, and Visa.

Local calls made from most pay phones cost 50¢. Most long-distance and international calls can be dialed directly from any phone. **To make calls within the United States and to Canada,** dial 1, followed by the area code and the seven-digit number. **For other international calls,** dial 011, followed by the country code, city code, and the number you are calling.

Calls to area codes **800, 888, 877,** and **866** are toll-free. However, calls to area codes **700** and **900** (chat lines, bulletin boards, "dating" services, and so on) can be expensive—charges of 95¢ to $3 or more per minute. Some numbers have minimum charges that can run $15 or more.

For **reversed-charge or collect calls,** and for person-to-person calls, dial the number 0, then the area code and number; an operator will come on the line, and you should specify whether you are calling collect, person-to-person, or both. If your operator-assisted call is international, ask for the overseas operator.

For **directory assistance** ("Information"), dial 411 for local numbers and national numbers in the U.S. and Canada. For dedicated long-distance information, dial 1, then the appropriate area code plus 555-1212.

Time   The continental United States is divided into **four time zones:** Eastern Standard Time (EST), Central Standard Time (CST), Mountain Standard Time (MST), and Pacific Standard Time (PST). Alaska and Hawaii have their own zones. For example, when it's 7am in Honolulu (HST), it's 9am in Los Angeles (PST), 10am in Denver (MST), 11am in Chicago (CST), noon in New York City (EST), 5pm in London (GMT), and 2am the next day in Sydney.

Daylight saving time, in effect in most of the United States from 2am on the second Sunday in March to 2am on the first Sunday in November, is not observed in Hawaii, Arizona, the U.S. Virgin Islands, and Puerto Rico. Daylight saving time moves the clock 1 hour ahead of standard time.

Tipping   Tips are a major part of certain workers' income, and gratuities are the standard way of showing appreciation for services provided. (Tipping is certainly not compulsory if the service is poor!) In hotels, tip **bellhops** at least $2 per bag ($3–$5 if you have a lot of luggage) and tip the **housekeepers** $2 per person per day (more if you've left a disaster area for him or her to clean up). Tip the

doorman or **concierge** only if he or she has provided you with some specific service (for example, calling a cab for you or obtaining difficult-to-get theater tickets). Tip the **valet-parking attendant** $2 to $5 every time you get your car.

In restaurants, bars, and nightclubs, tip **service staff** and **bartenders** 18 to 20% of the check, and tip **valet-parking attendants** $2 per vehicle.

As for other service personnel, tip **cab drivers** 15% of the fare; tip **skycaps** at airports at least $2 per bag ($3–$5 if you have a lot of luggage); and tip **hairdressers** and **barbers** 18 to 20%.

Toilets You won't find public toilets or "restrooms" on the streets in Hawaii but they can be found in hotel lobbies, restaurants, museums, department stores, railway and bus stations, service stations, and at most beaches. Large hotels and fast-food restaurants are often the best bet for clean facilities. Restaurants and bars in heavily visited areas may reserve their restrooms for patrons.

Travelers with Disabilities Travelers with disabilities are made to feel very welcome in Hawaii. Many hotels are equipped with wheelchair-accessible rooms and pools, and tour companies provide many special services.

For tips on accessible travel in Hawaii, go to the **Hawaii Tourism Authority** website (www.gohawaii.com/oahu/about/travel-tips/special-needs). The **Hawaii Centers for Independent Living,** 200 N. Vineyard Blvd., Bldg. A501, Honolulu, HI 96817 (www.cil-hawaii.org; © **808/522-5400**), can provide additional information about accessibility throughout the Islands.

Access Aloha Travel (www.accessalohatravel.com; © **800/480-1143**) specializes in accommodating travelers with disabilities. Agents book cruises, tours, accommodations, and airfare (as part of a package only). On Maui and Kauai, **Gammie Homecare** (www.gammie.com; Maui: © **808/877-4032;** Kauai: © **808/632-2333**) rents everything from motorized scooters to shower chairs.

For more on resources for travelers with disabilities, go to www.frommers.com.

Visas The U.S. State Department has a **Visa Waiver Program (VWP)** allowing citizens of the following countries to enter the United States without a visa for stays of up to 90 days: Andorra,

Australia, Austria, Belgium, Brunei, Chile, Czech Republic, Denmark, Estonia, Finland, France, Germany, Greece, Hungary, Iceland, Ireland, Italy, Japan, Latvia, Liechtenstein, Lithuania, Luxembourg, Malta, Monaco, the Netherlands, New Zealand, Norway, Portugal, San Marino, Singapore, Slovakia, Slovenia, South Korea, Spain, Sweden, Switzerland, Taiwan, and the United Kingdom. (**Note:** This list was accurate at press time; for the most up-to-date list of countries in the VWP, consult http://usvisas.state.gov.) Even though a visa isn't necessary, in an effort to help U.S. officials check travelers against terror watch lists before they arrive at U.S. borders, visitors from VWP countries must register online through the Electronic System for Travel Authorization (ESTA) before boarding a plane or a boat to the U.S. Travelers must complete an electronic application providing basic personal and travel eligibility information. The Department of Homeland Security recommends filling out the form at least 3 days before traveling. Authorizations will be valid for up to 2 years or until the traveler's passport expires, whichever comes first. Currently, there is a US$14 fee for the online application. Existing ESTA registrations remain valid through their expiration dates. **Note:** Any passport issued on or after October 26, 2006, by a VWP country must be an **e-Passport** for VWP travelers to be eligible to enter the U.S. without a visa. Citizens of these nations also need to present a round-trip air or cruise ticket upon arrival. E-Passports contain computer chips capable of storing biometric information, such as the required digital photograph of the holder. If your passport doesn't have this feature, you can still travel without a visa if the valid passport was issued before October 26, 2005, and includes a machine-readable zone; or if the valid passport was issued between October 26, 2005, and October 25, 2006, and includes a digital photograph. For more information, go to **http://usvisas.state.gov**. Canadian citizens may enter the United States without a visa but will need to show a passport and proof of residence.

Citizens of all other countries must have (1) a valid passport that expires at least 6 months later than the scheduled end of their visit to the U.S., and (2) a tourist visa. For information about U.S. visas, go to **http://usvisas.state.gov**. Or go to one of the following:

Australian citizens can obtain up-to-date visa information from the **U.S. Embassy Canberra,** Moonah Place, Yarralumla, ACT 2600

(☎ **02/6214-5600**) or by checking the U.S. Diplomatic Mission's website at http://canberra.usembassy.gov/visas.html.

British subjects can obtain up-to-date visa information by calling the **U.S. Embassy Visa Information Line** (☎ **09042-450-100** from within the U.K. at £1.20 per min.; or ☎ **866/382-3589** from within the U.S. at a flat rate of $16, payable by credit card only) or by visiting the American Embassy London's website at http://london.usembassy.gov/visas.html.

Irish citizens can obtain up-to-date visa information through the **U.S. Embassy Dublin,** 42 Elgin Rd., Ballsbridge, Dublin 4 (http://dublin.usembassy.gov; ☎ **1580-47-VISA [8472]** from within the Republic of Ireland at €2.40 per min.).

Citizens of **New Zealand** can obtain up-to-date visa information by contacting the **U.S. Embassy New Zealand,** 29 Fitzherbert Terrace, Thorndon, Wellington (http://newzealand.usembassy.gov; ☎ **644/462-6000**).

Water   Generally the water in your hotel or at public drinking fountains is safe to drink (depending on the island, it may have more chlorine than you like).

Wi-Fi   See "Internet & Wi-Fi," earlier in this section.

Index

Accommodations

Restaurants

PHOTO CREDITS